Richard Trevithick

Richard Trevithick

GIANT OF STEAM

ANTHONY BURTON

AURUM PRESS

First published in Great Britain 2000
by Aurum Press Ltd
25 Bedford Avenue, London WC1B 3AT

This paperback edition first published 2002
by Aurum Press Ltd

A catalogue record for this book is available from the British Library.

ISBN 1 85410 878 6

3 5 7 9 10 8 6 4
2004 2006 2005

Text design by Roger Lightfoot
Printed in Great Britain by
Bookmarque, Croydon

Contents

For Frank Trevithick Okuno

Preface

There are some books where the idea strikes and before you know where you are, you are up and running, dashing towards the finishing-line. There are others that jog along at a steady, even pace. This has been a marathon, run by snails. It began with a suggestion from a reader in 1980, and shortly afterwards I literally took the first steps when I went walking the track of the Penydarren tramway for my book, *Walking the Line*. Somehow the idea of a biography remained on the shelf, though two other Trevithicks, the grandsons, popped up when I was working on the story of British-built railways overseas, *The Railway Empire*. It was then that I met Frank Trevithick Okuno, a direct descendant of the great engineer. The final nudge came when I went to a lecture given by Stuart Owen-Jones on the building of the Penydarren replica. So I owe a special thanks to him for finally getting me started.

Inevitably, in a project of this kind one builds up a long list of debts to individuals and institutions. I am especially grateful to those in Cornwall who have done so much to help keep the Trevithick name alive. In particular I should like to thank Philip Hosken of The Trevithick Society for all he has done and especially, together with John Sawle, for reading the manuscript. As always, the faults that have survived are all my own. Stuart B. Smith of The Trevithick Trust has been most encouraging and Mrs Lois Humphrey, of Penponds, dealt most patiently with my many enquiries. One of the most difficult areas to research was the eleven-year period when Trevithick was in South America. Sharron Schwartz of the Cornish Global Migration Programme has been doing her Ph.D. on the Cornish in Latin America, and she passed on the results of her hard work. This section would have been the poorer without her help. Tom Brogden, who built the replica of the London steam carriage let me look over his splendid machine.

Much of the research obviously had to take place in Cornwall, and I am very grateful to Angela Broome, Librarian of the Courtney Library and Cornish History Archive for hunting down obscure material and to Roger Penhallurick, Curator of the Royal Cornwall Museum. I also had a great deal of useful assistance from the Cornwall Record Office and the Cornish Studies Library. The Birmingham Central Library gave me access to the Boulton and Watt papers, and Dartford Library helped by supplying a good deal of new information on the end of Trevithick's life, as did J. & E. Hall Ltd. The remainder of the documentary evidence used in writing this book came from the Science Museum Library in London.

I have one last special thank you to make. My wife, Pip, has helped me with everything I have written in one way or another but this time she had a special interest, as her forebears worked in the Cornish mining industry. She joined me in searching the archives and did all of the picture research for the book.

After all that help, there was very little left for me to do, apart from sit down and write the book, nearly twenty years after the idea was born.

Anthony Burton
Stroud, February 2000

CHAPTER ONE

West Barbary

Richard Trevithick was a man of such an extravagant and flamboyant personality, so bursting with ideas and plans, that it is impossible to imagine him having anything other than an extraordinary life. Yet, paradoxically, few men have had a career whose development can be more clearly traced back to the simple facts of where and when they were born. So strong were those influences that it is literally impossible to understand Trevithick's life without knowing what Cornwall, and in particular the region round Carn Brea, was like when he was born there on 13 April 1771.

Cornwall was known as "West Barbary" to some, partly because it was almost an unknown country as far as the rest of England was concerned, a strange Celtic land stuck out into the Atlantic waves. It was inhospitable whichever way you approached it. The roads west of the River Tamar were poor, quite bad enough to discourage travellers other than those who had an absolute necessity to be there. The sea passage was worse: it was fearsome. The rough, rocky coastline where a few narrow inlets gave access to a disturbingly small number of anchorages, offering shelter from the storms that whistled across the Atlantic, was rightly feared. However, bad as its reputation was, it was made infinitely worse by the horrific stories of smugglers and wreckers. Some may have been exaggerated, but there was a hard kernel of unpalatable truth inside the tales. Wrecking was a reality, though enough vessels foundered in the storms to make any extra effort on the part of the Cornish people almost unnecessary. The grim part grew with a horrible inevitability out of the law itself, which strictly defined a wreck as "any ship from which no living creature escaped to shore". To the shipwrecked sailor, clinging to a broken spar and crying for help, the sight and sound of crowds on the shore might have offered a last hope of rescue. How could he know that, to them, he was all that stood between a wretched, impoverished people and a dream of riches? And once a vessel was officially a wreck, then the men could get to work. According to George Borlase, writing in 1753: "They'll cut a large trading vessel to pieces in one tide, and cut down everybody that offers to oppose them."[1] Not all the stories concern atrocities. John Carter was a notorious smuggler, known throughout the area as "The King of Prussia Cove" who operated from 1770 right through to 1807, but who had a reputation for courtesy and honesty. It was, after all, generally accepted among the Cornish that the taxes and duties imposed by far-off Westminster had little or nothing to do with them, and their evasion was no more than a matter of good commercial common sense. Carter certainly did not regard himself as a thief. On one occasion the customs men seized some smuggled goods which he had agreed to deliver to a customer. This posed something of a dilemma for Carter, who regarded it as a matter of personal honour to produce goods as ordered. So he broke into the Customs House, removed his "own" property, but left everything else untouched. The customs men sanguinely accepted that Carter had paid them a visit, and took the matter no further. The point about all these stories is not that Cornwall was necessarily a barbarous place, but that it operated by its own set of rules, very different from those of the rest of England. And what was true of the lawless was equally true of those in the legitimate trade from which the Trevithicks made their living: the centuries-old industry of mining for metals.

Tin extraction was being practised before there were written records and, in legend at least, the Phoenicians sailed all the way from the Mediterranean to trade in the metal. In early times, it was obtained by "streaming", which initially involved no more than working a "stream" of loose ore that appeared on an open hillside. This was an alluvial deposit, fanning out from a vein or lode which could then be attacked where it lay close to the surface by digging open trenches or "coffins". The ore might appear as sizeable chunks, but more often had the consistency of gravel. Removing the valuable ore from the waste stone was simply a matter of washing in running water, when the heavier tin would separate out. The rights to a stream were passed on from generation to generation. Many tinners earned a meagre amount from the workings, but they represented their most cherished assets. My wife's forebears were Cornish and the 1732 will of the resoundingly named Melchizedich Rogers has an item for a "bound", an area roughly marked out on open land, for which he had streaming rights. These, together with his working tools, were valued at £4-15-0, around a third of everything he owned. It was not much but it brought at least the idea of independence. However, by the eighteenth century such easily acquired ore had mostly been taken. Now the only way to reach big deposits was to burrow deep underground. And by the time Trevithick breathed his first, tin mining had largely been replaced by mining for copper.

Deep mining requires capital, a good deal of capital, which might suggest that the age of the independent miner was at an end. But the Cornish contrived a system quite unlike that which existed in any other industry. At the top of the hierarchy was the landowner, who was in a very happy "heads I win, tails I don't lose" situation. He granted the right to mine a section of land, called a "sett", to a mining consortium, known as "adventurers". He had no need to put up any of his own money, for all the costs of exploration and working the mine fell on the adventurers, who were normally given a twenty-one year lease. If the venture failed, the landowner lost nothing, if it succeeded he was entitled to the "lord's dues", which could be anything from one thirty-second to one fifteenth part of the value of the ore raised. He stood to gain a regular income that might be several thousands of pounds if the mine proved profitable, with absolutely no risk at all. The adventurers, on the other hand, risked everything, and well deserved their name. For all practical purposes, they were the mine-owners, and the number of adventurers in a consortium varied considerably. There were generally sixty-four shares, and any individual could hold any number of shares. Given the number of mines in the region, this meant that interest in the success of mining was widely spread throughout the community.

When it came to the working of the mine, the unique character of the Cornish system appeared. The adventurers appointed mine "captains" to oversee the actual work. In the larger mines, there would be different captains to overlook the work underground and the preparation of the ore at the surface. These were men of considerable status, who were regularly referred to as "Captain", just as they would have been if they held a commission in the army or commanded a ship. They almost invariably rose up from the

ranks of ordinary miners on the basis of both a good understanding
of the technicalities of mining and an ability to control an often
rough and fractious work force. It was a job that depended as
much on character as on skill and intellect. And the captains had
one other vital role to play: in the "settings". The miners were paid
no wages as such, but had to negotiate contracts afresh at each of
the settings, which were generally held at two-monthly intervals.
They gathered at the mine count house, where the captains stood
on a raised platform, and negotiated the terms for the different
types of work. The least complex part of the work to be let was the
"dressing", separating the ore from the useless waste, and breaking
it up ready for sale. Much of the actual work was done by women,
known as "bal maidens", a romantic sounding name for a singularly unromantic job of breaking up and picking through slimy,
muddy piles of rock and ore. Next came the "tutwork". This
involved payment for the basic work of sinking shafts and driving
levels far underground. These would have been measured up in
advance by the captain, and the work was paid accordingly.
Measurement, very appropriately for this county all but
surrounded by sea, was in fathoms (6 ft or 1.8 m) and the work
was allocated, in theory, to the lowest bidder. It was not quite as
simple as that. It was commonplace for groups of men to offer for
more work than they could possibly perform and at a higher price
than they ever expected to get. There was a great deal of bargain-
ing to be gone through, even if it did have a certain ritual element
to it. To add to the confusion of terminology, a group taking a
particular piece of work was known as a "pair" or "pare", no
matter how many men were in it, but there was a minimum of six,
to allow for three shifts, with at least two men per shift, throughout
the twenty-four-hour working day. Tools were supplied by the
company, but they then became the responsibility of the men, who
had to look after their sharpening and repair; while essential materials, including candles and gunpowder, were charged against the
final settlement, which usually came round two weeks after the end
of the period. The final work was "tribute". This was the crucial
work of wrenching the mineral-bearing ore from the underground
seams and bringing it to the surface. Once again the work was
auctioned out, but here the men had to make shrewd judgements,
for the rate they got for the job was not determined by how much
rock and ore they shifted, but depended on the value of what was
brought to the surface, based on samples of the ore collected by

the captains. A miscalculation of the quality of the ore, or the discovery of unexpected problems, could lead to a whole gang working for weeks and seeing no reward at the end of it. Conversely, if the gang had made a more astute judgement than the captains, they could make a very considerable profit. The men who got the ore were, in their own way, as much adventurers as those who put up the capital. It is fair to say that almost everyone who worked in a Cornish mine had a direct interest in its success, and the miners in particular were never mere wage earners, but depended on their own judgement and experience as much as on their hard muscles. It was not a system that bred subservience: as a popular saying of the time had it, "the whole art of mining is fooling the captain".

What of the work itself? At the beginning of the eighteenth century, mechanisation was almost unknown. The main piece of equipment above ground was the horse gin or whim, a simple device by which a horse or mule, walking a circular track, turned a drum around which a rope was wound. This was used to lower materials down the mine, haul up the ore and, sometimes, to raise and lower the men. William Beckford of Fonthill Abbey, a gentleman best known for his accounts of travel in Europe, had time on his hands while waiting for a packet to Lisbon, where he intended to make yet more notes for an account of foreign travel to exotic places. He was persuaded to visit the mining region of Gwennap, and his description of the place and its people might have come straight from the pages of a Gothic novel. This was Consolidated Mines in the eighteenth century.[2]

They are situated in a bleak desert, rendered still more doleful by the unhealthy appearance of its inhabitants. At every step one stumbles upon ladders that lead into utter darkness, or funnels that exhale warm copperous vapours. All around these openings the ore is piled up in heaps ready for purchasers. I saw it drawn reeking out of the mine by the help of a machine called a whim put in motion by mules, which in their turn are stimulated by impish children hanging over the poor brutes and flogging them without respite. This dismal scene of whims, suffering mules and hillocks of cinders extends for miles ... Two strange-looking beings, dressed in ghostly white, conducted me about and very kindly proposed a descent into the bowels of the earth, but I declined the invitation. These mystagogues occupy a tolerable house with fair sash windows where the inspectors of the mine hold their meetings and regale upon beef,

pudding and brandy. While I was standing at the door of this habita-
tion several woeful figures in tattered garments with pick-axes on
their shoulders crawled out of a dark fissure and repaired to a hovel,
which I learnt was a gin-shop. There they pass the few hours allotted
to them above ground and drink, it is to be hoped, in oblivion of
their subterranean existence.

Perhaps it is as well that he did not go underground, as he would
certainly have found that experience even less enjoyable. The
descent would either have been by means of the whim, with a foot
looped into the rope or, just as alarmingly, by vertical ladders –
with the unhappy thought that for every rung descended, the same
rung would have to be tackled again on the way up. Once down,
the darkness would have seemed all but overwhelming, with no
light apart from a stub of candle stuck on the front of a stiff, round
hat. The dark at the bottom of a mine is not the dark of a moonless
night, but an absolute velvet hood of darkness. What little light
there was would have revealed no very encouraging sight, simply a
roof of rock holding up who could tell how much solid, or not so
solid, earth overhead, shored up by timbers that, to the inexperi-
enced eye, seemed to bend under the heavy load. Then there was
the heat with temperatures in the deepest mines rising to a stifling
40°C, while the heavy, acrid air might still be scented with the
whiff of burnt powder from the last blasting. Then, most alarming
of all, there would have been water – water that seemed to come
from everywhere, flowing round the feet, dripping from walls and
roofs, as though the whole mine was oozing into the darkness.
Underground was a world of its own, a three-dimensional village of
narrow alleys and broad streets, crossing and recrossing at different
levels, full of alarming junctions where a single plank might lead
across an abyss, a dark space where no light penetrated, where
there was no means of even guessing the depth. A visit to an eighteenth-century copper mine was not for the faint hearted.

The darkness, the heat and the discomfort were so much a part
of the everyday life of the miner that they were scarcely registered
after a time – but water was an ever-present enemy. And the
deeper one went, the stronger the enemy became. In the early part
of the century, mines were kept drained by pumps worked first by
hand, then by animals, then later again by water wheels. But there
was a limit to the depth from which such primitive devices could
lift water. Where these methods failed, then the next remedy was

the drainage tunnel or adit. Some of these were immense affairs, as complex as the mine-workings themselves. One of the most impressive of all was the Great County Adit begun in 1748 by the chief adventurer of Poldice mine, Sir William Lemon. Once begun, it was extended throughout the century, and from draining one mine it spread through Gwennap, Chacewater, St Day and Scorrier. By the end it was taking water from as deep as 70 fathoms, and the longest distance from the outflow at Bissoe was to Wheal Cardew,[3] an astonishing 5 miles away. It was an immense undertaking, but it was estimated that when completed it was saving the adventurers nearly £20,000 a year in pumping costs. Its importance did not diminsh with the coming of the steam age, because the great engines were not required to lift water right up to the surface, but only to the level of the adit. It was estimated that, by the end of the eighteenth century, half the most advanced steam engines in use, not just in Cornwall, but in the entire world, were discharging into the Great Adit. It may have been worth it in financial terms, but there was often a heavy human price to be paid, as a contemporary account makes all too clear.[4]

> Few operations can be conceived more unpleasant and dangerous to the workmen, than the execution of these adits, especially when, as is sometimes the case, they are barely wide enough to allow the sinker to creep along. The dangers which are created by blasting the solid rocks with gunpowder in such confined spaces, will be easily conceived.

The greatest danger of all came from the possibility of breaking through to a submerged area, where the water was under considerable pressure. One stroke of the pick-axe or drill might be all that was needed to release a huge wave that would rush out, filling the narrow passageway. Just such an event occurred in one of the St Just mines in the nineteenth century, and resulted in four miners losing their lives. It was remembered by an old man.[5]

> They say the end they was driving had been bone-dry all along. When the men got down that day they stopped out at the beginning of the level to touch a pipe of bacca, and told the boy to go in and clear up the end 'gainst they started to work. Over a while the boy came out and said: "We ain't far off the water now, Uncle Nick, for tes running through in the end." "Git away," said the man, "theest took fear, booy," What happened after that they don't know, but 'tis

supposed the men went in to work and the first blow they struck on the drill, the water burst through upon them. One man was found afterwards with the tram thrown on top of him yards back in the level, and one they never found for a week. The two other men, as I said, I seed myself broft into the carpenters' shop and laid out pon the binch.

Adit-driving was dangerous but necessary work, but even so, not every mine could be drained in this way and an alternative was desperately needed. It was that need that gave birth to a new age, an age where the name of Trevithick was to shine out – the age of the steam engine.

The first steam-pumping engine, invented by Captain Savery in 1698, was known variously as a fire engine and as "The Miner's Friend" – dubiously, because it involved setting a fire underground, which would have been disastrous in the gaseous mines, particularly those of the coal fields. It worked by condensing steam to create a vacuum, which drew up water into a receiving vessel. Steam under pressure was then used to force the water out of the receiver and up to a higher level. It was limited to comparatively short lifts, no more than 5 or 6 fathoms. It did not excite much interest in Cornwall, but the next inventor on the scene was a local man, who thoroughly understood the needs and problems of mine drainage.

Thomas Newcomen was born at Dartmouth in 1663, was trained as a blacksmith and had a brisk trade in providing metal tools for the local mines in Devon and across the Tamar in Cornwall. His travels made him very well aware of the problems of mine drainage, but not it seems of Savery's engine – a good measure of just how little it was regarded in the region. But not knowing about it did not mean that he had a free hand as an inventor. Savery had taken out a patent which was so broadly worded that it effectively covered any use of steam to raise water. So when Newcomen came up with his own far superior and entirely different engine, he still had to reach an accommodation with Savery the patent holder. This was to be a story that was to be repeated in the Trevithick saga, but in a far less friendly manner, and without a happy ending.

Newcomen's engine was very simple, but limited. In essence it consisted of an open-topped cylinder fitted with a piston. Steam was admitted below the piston, then condensed by a cold-water spray. This created a vacuum inside the cylinder, and atmospheric pressure on top of the piston forced it down. Now all Newcomen had to do was suspend his piston by chains from one end of an overhead pivoted beam and attach pump rods to the opposite end. As the piston went down, so the pump rods were raised. Then, when the vacuum was broken and the pressure equalised, the weight of rods would drag that end of the beam down and up would come the piston. The steam valve would then be opened and the whole cycle could start again. The engines were massive and cumbersome. The cylinder sat on top of what looked like, and in effect was, a giant copper kettle, from which the piston rose to a massive beam of timber, strapped with iron. All this was contained in an engine house, specially built for that particular engine. One half of the beam was inside the house, the rest passed out through a hole in the wall, to end above the rods descending down the pumping shaft. The first Newcomen engine was set to work at a coal mine at Dudley in the Black Country in 1712, and by 1720 it had made its first appearance in Cornwall at Wheal Fortune. It had a 47-in. (120 cm) diameter cylinder,[6] and the huge beam slowly nodded up and down at half a dozen strokes a minute. But the work it did was immense, raising water from a depth of 30 fathoms. The Cornish were suitably impressed. Here was a machine that could bring water from deep underground, and was safe, since the steam was at very low pressure. Other engines were ordered and soon spread throughout the mining districts, and the region acquired primitive versions of some of its most distinctive features, the Cornish engine houses, those crumbling ruins with their tall chimneys, that stare blankly out over moor and cliff.

Here, it seemed, was the answer to the problem of the deep mines, and one that fitted well with the Cornish taste for keeping as much work as possible in their own backyard. Apart from the cylinders, which had to be accurately cast – often by the well-known Darby Company of Coalbrookdale – everything could be done locally. The various parts were put together by blacksmiths and plumbers: the Newcomen engine was not a delicate machine. But there was a serious problem – the engines consumed vast amounts of coal. The science of the steam engine had not even begun to be formulated, and concepts such as latent heat had yet to appear. No one had realised just how inefficient it was to repeatedly heat and cool, heat and cool the giant cylinder.

This was not a problem in the coal fields where the Newcomen engine was first put to work, since coal was the one thing that was available in vast quantities. Cornwall did not enjoy this luxury. There is no coal in the far south-west, and the cheapest way to bring fuel to the mines was across the sea from South Wales, then overland along rough pack-horse trails. As a result, coal that cost around 4 shillings (20p) a load at the pithead cost the Cornish mine owners £1 in the mid-1770s. It was a cost that could be carried as long as the price of copper was high – a cost that had to be borne and passed on if deep mining was to continue at all. Paradoxically, it was the very lack of coal in the south-west that helped ease the burden.

The one aspect of copper mining that has not been touched on is the extraction of the metal from the ore. This is done by smelting, a process that requires a great deal of fuel for a small amount of ore, so it made good sense to send the ore to a smelter near a source of fuel rather than bring fuel to a local smelter. Early furnaces were set up in the Wye valley, then in Neath, but soon became increasingly concentrated in the area round Swansea. The ore ships, that would probably have returned in ballast, could now come back laden with coal to keep Mr Newcomen's giants nodding. It was a system that worked well for a time. The ore was sold at regular "ticketings", a weekly event in the biggest mines. The ore was set out, samples provided and the smelters' agents attached tickets naming the price they intended to pay. It was a form of blind auction, though suspicions of price rigging among the small group of smelters were almost certainly well-founded.

All seemed set for a prosperous future until, as far as Cornwall was concerned, disaster struck. Copper ore was discovered on Anglesey, not in small quantities, but a whole hill of it. Soon miners were swarming all over Parys Mountain, eating at the sides in huge open cast quarries, or burrowing deep into its heart. The ore was not as high a grade as that of Cornwall, but it was available in such vast quantities that that scarcely seemed to matter. And costs were so much lower. No need for very expensive drainage pumps, and even transport costs were low, for there was a splendid harbour at Amlwch, practically at the foot of the mountain. If Cornwall was to compete, then Cornish costs would have to come down, and the first likely candidate for cost cutting was the coal-guzzling Newcomen engine. Considerable improvements were made by one of the great engineers of the day, John Smeaton. Engine efficiency was measured in terms of "duty", the number of pounds of water that could be raised by one foot for the consumption of one bushel of coal – not a perfect measure, since not everyone agreed how much coal there was in a bushel. The best of the Newcomen engines had a duty of around 4 million, which Smeaton was able to raise to over 12 million. His efforts were largely concentrated on improving manufacturing techniques. One problem that we now have in discussing engine efficiency is that there is no way of working out how much of an improvement might be due to the engine and how much to increased boiler-efficiency. An efficient boiler will produce more steam for a given weight of coal, so that even if nothing at all is done to the engine itself, duty will rise. Smeaton built the biggest engines of the day, culminating in a 72-in. (183 cm) engine at Chacewater. It was all very impressive, but a limit had been reached set by the fundamental flaw in the Newcomen engine, and until something could be done about that, the problem of really efficient and cheap pumping could not be solved, and the competition from Anglesey could scarcely be faced.

This was a world where independence was valued, a world in which men were expected to think for themselves and to reach their own decisions. It was a world in which the Trevithick family held a respected place. Both Richard Trevithick Senior and his brother John were mine captains from an early age, and in 1760 Richard felt he had reached a position where he was able to approach the Teague family, equally highly-respected mine managers in Redruth, to seek permission to marry their daughter Anne. Not a great deal is known about the Teagues, other than that they had originally come to Cornwall from Ireland, but it is fair to assume they must have been a strapping lot. Richard and Anne were married that year and a year later the first daughter appeared, Elizabeth, to be followed over the next seven years by Anne, Prudence and Mary – all well above average height, almost touching the 6 ft mark. Meanwhile the father was making steady progress in the world. As a mine captain he was involved over the years with a number of concerns, and by the time he was thirty he was engineer and assay master at Cook's Kitchen, Stray Park and one of the mightiest of them all, Dolcoath. And his responsibilities did not end there, for he was also agent for one of the most important landowning families of the region, the Bassets of Tehidy. Their land contained some of the most profitable mines in the county, including Carn Brea, East Pool, South Crofty and, named after themselves, Basset mines. William Basset married an heiress and in 1796 became Lord de Dunstanville. This was the family who looked to Trevithick to take care of their interests.

It is difficult to place Trevithick in the social world of the eighteenth century, for there is no real equivalent. He was a man who had worked with his hands in the harsh and cruel environment of the mine, but as mine captain and agent he could sit down to dine with the lord of the manor with no sense of inferiority. It was part of the curiosity of the system that adventurers, captains, landowners and agents would all meet once a quarter at the count house to go through the mine accounts, an event considered a good deal less important than the dinner that ended the proceedings. Quite how much of the profits went on these junketings is simply not known. When one of the investors, new to the area, remarked to the mine accountant that he could find no reference to the costs of the feast, the latter took it as a compliment. The costs were all in there, but no one was expected to be able to find them. A correspondent writing in the *Cornish Telegraph* looked back with nostalgia on the count house dinners of the early nineteenth century.[7]

> You might years ago enter the "account house" of a mine at one of these meetings and find its kitchen like a fiery furnace, and redolent of savoury smells. And as the shareholders rode or walked up for the business of the day they would enter the cookery and critically survey the contents of a cauldron in which there would be a huge joint of beef, simmering in a broth of greasy water, with cabbage and every other available vegetable simmering around it. And as these visitors arrived the "count house woman" or cook would take basins and dip them into the savoury liquor and set them before her guests, who would thus take their preliminary and appetising whets.
>
> Then the meeting would open, a statement of cut and dried accounts would be read, some shareholders might probably grumble over the price of a pennyworth of nails, and pass over without comment the price charged for a steam-engine, but all would end happily in the usual way, and the real business commence in a splendid dinner, and its varied accompaniments of punch and grog.

Those who did business together in such circumstances were not likely to stand on ceremony, if they could stand at all, and there was a certain easy familiarity between these men who, in different circumstances, would never have met at all.

We know something of the working life of the elder Trevithick because a few of his old account books have survived, and they give more than a hint of the importance of what he was doing. Among the entries for Dolcoath at the time of his marriage are a number of large sums for a new deep adit. Between September 1765 and August 1766 costs of £316-12-6 are recorded but then they began to rise, reaching a monthly high point of £106-12-10, before falling away at the end of 1767 to little more than £20 a month, when one can assume the main work was completed. Names crop up in the accounts which are to recur throughout the Trevithick story. Arthur and John Woolf are shown on the payroll and a local blacksmith called Harvey is paid ten shillings for shovels: the Woolf family were to find fame as engine designers, while the Harveys were to become one of the greatest of all manufacturers of steam engines. Dolcoath and the surrounding mines were great breeding-grounds of talent.

Trevithick appears to have been a careful and methodical businessman, characteristics which he singularly failed to pass on to his son. The few anecdotes about his personal life, however, do suggest that, in some respects, father and son had similar temperaments. John Vivian, another of the names to appear regularly in the ledgers, described a dinner they had together in Bristol.[8]

> When dining at the inn the waiter remained in the room after the dinner had been placed on the table. Trevithick, not wanting him, said, "What are you doing here?" "Oh, sir! it is my business to wait upon you, sir!" "Well, but I do not want you here; peeping upon every bit I put in my mouth. Will you be off now?" "Oh no, sir, I am ordered to remain!" "You won't be off won't you? We'll soon see then!" and striding towards the waiter with an evident inclination to shake him, he drove him out.

Richard Trevithick Senior, then, was a man of considerable standing, recognised from an early age as an expert in all aspects of mining technology – and a man of decided views and unpredictable temper. He passed on these characteristics as well as his name, when the four daughters were followed by the first and only son, who was destined to make the name Richard Trevithick famous far beyond the boundaries of his native Cornwall.

CHAPTER TWO

The Captain's Son

Richard Trevithick was born in the parish of Illogan on 13 April 1771, in a house that lay between the village of Pool and the hill of Carn Brea. Had you visited the area at the time, you would have had two very different views to contemplate. Turn towards Carn Brea, and you would have seen a hill bearing evidence of a long history. Stone Age man came here to live, and Iron Age settlers surrounded their simple huts with the massive ramparts and ditches of a fortress. A thousand years later, the Normans arrived to build their own castle on the hill. All these remains, crumbling but still visible, were reminders of distant times, of warring tribes and knights in armour. Turn from the hill to the valley, and a very different scene appeared; engine houses, spoil heaps, whims, headstock gear – all the clutter, noise and dirt of a great mine. The young Richard was born half-way between romance and industry: not a bad metaphor for his life. A photograph survives, taken around 1870, showing a pleasant, thatched building with whitewashed walls, but sadly forlorn, all but overwhelmed by the mining landscape. It was always assumed that the house had long since gone, but recent research by the Trevithick Society has identified it as a house in Station Road, Pool.[1]

Shortly after the birth, the family moved three miles away to Penponds on the outskirts of Camborne. This house has been preserved, much as it was two centuries ago, and to modern eyes it seems a place of immense charm, stone built with thatched roof, a house of solid worth that owed nothing to fashions and everything to a long vernacular tradition. Once inside, however, it becomes clear that this was a family several rungs up the social ladder. The kitchen, to one side of the front door, is simple enough, plain but spacious. It is the parlour on the other side that proclaims superiority, with elegant wooden panelling covering the bare plaster. It is a comfortable family home, but home to a family of some consequence.

The first we hear of the child is a less than flattering report from the master of the little school at nearby Camborne, who described him as a "disobedient, slow, obstinate, spoiled boy, frequently absent, and very inattentive".[2] Some of the remarks are not too surprising. With four elder sisters to look after him, there is every chance that the little boy did come in for a good deal of spoiling, though that was probably reduced, even if it did not come to an end, with the arrival of the last of the children, Thomasina. The education in such schools consisted of little more than rote learning, limited to the three Rs, with work proceeding at the speed of the slowest. A bright child, and young Richard was certainly that, whatever the schoolmaster might have said, would soon have got bored. There is ample evidence from his later correspondence that reading and writing were thoroughly learned, though his spelling remained interestingly wayward throughout his life. It seems likely that it was often a direct representation of his own strong Cornish accent. He would have said a simple word like "they", for example, with a long, drawn-out "e", so he always wrote it simply as "the". He is likely to have received as much education at home as he did in the classroom. Arithmetic, however, is a very different matter. He seems to have developed his own way of doing things – a trend which certainly continued throughout his life. The teacher told him off because although he had got the right answer to the sums, he had used the wrong methods. Young Richard is said to have replied "I'll do six sums to your one", which might well have been true but it is not hard to see why his schoolmaster should consider him a particularly unpleasant and egotistical small boy. One has to take such stories with a pinch of salt, since they never seem to surface until after the subject has become famous. Henry Vivian, another mine captain whose family was to be heavily involved with the Trevithicks, recalled his own father working out engine duties, figures represented in millions, by multiplying a four-figure sum by a six-figure sum in his head – and always getting the right answer. Of Trevithick he wrote that he "was a man of still greater powers of mind, but would too often run wild from want of calculation". Perhaps his own methods were not quite so good as he thought. It seems likely that even as a small boy he realised the limitations of the local school and soon reached them. There was one other source of education, the chapel. His father was a regular worshiper at the Adjewhella Methodist Chapel at Penponds, where he was also a class leader at the Sunday School. There was not much chance of the young boy shirking his lessons when father was in charge. Equally, however, there is very little evidence that Methodism played any great part in his later life. There were, in any case, far more interesting things to learn and absorb outside the classroom door.

Information on the boy's early years may be scant, but we know that this was a time of immense importance to his father, and also a period of great excitement throughout the area. Today we look at the ruined engine houses of Cornwall as romantic remains speaking of a world long gone. It requires something of an act of imagination to comprehend what it meant to be in Cornwall when those gaunt buildings were home to a technology that was not only new but was the most impressive thing the people of the time had ever seen. Instead of mules or horses stumbling slowly round a circular track, a water wheel or even a hand-operated winch, a new monster appeared, soaring high above the surrounding houses, huffing, wheezing and puffing in its ponderous motion and with each nod of its giant head hauling tons of water from deep underground. It would fascinate any small boy, and what would be doubly exciting was the news that his own father was in charge of bringing one of these mighty machines to the region.

Trevithick's ledgers for 1775 give detailed costings for a Newcomen engine that was to be installed at Dolcoath. It is described as the "new engine", but in fact it was secondhand and had to be almost entirely rebuilt, and in the process many improvements were made. One of these was down to Trevithick Snr. The original boiler had been constructed with a flat top, weighed down with granite blocks. The joints were a source of weakness and leaks, and where coal was so expensive any steam escaping uselessly into the outer air was costing a good deal of money. Trevithick redesigned the boiler with a curved top, a shape better able to withstand pressure and greatly increasing its efficiency. The detailed accounts show what a complex affair it was installing the engine. It had been bought for £414-12-3, but the final cost by the time it was set to work came out at three times as much, £1348-14-5. The new boiler had to be built and pump-work had

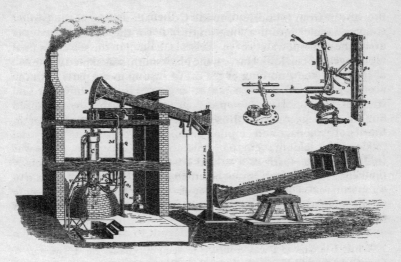

Fig 1: *Newcomen engine installed and improved by Richard Trevithick senior at Dolcoath in 1775. The inset diagram shows the working beam (qq) suspended from the main beam. It moves up and down through a hole in the floor, and pins in the central slit engage with a simple system of levers to operate the steam valves and condensing spray.*

to be supplied from outside the region. Iron pumps were sent from Jones of Bristol and from the famous Darby works at Coalbrookdale, who were then just in the process of finalising plans for what was to be the world's first iron bridge. The actual erection of the engine was entrusted to the most experienced steam engineer in Cornwall, John Budge. The setting of the boiler was the responsibility of the local blacksmith John Harvey, who, on this occasion, showed his versatility by also taking charge of the brick-laying and masonry. Arthur Woolf was the other leading figure consulted at the time. It would make a good story to be able to report that the little boy was taken along to see the building of the steam giant and developed a lifelong passion for steam as a result but, alas, all we have are the bare details laid out in account books. Steam engines, however, were, for many years, to dominate the lives of all the men whose names appear in connection with the Dolcoath engine.

One reason for the great expense of constructing an engine was the need to get all the cast iron work for pumps, cylinders and pipes brought in from foundries outside Cornwall, which, in the case of Coalbrookdale, meant a long journey down the Severn, a voyage down the difficult waters of the Bristol Channel to the sea and a final leg by pack-horse. John Harvey, the blacksmith, was skilled in the use of iron, but knew nothing of the art of casting metal parts with the accuracy demanded for a steam engine. He was, however, no stranger to foundries. A popular legend has it that he disguised himself as a beggar to steal the secrets from an iron works near Neath. Stories of espionage and cunning disguise have passed into industrial folklore, but seldom seem to be true: this is no exception. As he was well known at Neath as a valued customer, this tale is especially unlikely. He did certainly visit Neath in July 1776, bringing a cargo of scrap iron to be converted into wrought iron for his forge. It was quite a little adventure, as he explained in a letter to his wife.[3] He set off from Hayle.

> When I left hayle I was troubled to see you Greaveing. I saw you walking up and Down the beach but culd not Speake to me. About ten o'clock I had a little Quame which hould till two, at which time we almost lost Sight of Land with a fresh Gale & a very great Sea. I for amusement imployd my Self in catching of Mackrill. The Next Day we made the land, and at Night ankerd at Neath.

Perhaps the sight of the furnaces did inspire him for he soon began to plan a foundry of his own that would serve the local mines. He needed to import his raw materials and coal, so a site near an established port was essential, and Hayle, from which he set sail for Wales, seemed ideal. He was not the only one with his eye on that particular site. John Edwards was another young Cornishman who resented work being done outside the Duchy, and he was the leading force in establishing the Cornish Copper Company to smelt ore. Edwards looked across the estuary from his base at Copperhouse to Harvey in Hayle. They were not obvious rivals, but whoever controlled the harbour could control trade in all kinds of valuable commodities, especially coal, and, before long, quarrels developed, each of which led to more bitterness. For decades the two concerns fought, sometimes through the courts, sometimes by more violent means. Yet both prospered, and contacts between the Harveys and the Trevithicks were to grow and strengthen through the years. Both families had the same fierce patriotism and both of them saw themselves as committed to finding local solutions to local problems and local supplies for local demands. Into this tight, clenched little community a new force erupted in 1776 which was to mark the start of a new age in the history of mining and steam in Cornwall. The man who began it was a Scotsman and what he did and who he was forms one of the crucial elements in the Trevithick story.

Older popular histories, and some modern ones that should know better, often refer to James Watt as "the father of the steam engine". It should be clear by now that steam engines were at work even before he was born in 1736, but what he did do was move the steam engine onwards into its second age. He showed an early aptitude for mathematics, and apparently as a small boy he really did try experiments with a kettle, moving a plate around in front of the spout to check on condensation – so that old story at least has a foundation in truth. But his real introduction to the steam engine came in adult life when, as an instrument maker, he was asked to repair a working model of a Newcomen engine for a professor at Glasgow University. It was inefficient, and increasing the supply of steam simply stopped it altogether. It made an interesting puzzle, and Glasgow was the ideal place in which to find the key to its solution. James Black was an eminent chemist at the university, who had been doing a good deal of research into the nature of heat. His first major discovery was that heat and temperature were not simply different names for the same thing. He then took his experiments a step forward, and discovered that extra energy is needed when matter changes its state, the conversion of water into steam being a perfect example. In such a case, heat has to be added to effect the change, but there is no rise in temperature. He called this "latent heat". He first expounded his idea in 1763, and if practical engineers had been in the habit of attending science lectures they would have seen at once where the fundamental problem lay with the Newcomen engine. Because the steam was being condensed at each cycle, extra heat had to be applied which had no value in terms of the actual work of the machine. Watt claimed later that he did not know about Black's work – which seems a little strange, since it was considered one of the major scientific discoveries in the university where Watt himself was employed. There is, however, no doubt at all that it was Watt who understood the significance of latent heat in the working of the atmospheric engine – and it was Watt who made the great breakthrough. The story was told by Professor John Robison of Glasgow, who at that time was simply a student and friend of Watt. He wrote down his memories of those days in 1796, thirty years after the event.[4]

> At the breaking up of the College (I think in 1765) I went to the Country. About a fortnight after this I came to town, and went to have a Chat with Mr. Watt and to communicate to him some observations I had made on Desaguiliers and Belidore's Account of the Steam Engine. I came into Mr. Watt's parlour without Ceremony, and found him sitting before the fire, having lying on his knee a little Tin Cistern, which he was looking at, I entered into conversation on what we had been speaking of at last meeting, something about Steam. All the while Mr. Watt kept looking at the fire, and laid down the Cistern at the foot of his Chair – at last he looked at me and said briskly "You need not fash yourself any more about that Man, I have now made an Engine that shall not waste a particle of Steam. It shall all be boiling hot, aye and hot water injected if I please". So saying Mr. Watt looked with Complacency at the little thing at his foot.

The little thing was a model of the separate condenser, the device that was eventually to make his fortune. Watt had realised that the secret to greater efficiency lay in always keeping his steam cylinder at a high temperature. To do this he condensed the steam in a separate vessel that could always be kept cold. He then took the whole process a stage further, and closed off the top of the cylinder. He no longer relied on air-pressure to force the piston down, but used the vacuum beneath the piston, combined with steam at a pressure of around 10 pounds creating pressure from above, to make it move. And it did not end there. The Newcomen engine relied on the weight of the pump rods to drag the beam in the opposite direction to raise the piston ready for the cycle to start again. But with a closed cylinder, the steam could be admitted on either side so that the piston could be moved up and down entirely by steam. The change was no longer just that from atmospheric engine to steam engine, it was also a change from a device limited to pumping to a versatile power source. The implications were enormous.

Like many an inventor, Watt was to discover that the idea might be brilliant, but that did not ensure a rush of investors eager to advance the money to put it into practice. One trouble was that, as an instrument maker, he had no experience of working on a large scale – or in his own words: "The necessary experience in great was wanting". After a troublesome time which is not relevant to our story, he made the connection that was to ease his way to success; he was introduced to a successful Birmingham manufacturer, Matthew Boulton, who made no personal claims to any skill in engineering, but did understand how to produce for profit. He set out his views with brilliant clarity: it was the genius of Watt that had produced the new idea, but it was Boulton who knew how to make it a working reality. His letter to Watt in 1769 is worth quoting at some length, for what he had to say would echo and re-echo down the years, not least among the engineers of Cornwall.[5]

> I was excited by two motivs to offer you my assistance which were love of you and love of a money-getting ingenious project. I presum'd that your Engine would require mony, very accurate workmanship, and extensive correspondence, to make it turn out to the best advantage; and that the best means of keeping up the reputation, and doing the invention justice, would be to keep the executive part out of the hands of the multitude of empirical Engineers who from ignorance, want of experience; and want of necessary convenience, would be very liable to produce bad and inaccurate workmanship; all which deficiencies would affect the reputation of the invention. to remedy which and to produce the most profit, my idea was to settle a manufactory near to my own by the side of our Canal where I would erect all the conveniences necessary for the completion of Engines and from which Manufactory We would serve all the World with Engines of all sizes; by these means and your assistance we could engage and instruct some excellent workmen who (with more excellent tools than would be worth any mans while to procure for one single engine) could execute the invention 20 Per Cent cheaper than it would be otherwise executed, and with as great a difference of accuracy as there is between the Blacksmith and the mathematical instrument maker: it would not be worth my while to make for three Countys only, but I find it very well worth while to make for all the World. What led me to drop the hint I did to you was the possesing an idea that you wanted a midwife to ease you of your burthen, and to introduce your brat into the world.

The partnership of Boulton and Watt did indeed bring steam engines to the world, engines of great power and durability. And one reason for their success was that they were able to exercise precisely the sort of close control that Boulton had suggested in his letter. A patent protected the new ideas right through to the end of the eighteenth century, and effectively prevented anyone else either using the true steam engine or indeed developing it in new and possibly better ways. The partners also made it impossible for anyone to erect a Boulton and Watt engine anywhere without their permission and without the service of an engineer of whom they approved. This was all very different from the days when the Newcomen engine was being installed at mines around the country, where locals were allowed to make their own arrangements. In the long-term it was to lead to acrimonious arguments between the Birmingham manufacturers and Cornish engineers, a battle in which the Trevithicks were soon to become heavily involved. But first Boulton and Watt had to establish themselves in Cornwall.

Boulton and Watt did not, strictly speaking, build the engines that carried their name, but they did provide the more complex parts, notably the valve arrangements. Cylinders would, as before, be supplied by a specialist foundry and the simpler parts could again be made by a local smithy. The manufacturing profits would hardly have made the enterprise worth the trouble, but there was a second and far more important source of income – and, in time, of contention – the premium. Boulton and Watt were to be paid one third of the savings in fuel made by conversion from the old style of atmospheric engine to the new, separate condenser steam engine. On the face of it, this was a very good deal for everyone. The biggest cost that faced the mine-owners on a day to day basis was fuel, which in Cornwall was purchased dearly. They were promised a huge saving and were to keep two-thirds of it. That Boulton and Watt should keep a modest third seemed no more than a fair reward for genius and enterprise. Jumping ahead a little in the story to 1779, when the first of the new engines had already been built, an observer, a Mr Dalton, was despatched to Cornwall to report on the performance of the engine at Wheal Busy at Chacewater. This is what he found. The mine had previously been drained using two Newcomen engines, costing £5000 the pair. In a twenty-four-hour period they had consumed 6½ weys of coal at £2-11-6 a wey. The new engine cost £2500 and lifted the same amount of water as the two atmospheric engines together using just 2½ weys. Those were impressive figures and the adventurers were happy with their share of the savings, which worked out at well over £6 a day. As the engine was generally kept going continuously they were saving over £2000 a year on a £2500 investment, excellent figures in anyone's accounts. But, of course, nothing could happen in Cornwall until the first mine-owner took the plunge.

Boulton and Watt were well aware that Cornwall was potentially one of the most important areas for them to develop and they set about the often frustrating business of getting started. An obvious first step was to invite some of the leading engineers to their Soho works in Birmingham to see the new machine for themselves. They came, Trevithick Snr among them. They not only liked what they saw, but someone had the bright idea of taking home a souvenir in the form of a working drawing, no doubt with the idea of a little industrial piracy in mind. The culprit was never actually named, but Boulton wrote to a Redruth engineer, Thomas Innes, and left him in no doubt as to what he thought of it all.[6]

It came out that he had been prevailed upon by you to leave the Drawing at the Castle Inn in Birmingham under a promise that it should be returned when you come to Soho the next morning but we find you have take the Drawing with you ... We do not keep a school to teach Fire Engine making but profess the making of them our-selves. When you reflect on this matter you will readily perceive that there was an Impropriety in taking the drawing without our Knowledge & consent and as I am persuaded you would not deviate from the Character of a Gentleman I doubt not but you will return the drawing with every copy that hath been taken of it and which I hear have been exhibited in Cornwall.

That little matter settled, negotiations were opened with one of the leading engineers of the day, Jonathan Hornblower Snr, who was offered a special deal, that if the engine was not found to be satisfactory Boulton and Watt would take it back and refund all the money. Negotiations continued, and by the end of 1776 they got as far as ascertaining that a new engine could easily be installed in the old engine house at Ting Tang mine. But a problem arose that was to recur over the years: persuading or, failing that, forcing the Cornish to accept Boulton and Watt rules.[7] "I must once and for all beg that you would not take amiss my insisting upon your strict adherence to my plans & directions even though contrary to common practice." By January 1777 working drawings had been prepared and arrangements made for supplying the parts. But by 1 May they were writing to another engineer, Thomas Wilson,

offering a very similar "one off" deal, because so little progress was
being made with Hornblower. In the end, in spite of all the delays,
Ting Tang was to see the first small Boulton and Watt engine
installed in Cornwall.

What Boulton and Watt now needed was the support of the men
acknowledged as the leading engineers of the day who were
engaged with the most important mines, which meant in effect,
winning over John Budge and Richard Trevithick. It was John
Edwards of the Copperhouse works who first recommended
Budge.[8] "Though perhaps you may not find Mr Budge inclined to
talk very scientifically even on the subject of Engines, yet almost
one half of those in this County are under his Care, and were built
by his direction; He is esteemed one of the best practical Engineers
in it." Budge, however, did not perform as expected and expressed
doubts about the new machines, an attitude which infuriated Watt
in particular. Budge was polite but unmoved in his opinion.[9]

> I am sorry to hear that you are so much offended respecting my
> report of your Engine near Coventry – by every experiment & calcu-
> lation that I have made to prove the difference I have ... adjusted
> everything without prejudice as my small ability will admit of. I did
> not think that Mr Watt wod cast a reflection on a man when Oblige
> to give his sentiments.

Budge turned down the offer to construct an engine, at which
point Edwards promptly reversed his earlier judgement and
declared him "a simpleton". Trevithick, who knew Budge well and
respected his opinion, now proved equally reluctant to accept the
superiority of the new engines, so that he and his associates
became known to Boulton as "The Infidels of Dolcoath". Watt was
even more damning, writing of Trevithick Snr, after an acrimonious meeting at Wheal Union in 1779: "During this time I was so
confounded with the impudence, ignorance and overbearing
manner of the man that I could make no adequate defence, and
indeed could scarcely keep my temper". Watt was, in fact, notoriously bad at keeping his temper, and tended to regard even a hint
of criticism of his inventions as a personal insult.

Budge has been heard in his own defence: he reported as he
found. What of Trevithick? Nothing has survived which spells out
the grounds for his opposition, but apart from being influenced by
Budge, one can hazard a few guesses. He was by now a man of
considerable standing in Cornwall and had shown himself to be

adept at improving existing engines. It could not have been easy to accept that an outsider had something far better than he could offer, and the fact that the outsider wanted complete control would have made it even harder to bear. He was not going to be rushed into the unknown: he needed convincing. And, inevitably, in time he was convinced. The evidence simply could not be ignored: by 1780 Dolcoath had succumbed, and by 1783 not a single Newcomen engine was to be found at work in the whole of Cornwall. Boulton and Watt had triumphed. Not everyone, however, was prepared to accept the victory.

There were stirrings among the Cornish, who began to feel that whatever the Birmingham Company could do, they could probably do as well if not better for themselves. Jonathan Hornblower may have received a stern lecture about doing just what he was told and no more, but as early as 1778 he was experimenting on his own behalf, and he was not alone.[10]

> Jabez Hornblower is trying an Experiment at Wh. Maiden mine which he says will be a Considerable improvement in the Engine branch, in every way preferable to what has been shown in this County but what it is no other yet knows but the greatest part judges it to be the last shift. Mr Budge has been making no Experiments lately his Engine at Wh. Prosper is in the Common one – had its small cylinder fixed to the side of the other in order to Increase the power.

The idea of having two cylinders instead of one, a process known as "compounding" was something quite new, but the first crude attempt was not a success. A gratifying report of the first experiment reached Birmingham in March 1778 that the piston had only moved about 6 in. and seized. That did not mean that Boulton and Watt were prepared to sit back and let anyone try for other improvements. Boulton wrote in vehement terms to Watt, "No man shall use any of these principles in Fire Engines to our prejudice by God", and then went on to explain just how they could protect themselves at law by patenting every single thing they could think of.[11]

> Hence you see a sort of reason for our executing every Idea that may seem plausible to Strangers such as putting the Cylinder in the Boiler, such as applying a sinking pipe 35 feet long – Such as using second hand Steam, such as working the Condenser by the least

power possible and any other thing that may seem likely in order to shut the mouths of ignorant boasters ... I think all the possabilities of a good Steam Engine lye within a little compass & therfore we should execute all.

This all sounded very good to the Birmingham manufacturers, but what they were proposing amounted not just to the protection of an existing patent but was, in fact, an extension, intended to prohibit all steam engine development that did not emanate from Soho. This was a view that was never acceptable in Cornwall, and among the most enthusiastic challengers of the monopoly was to be the young Richard Trevithick whose school days were soon to come to an end.

The little we know about his early boyhood tells of his enthusiasm for wandering about the mine-workings and picking up the mine gossip. Even if he was not sure of the principles, let alone the subtleties, of steam engine design, he could not have been deaf to the sounds of argument nor unaware of the passions that had been roused. His own father was, after all, at the heart of the drama. All this excitement was happening at a time when he was ready to leave school, having long since absorbed all it had to teach him. The next phase of his education seems to have been conducted by himself on his own terms, learning what he could about the great engines by talking to those who built them and worked with them and getting as much practical experience as he could persuade practising engineers to give him. This was a path followed by many of the great engineers of the age, for whom formal education was not just unknown but unwanted. It gave him a good start and confirmed a belief that what he could learn for himself was infinitely more useful than what others thought they could, or should, teach him. It was an attitude which, for good and evil, was to stay with him all his life.

CHAPTER THREE

The Young Giant

Quite when young Trevithick left school is not known, though it was no doubt an event that was greeted with as much enthusiasm by the exasperated teacher as it was by the bored pupil. There is one brief account of that period, written by Richard Edmonds, who was said to have known him well.[1]

> With scarce any schooling, and with no books, he acquired such practical knowledge of steam-engines and mine-machinery that long before he attained his majority he was, to the utter astonishment of his father, appointed engineer to several mines. The father begged the mine-agents from whom the appointment had proceeded to reconsider what they had done, as he was sure his son could not, at so early an age, be qualified for so responsible an office. But having had sufficient proof to the contrary, they merely thanked him for his disinterested advice.

It has to be said that there are very good reasons for doubting the accuracy of this report. For a start, it was published in 1862, some eighty years after the event, so can hardly have been based on first-hand observation. Secondly, the Trevithicks were a mining family through and through, with widespread interests throughout western Cornwall. His uncle John was a mine captain of considerable reputation, whose own son, also John, was to work alongside his cousin. That this extended family, all totally committed to the world of mining, should be unaware of what young Dick was doing defies belief. And evidence has emerged that the boy was not only earning his living at a far younger age than had previously been supposed, but was doing so under family supervision.[2] Richard's name first appears in mine ledgers as working at Dolcoath in 1786, when he was fifteen years old and by 1790 he appears in the books of East Stray Park, during which time his monthly pay rose from £1-4-0 to £1-6-0. Looking at the East Stray Park books, one finds the whole Trevithick clan involved: John and Richard Snr as mine captains, with young John working there as well. At first sight it would appear that the boy was valued almost as highly as his well-respected father and uncle, since they were only receiving £2 a month each. But one has to remember that the older men held other appointments, and that the East Stray Park fees represented only a part of their income. Nevertheless, young Richard Trevithick was receiving what many would regard as a handsome salary for a lad of his age, somewhere between that of an ordinary miner and a specialist such as the engine man.

How much of his success was down to family influence? The answer must be that it certainly did nothing to hurt his chances, and the old story of his father trying to prevent mine owners employing him must be added to the long list of fables that tend to be tacked on to the lives of famous men. It is now clear that all his early mining experience took place under the close supervision of his father and uncle. But no amount of patronage would have helped him survive in the mining world of the 1780s if he had not possessed that natural ability and genius that was to shape his life. For these were desperate times when mine adventurers saw prices and profits tumbling, so that they were constantly on the look out for ways of cutting costs. Finding easy, well paid jobs for youngsters did not feature on their agenda, whoever their parents might be.

We do not have a detailed account of just how the boy was employed in the first years after leaving school, though it is safe to assume from the evidence of later years that he was given a thorough grounding in all aspects of mine engineering. We do, however, know that what was happening in the Cornish mines at the time was to have a profound effect on the way in which Trevithick's career was to develop, and in particular on his usually torrid relationship with those giants among steam engine manufacturers, Boulton and Watt.

The crisis in the mining industry was a direct result of the vast amount of cheap ore coming from Parys Mountain on Anglesey, as James Watt made clear in a letter to his Cornish agent in 1784, when he was looking at the possibility of investing in the mines.[3]

The greatest objection however is the extravagant rate at which the anglesea compy are getting ores, which on any demurr in sales must over stock the markets and infallibly lower the price of copper so much that nothing but loss can be got by it, which indeed makes one tremble for the business in general, but to do these gentlemen justice they are indefatigable in seeking out forreign markets, which will throw the backwater of sales on some of the foreign mines and probably stop some of them entirely – there were mines wrought in Switzerland in the time of the war which are now stopt.

In their desperation to cut costs in order to compete with the Welsh, the Cornish mine owners inevitably looked at the premium paid to Boulton and Watt. The euphoria they had felt at having a cheap and effective steam engine available was now no more than a memory. They had paid for their engines, they had been at work for some time, yet they were to go on paying, it seemed, for ever. Resentment grew, even though it had been clear from the start that the terms to which they had cheerfully agreed were designed to favour both parties. The manufacturers were rewarded for their enterprise, while the adventurers were only being asked to pay over a portion of the considerable savings resulting from the use of the engines. The adventurers were free to stop using the engines, but they knew very well that they were a great deal better off keeping them at work and paying the premium. The manufacturers were far from insensitive to the adventurers' problems, and indeed one of the ways in which they helped with finance in the difficult years was to take mine shares themselves. It was not in their interest to see mines close and engines stand idle. Although the Cornish engines only represented a part of their output, it was a substantial and valued part. They made this medical analogy: "The Physician has a right to take his fees from all his patients, but if he is wise and benevolent, he will take them from the rich that he may thereby be better enabled to be kind to the poor". They were prepared to help out mines in trouble by adjusting the premium payments, but that was not enough for everyone. John Vivian of Poldice indicated that he needed a new engine, but was not prepared to pay any premium for some time. The idea was not enthusiastically received at the Soho works, as was made clear to their Cornish agent, Thomas Wilson.[4]

JW wrote you last post informing you of the proposition made by Mr Vivian & others that unless the Lords of Poldice & ourselves would agree to give up entirely all manner of dues of premium arising from that mine, until it should have repaid £7000, which they say the new engines will cost, they would vote for stopping the mine entirely As they did not seem disposed to make the same demand in regard to the merchants profits we look upon the proposal as partial & unjust And even setting that consideration aside we cannot agree to the proposal without receiving a far greater injury than the stopping of the mine can do us, by setting a precedent for demand which must end in the annihilation of our income; & therefore as we must make a stand somewhere it is best that it be understood by every body that we will upon no occasion agree to pay for or contribute towards Engines or those repairs or costs of mines. But in this present case as Poldice mine has not been profitable nor is soon likely to be so, from the current expences of working the mine independant of any new erections, we will make them an abatement of part of our dues untill the mine shall have repaid the losses she has made from the 1st of May last.

It was not an unreasonable answer, but others were already writing, demanding better terms. Watt, always liable to be more irascible than his partner, was blunt:[5]

By our last letter to Mr Daniel we absolutely refused giving any Abatement beyond the 1/3 come what will. We have certainly showed a disposition favourable to the Mines even *beyond* our interest, but we neither can nor will be any more the only persons to make up their deficiencies.

The demands, however, continued unabated to the growing annoyance of the Birmingham partners.[6]

Mr H sais, he is out of Pocket £500 for his 1/11 share whilst we are carrying off large sums clear of Risk –
We are very sorry for the loss of the Adventurers, & would do every thing in our Power to assist, or prevent such Losses, except giving them the Profits of our Trade, and they may with as much propriety ask the Merchants, the Captains and all other Persons to give up their Profits as to ask us, to give up ours. –
Mr H sais, surely it was never the Design for B & W to be paid *out of the Pockets* of Gentlemen unless the Profits of the Mines whereon the Engines are erected are sufficient for that Purpose –
This we must say is a New Doctrine to us, & such as we never can subscribe to – If the Adventurers purchase from Swansey 4 Bushl. of coal they must pay for the same, whether the Mine is gaining or loosing, & if B & W save them 3 Bushl. surely they can better afford

to pay B & W, one, for saving 3, than pay the Coal Merchant for the whole 4: As to how much we are Gainers, it is impossible for Mr. H. to judge, because if we had not applied our Time, our Thoughts, & our Money in perfectioning Fire Engines we might by other applications of them perhaps have gained more money – the Lords take their dues, the Merchants take their Profits & the Captains & Workmen their Wages, whether the Mine gains or looses, then why should *we* (who are the sole Persons that have found the means of working the Mines cheaper than before) be deprived of our fair Profits –

You may Assure Mr. H. that we will on all occasions shew ourselves as Liberal towards the Mines, as any Lords, Merchants or Servants, belonging to them, but when we reflect that we have been urgently press'd to give up our Profits on Account of the poverty of some Mines (that you know of) which were at the same time gaining Profits; we must own that such like Circumstances have chill'd our Generosity, but we shall never suffer it to be absolutely froze in cases of real Necessity; however we reserve to ourselves the right of being sole Judge in these cases.

In spite of their exasperation, it is clear from this and other similar letters that Boulton and Watt were serious in their efforts to keep the mines open, but had a very justifiable suspicion that if they made too many concessions they could find themselves faced with a general onslaught on the whole question of payments.

As the recession deepened, there was indeed a general resentment against Boulton and Watt. The locals preferred, as so often happens, to put the blame for their problems on outside forces. There was nothing to be done about the Welsh mines, but the Birmingham representatives in Cornwall began to feel the full weight of local resentment. There were even fears of physical violence, and James Watt, though he expressed sympathy for the plight of the agent Wilson and his family, was still determined to yield nothing to threats.[7]

I am just now faced with yours of 14th and am very much alarmed at this fresh rising of the miners, who certainly are instigated by some enemy to the country & to you. I hope you will avoid going in their way again & to prevent surprizes that you will pack up your books & papers & send them to Truro or at least have them in a chest ready to put on a horses back. Indeed I wish you would remove yourself & family there until matters are quieted I hope no improper concessions will be made to them & that some body of authority will interpose in time, soldiers should be quartered at Truro & at Redruth.

A detached observer would have felt that Boulton and Watt had acted reasonably in dealing with the financial crisis by making the concessions that they did, while refusing to be browbeaten into giving away more than they could reasonably afford. This was not, however, by any means the only point at dispute between them and the Cornish. The all-embracing Watt patents had received little comment when they first appeared, probably because no one in Cornwall knew much about them at first, but now things were changing. One obvious way to avoid paying a premium to Birmingham was to design an engine of one's own, but it soon became apparent that it was all but impossible to build anything which did not fall foul of the patent – which was exactly what Boulton and Watt had intended from the first. Any attempt to build any type of engine, without paying royalties, was greeted with outraged cries of "Piracy!". In a county which tended to regard smuggling as a perfectly justifiable way of avoiding unwanted taxes, this was not always taken very seriously. But even among those who prided themselves on strict adherence to the law, there was a feeling that all was not fair in relation to the patents. This was especially true of those who had been working on steam engine experiments at much the same time as Watt, and foremost among these was Jonathan Hornblower of Penryn.

History has not been kind to Hornblower, largely, one suspects, because he was so widely and regularly condemned in the voluminous correspondence of Boulton and Watt, and because little has survived in the shape of letters putting the case for the defence. What is all but irrefutable is that Hornblower was the first to design a compound engine, in which the exhaust steam from the first cylinder, still under pressure, was fed on to work in a second cylinder. He did, in fact, take out a patent for that idea in 1781. This engine first came to the notice of Boulton and Watt when Hornblower and his partner, the Bristol iron founder John Winwood, built an engine at Radstock Colliery in Somerset. Observers were quickly dispatched to Radstock, who declared it a poor thing, little better than the old Newcomen engines. That did not prevent Watt from issuing strict warnings to the colliery owners, that "he came as a Gentleman to open their Eyes and

make them sensible of circumstances that shou'd not leave them in
ignorance of the Infringements upon his property".[8] To drive the
point home, Watt put out an advert listing all the features of steam
engines that were covered by his patent. There were six in all, two
of which were enough by themselves to prevent anyone making
improved designs of their own – closing the top of the cylinder and
using a separate condenser. He also threw in "double acting
engines", even though these were covered by Hornblower's own
patent. He gave serious consideration to taking Hornblower to
court, but decided that as long as his engine was not performing
well it was safest to let things lie – "One should not warn a man
that we mean to break his head, lest he put on a helmet". In Watt's
view the case was simple. Hornblower had made no real advances,
simply stuck a second cylinder alongside the first to avoid his
patent. It was a clear case of arrant piracy. Recently, however, a
letter has come to light, written in March 1789, putting
Hornblower's version of events. The interesting point about this
letter is that it was not arguing a case in public, but simply setting
out the facts as Hornblower saw them for the benefit of his uncle
Josiah Hornblower in America. It could have had no influence on
events and opinions in Britain.[9]

> The engine for which I obtain'd a patent of late years is not to be
> consider'd as an improvement on W's because I made a model of it
> 13 years ago, which was before I had ever heard of such a man. It's
> advantages I believe I have pointed out to you namely that of
> working with 16 lbs on the square inch [p.s.i.], which is absolutely
> the case with an engine I have now in my yard the small cylinder of
> which is 9 in. diamr. the large one 11 in. The mechanism is similar
> to Watt's in most respects.

He goes on to add that "We have hitherto had no success as the
copper trade is so low, and tin too as to entirely check the spirit of
mining." Had Watt seen this letter, he would certainly have found
it alarming reading, for it was a clear indication that as soon as
trade improved, Hornblower was going to be trying to break his
monopoly in Cornwall. And where Hornblower tried, others were
sure to follow. And that is precisely what he did and just what
happened. There is another interesting point in the letter, that
Hornblower was then working with steam at 16 p.s.i., which was
half as much again as Watt considered advisable. "Strong steam"
was the ogre that stalked James Watt in the shadows. So here we

have Hornblower preparing to fight Watt in Cornwall and moving, if only tentatively, towards the use of high-pressure steam. This was an idea that was seized upon by a young man who was to play a crucial part in the Trevithick story. He was born Davies Giddy, but was to be known for most of his life as Davies Gilbert.

Gilbert was born in 1767 at St Erth near Hayle. His father was a curate who dabbled in tin, but his mother came from an aristocratic background. As an undergraduate at Oxford he was heavily influenced by Thomas Beddoes, the University Reader in Chemistry and although in later life he was to settle into a comfortable routine as one of the land owning gentry, he never lost his interest in science. He was no mere dilettante. He was always eager to see how science could be applied to technology, especially in his native county. He advised Hornblower and encouraged him in his experiments, and tried to move him in ever more radical directions. Like Watt, he was familar with Black's work on latent heat and pointed out to Hornblower just what it could mean for steam engine development.[10]

> I am inclined to think it advantageous to work with steam considerably stronger than the Atmosphere and for these Reasons. Dr. Black and others have found that the same quantity of heat or Fire necessary to melt a given quantity of Ice will carry the Water up to 60 degrees of Fahrenheit's Thermometer. And the quantity of Heat or Fire necessary to convert one part of boiling water into steam will carry 405 parts of water up one degree. I believe the capacity of Steam for heat and the increase in its elasticity in consequence of its increase of temperature have not been sufficiently ascertained; but from the great quantity of Fire absorbed in converting water into Steam, it seems highly probable that a much less quantity of Fire or heat will be necessary to increase in any ratio the Elasticity of the steam already produced than to generate a proportional quantity of fresh steam, whilst the Friction is no more in a powerful stroke than a weak one.

Or to put it another way, it requires a good deal less heat to increase steam pressure than it does to convert water into steam in the first place. Hornblower was not prepared to follow the line suggested by Gilbert, but even so, he received enthusiastic support for his compound engines in Cornwall. Indeed anyone who looked to have found a way to smash the Birmingham monopoly would have had a warm reception. There was no shortage of mine owners ready to put the Hornblower compound to the test. In 1791 he installed his first Cornish compound at Tincroft mine, and it was rapidly followed by nine others. This was quite enough to provoke Watt into a typical outburst against not just Hornblower but the entire mining community of Cornwall.[11]

> On Thursday I rec'd a letter from Capt. Gundry, that the advrs had determined to build a 21 Inch cylr of Hornblowers construction that both Jethro & Jonathan was there, & that the advrs were unanimous for them This is the most mortifying circumstance, to have them to build on a place where we are so largely concerned; & where the rotative Engine is so well calculated for, & to have ones property, sported with, which I look upon to be the case merely to gratify the Caprice, hatred, or Malevolence, of a set of people who really know nothing of the merits, it is almost too much to bear.

Battle had commenced, and the younger generation of engineers was eager to enlist. Prominent among these was Richard Trevithick, who was to prove a good deal more enthusiastic about using high-pressure steam than Hornblower had ever been. Not only did he listen carefully to Gilbert's arguments, but over the years he was to make him his scientific mentor and teacher, the man he would turn to time and again when he needed to understand the theory behind any practical problem that troubled him. It is interesting to see how Trevithick, who in general went his own way regardless of accepted opinion, would always defer to Gilbert, a man only four years his senior.

These crisis years, when the Cornish grew ever more resentful of the influence of Boulton and Watt and what they saw as the dead weight of the patents that held down all prospects of development, form the background to Trevithick's youth and early manhood. He was seen as a young man of promise, but what most people who knew him recalled was neither his intellect nor his practical skills, but his immense size and strength.[12] Anecdotes abound of his feats, most famously in lifting the blacksmith's mandril, a cast-iron pipe weighing half a ton (500 kg). The story was described by Hugh Hunter, a foreman at Cook's Kitchen mine, and, according to him, the event always attracted a large crowd.

> He used to put a bar of iron inside the mandril and fasten another bar to it so that he could get a good hold. A strong stool was

placed on each side of the mandril, upon which he would stand with the mandril between his legs, and would lift it off the ground. He was an uncommon quick-spirited man and the strongest ever known.

His idea of a physical work-out was even more impressive and alarming: "Captain Dick would climb up the great shears, or triangles, fifty or sixty feet high, and, standing on the top of the three poles or shear-legs, would swing around a heavy sledge hammer". He was said to have picked up one of his fellow diners at a Dolcoath count house dinner, turned him upside down and stamped his boot prints on the ceiling, just for fun. Other party-pieces included writing his name on an overhead beam with a hundredweight (51 kg) weight hung off his thumbs, and hurling a sledge hammer over an engine house roof – hopefully, but not necessarily, checking to see if there was anyone standing around on the other side. His fame spread far beyond the mining community, and a member of the College of Surgeons came especially to measure his "strong frame" declaring that he had never seen such well-developed muscles. It was this remarkable physique that first brought him to the attention of Davies Gilbert: "about the year 1796 I remember hearing from Mr Jonathan Hornblower that a tall and strong young man had made his appearance among engineers, and that on more than one occasion he had threatened some people who contradicted him to fling them into the engine-shaft".[13]

This quick-tempered impetuosity was a side of his character that was to play a decisive role in determining the course of his life. In these early years, his immense strength and willingness to take on all comers, physically if necessary, did him no harm at all. No mine captain could succeed unless he had the respect of the men under him, and Trevithick earned that respect twice over, for his physical prowess every bit as much as for his engineering skills. Few captains were thought of with greater affection than Captain Dick, and his ability to form an easy relationship with his workforce remained with him throughout his life.

By 1792, the twenty-one-year-old engineer had worked at many of the region's mines and was considered sufficiently able to test and report on engines, including the Hornblower engine at Tincroft. He found it to be comparable in power to a Boulton and Watt of a similar size, a result which pleased neither party as each had been claiming vast superiority over the other. The occasion did, however, bring him to the attention of Davies Gilbert who was still heavily engaged with Hornblower and taking a keen interest in all the calculations regarding engine performance. Gilbert was sufficiently impressed by the work of Trevithick and another engineer, Morcom, to keep a copy of their report among his papers. It seems that Trevithick's enthusiasm for improving on existing engine designs had already been roused and the introduction to the scientific advocate of high-pressure steam whetted his appetite. But before that idea could be developed, he was to make the acquaintance of another innovator.

One of Trevithick's occupations was supervising the erection of new engines and this brought him into contact with another engine erector, Edward Bull. The latter had arrived in Cornwall from Bedworth Colliery near Coventry in 1781, and it is one of the ironies of the story that the man who was to give so much grief to Boulton and Watt should have worked as their erector for about ten years. But by 1791 he was declaring himself eager to erect engines in his own right, rather than as a mere employee. However, Watt caught a whiff of treachery in the air, and was by now convinced that Bull was no longer content to follow instructions to the letter as all his erectors were required to do, but had "improvements" in mind. Mr Watt did not approve of improvements other than his own, and the hint was quite enough for him to remove his approval from Mr Bull as well. He made his position perfectly clear in his instructions to Wilson.[14]

> In respect to Bull the less we have to do with him the better. If he applies to you on our terms & brings respectable persons as principals you will fix the premium with him & take his order for the size of the engine but we will not be directed how to make it.
>
> Had we agreed to let him make one of our Engines in such manner as he pleased, he would have made a bad thing & we should have had our share of the disgrace. As it now stands, his inventions must depend upon their own merit & unless he becomes more knowing than he has been hitherto, the merit will decide in our favour.

This was not to be the end of Bull as Watt must have hoped, but only the beginning of a campaign that was to culminate in a Bull-designed engine being set to work in Cornwall. And Bull had a young recruit more than ready to stand beside him to face the forces of Soho, Richard Trevithick.

CHAPTER FOUR

The Steam Wars

The skirmishes between Boulton and Watt and Cornish mining engineers and adventurers, that had begun in the 1780s, broke out into open warfare in the next decade. Leading the fight for the Cornish were Jonathan Hornblower and Edward Bull, and both had the support of the Trevithick family, with the father setting the example for the son. Watt noted sourly in the 1790s that Trevithick Snr had never really been won-over to Watt's engine and "even to this hour or at least very lately maintained that Newcomen's engines made by John Bouge [sic] were better." This seems unlikely, given that Trevithick had ordered Boulton and Watt engines for the mines where he had control, but it does suggest a continuing antagonism between the two men. The father was certainly not going to interfere when his son began to show defiance of the Birmingham men.

The first shots were fired when Hornblower applied to Parliament for an extension of the patent for his compound engine. Boulton and Watt promptly stepped in to oppose the application. The Hornblower camp argued that the extension was necessary because they had been unable to develop the idea fully, due to the time wasted in preparing for legal actions that never materialised: "Boulton and Watt held out threats of a Prosecution, and tired the Patience of the Public, with waiting to see them put into Execution".[1] Hornblower claimed originality for his ideas, and pointed out that he was not applying for a new patent, but simply an extension and, rather shrewdly, pointed out that "Mr. Watt's Grant for a Term of Thirty Years is an Example for him". The Boulton and Watt case was put with a good deal more vehemence.[2]

In 1781 Mr. Jonathan Hornblower obtained a Patent for a Fire Engine, alledged to be of his Invention. If there had been Merit and Novelty in that Engine, Messrs. Boulton and Watt would have readily acknowledged the Facts. – They were willing that Mr. Hornblower should bring his Engine to a fair Trial, and therefore have not hitherto interrupted him: But now, after *Eleven Years Trial*, Mr. Hornblower having erected only Two Engines, and those *upon the same Principles* as Mr. Watt's, in all essential Points; and attempting, as he is now doing, to procure the Sanction of the Legislature to his Proceedings, it becomes impossible for Messrs. Boulton and Watt longer to continue silent Spectators, or to permit an Imposition to be practised so injurious to their just Rights. They, therefore, undertake to prove, by competent Evidence, *that Mr. Hornblower's Engine is a direct and palpable* PLAGIARISM *of Mr. Watt's Invention.*

It is a curious argument that seems to say that Boulton and Watt were prepared to encourage Hornblower, until he became successful. Nevertheless, the application was rejected but, ominously for Boulton and Watt, all the Cornish members of Parliament voted against them, a sure sign of local sentiments. It was intended to follow up this result with injunctions against Hornblower to prevent him building any more engines, but as James Watt Jnr explained some years after the event, a more dangerous enemy was preparing to take the field.[3]

It was intended to have proceeded at Law against the Engines he had erected; but another person of the name of Edward Bull, who had also been employed by Boulton and Watt in the erection of their Engines, having in the meantime made other Steam Engines with the Cylinder inverted (which Mr. Watt had done before) and using the other Inventions of Mr. Watt, it was judged more expedient to proceed in the first instance against him, as his formed a cheaper and better Engine than Hornblowers and was spreading fast.

That Bull's engine was regarded as yet another example of steam piracy was inevitable, since that would have been true of virtually any new engine built by anyone at that time. But was the Bull engine no more than an attempt to bypass the patent or did it really work on a different principle? It certainly looked very different. For a start, it did away with the massive overhead beam. Instead the steam cylinder was inverted over the shaft and the piston rod was attached directly to the pit work, the rods and ancillary equipment in the shaft that activated the pumps. This had one immediate advantage. Anyone who has ever looked closely at a Cornish engine house will have noticed that one wall is shorter than the other three and considerably thicker. This was known as the bob wall and supported the massive beam which pivoted above it, so that one half was inside the house above the cylinder and the other half outside over the shaft. The engine house was not just something to keep off the rain, it was an integral part of the machine, providing it with a solid frame. As the Bull engine only had a light, small beam to activate the air pump and various connecting rods, this massive structure was not needed and the engine itself required a lot less expensive iron work. It did have one serious disadvantage. Most Cornish mines would have had two engines at the shaft: one for pumping, the other a winding engine for raising and lowering men and material. Once a Bull engine was in place, there was no space left for a winding engine. Did it infringe the Watt patent? There was no denying that it featured both a closed cylinder and a condenser, either of which was sufficient to condemn it in the Scotsman's eyes.

The first accounts reached Thomas Wilson, Boulton and Watt's leading man in Cornwall, in 1791 and the news was quickly passed on.[4] "We have heard that Bull has order'd his Engine, that he has agreed to build in Givindrow to be cast at Harveys & that it is to be an invented one but on what principles is still a secret." Watt at this stage was not really very concerned as he had a poor opinion of Bull's abilities. If he had known that what was proposed was an inverted engine he would have been even less worried, since this was an idea he had himself already considered and rejected. He wrote straight back to Wilson.[5] "In respect to Bull he must for the present take his swing, ten to one but he makes a very bad affair of it by dint of improvements, & I mistake if his employers will have any money." Just who those employers were is uncertain, but somebody must have been financing Bull, for he had no money of his own. He had only just been all but pleading with Boulton and Watt to let him erect their engines. The likeliest answer is that the Cornish adventurers were willing to finance almost anyone who seemed to have a chance of breaking the Birmingham monopoly.

Bull set to work with the enthusiastic support of almost everyone in Cornish mining, and among the young engineers who chose to march behind his banner was Richard Trevithick. Up to this time his reputation rested as much on his physical prowess as on his engineering achievements, and in siding openly with Bull he was taking a big risk, even if he was following a family tradition of backing Cornwall against the rest. If all went well, there was the chance of developing a range of Cornish engines for Cornish mines, which needed only to be comparable in performance to the Birmingham engines to appeal to local mine owners. If things went badly – and the Hornblower case was not an encouraging precedent – Trevithick could find himself expending a great deal of time and energy to no good purpose. Worse still, if Boulton and Watt chose to be vindictive, he could find himself effectively barred from working with any engine in any mines. Had it been anyone else, one could say that Trevithick was taking a calculated risk, but in his case he probably just took the risk without bothering too much about the calculation. Not for the last time in his life, it was the challenge of the new and unpredictable that appealed. For Bull it was a very different story. He was already out of favour with Boulton and Watt and so had little to lose.

Soho's early plan of sitting back and waiting for Bull to make a mess of things was soon abandoned when it became clear that, with Trevithick's very able help, he was doing nothing of the sort. The company sent out letters to all the adventurers pointing out that in their view the Bull engine was a piracy and that lawyers were gathering. This, they somewhat ingenuously claimed, was not a threat but a warning so that no one could later claim to be ignorant of the facts, a subtle distinction. The wait-and-see policy came under increasing strain as engines were built, proved successful and attracted new orders. Just when Trevithick became actively involved in their erection is uncertain, but he certainly made a detailed drawing of what is generally agreed to be the Dolcoath engine somewhere around 1792. He must at the very least have been a trusted confidante of Bull's to be allowed to do so, and as he was not a man much given to wasting time, it is more probable that he was actively involved rather than merely recording the design on paper. There was a certain amount of dithering in Soho about what should be done, while the company's representatives in Cornwall were under increasing pressure to cope with the unwanted competition. Thomas Wilson had already been joined by another engineer who was to achieve great things. His name only appears occasionally in the correspondence relating to Bull, but we shall be hearing a great deal more of him later. His name was William Murdoch.[6]* The group was completed by Simon Vivian, who worked under the supervision of the other two men.

By the end of 1792, the Bull group was loudly claiming that the new engines were better than Boulton and Watt's and were demanding comparative trials, which the Soho company refused to contemplate. They knew that if they agreed to any such thing they were acknowledging that the Bull engine was indeed different in some way from their own. That was a thing they could never do, if they planned to go to law. There is a, probably apocryphal, story that while giving evidence, Wilson, Boulton and Watt's agent in Cornwall, became exasperated with the claim that inversion made this a different machine. Putting his hat on the table, he asked what it was, and on receiving the answer, "a hat", he turned it upside down. "What is it now?" But this attitude did not go down well in Cornwall, where many believed that all questions of engineering merit should be settled by practical trials overseen by competent engineers, not by legal trials conducted by men in long wigs. Although Boulton and Watt were resolute in holding out against comparative trials, they were keenly aware of the resentment they had aroused. They were so concerned that, when the time came to try out one of their own new engines, they had to send Vivian in person to oversee the arrangements and seriously suggested that a guard should be mounted. The men in Soho were at least aware that their Cornish representatives were being put in a very uncomfortable position, and that they might even have put them into physical danger.[7] "I am really very sorry for you that you should meet with such mortifications in our cause but we cannot remedy them & the best is to be patient, perhaps you may have it in your power to piss upon *them* in your turn."

It turned into a dirty campaign, with anonymous letters and pamphlets attacking Boulton and Watt becoming all too common, and it could scarcely have surprised anyone that in 1793 the whole affair came to court. Watt was jubilant at the outcome, which resulted in Bull's engine being dubbed, as Watt put it, "a magnificent piracy". That was indeed the verdict, but there was a nasty sting in the tail in Lord Chief Justice Eyre's summary.[8]

But I think there is a question behind and that question is admitting it

* Murdoch's name was usually spelled "Murdock" in later years, but the older version is used here.

to be clear ... that there has been a pirating of that invention – admitting it to be clear too that there has been Letters patent yet it is the Language of the Law that these Letters patent can be of no avail unless there is a true Specification of that invention. I confess I have myself very great doubt whether this Specification is sufficient.

This left the way open for further attacks on the whole question of the validity of the Watt patents and yet more litigation. James Watt would have perhaps been advised to heed the words of his friend Dr Erasmus Darwin, who warned him against looking to the law to protect his patents.[9] "A lawsuit that pays well to the lawyers goes on like a snail creeping up a pole, which slips down again every 2 or 3 inches as he advances until he has beslimed the pole all over."

Losing the lawsuit deterred neither Bull nor Trevithick who continued to erect engines. There was nothing for it but to go to court again, this time to obtain injunctions against Bull to prevent his building any more, which, given the patent ruling, was pretty much a foregone conclusion. Bull asked if he might be allowed to finish the engines already begun at Ding Dong and Hallamannin, which was not just optimistic but really rather cheeky of him. The judge was not likely to agree to the completion of an illegal engine simply because it had been begun, any more than he would allow any other pirate to complete his piracy. There was great jubilation in Birmingham, but a warning was sent to Cornwall that no one should seem to be gloating. There was no need to antagonise the adventurers any further. But once again, the victory was not complete: the snail had slithered down the pole again.

Boulton and Watt had stopped Bull, but now the name of Trevithick had come back to plague them. Although they had their injunction, there was nothing to stop Trevithick quite legally carrying on where Bull had left off. At this stage, he was only known in Birmingham as Mr Trevithick Jnr, and Boulton and Watt were soon urgently sending to Cornwall to discover his Christian name, so that he too could be served with an injunction. And that, they must have thought, would settle matters once and for all. They had not allowed for Trevithick's character nor his somewhat fearsome reputation. They got their writ, but now they were faced with the problem of serving it on the man himself. It is at this stage that we get the first real account of Trevithick's involvement when he came to install an engine at Ding Dong mine.

If Trevithick and Bull were going to defy the law, then Ding Dong was as good a place to do so as any. The site is well away from the principal mining centres of Redruth and Camborne, set on a high, windy ridge overlooking St Michael's Mount. Surrounded by a wild moorland of bracken, brambles and gorse, it was difficult to reach except down the established mine tracks. The nearest village was some distance away, and the only buildings close at hand were the count house and a row of mine cottages. It was a place where strangers and unwelcome visitors would be instantly spotted and where the engineers could work undisturbed. It was going to take more than bits of paper to stop them. John Bolitho, whose father was at Ding Dong at the time, told Francis Trevithick just what happened when the two engineers got the mine engine work underway.[10]

> Boulton and Watt came down with an injunction printed out, and posted it up on the door of the engine-house, and upon the heaps of mine-stuff, and nobody dared to touch them. But Captain Trevithick did not care; he and Bull and William West came and turned the cylinder upside down, right over the pump rods in the shaft; they took off the cylinder top (it was the cylinder bottom before they turned it upside down).

The suggestion seems to be that they were looking for a new way of getting round the patent by using the steam expansively under the piston, and using air pressure and gravity combined for the down stroke once the steam was condensed: an ingenious idea, but scarcely more efficient than the old Newcomen engines. The same account also describes what seems to be Trevithick's first original contribution to the mining world, a "wind engine", and certainly the draughty moor would seem to be the ideal site, rather too good as it turned out. The mill raced along beautifully, but Trevithick had no idea how to slow it down, so he had to call in some sailors from the nearby port of Penzance to show him how to reef the canvas sails.

Trevithick had very little respect for bits of paper stuck on an engine house door, but that did not mean that he was happy at the thought that there were men at work in Cornwall who seemed determined to thwart his ambitions. He might claim that he was not concerned by the machinations of his opponents, but they obviously irritated him immensely, as Wilson was soon to discover.[11]

Trevithick fell furiously upon me, brought on the Affidavit business and his old calculations to prove your engines were little better than the common ones, gave me abuse very plentifully that I was an enemy to the county, had made a fortune in it, called me a fellow, and in short bespattered us all at a terrible rate, as I was in excellent spirits I defended myself well, and I believe had I impartial hearers should have done both you and myself some credit. This fellow Trevithick in return will certainly raise prejudice so strong against us as may perhaps make it dangerous to go West.

By 1795, Bull and Trevithick were inseparable as far as Birmingham was concerned and were considered as partners, though whether they were actually partners in any legal sense remained to be proved and, indeed, never was proved. This is perhaps not too surprising as Trevithick was not a great man for paperwork and documentation, and would have been quite happy working alongside Bull as an equal without entering into any formal agreement – a system which suited Bull perfectly well, but added to the frustrations of Boulton and Watt and their lawyers. They would have dearly loved to have been able to write him down as a partner, so that anything that could be proved against Bull could have been applied to him as well. Two years further on and they were still getting nowhere.[12]

I think the Affidavit of Simon Vivian will not be sufficient to prove the connection between Bull & Trevithick with sufficient certainty to intitle us to an *Attachment* against Bull *because* his Affidavit is *argumentative – & conjectural*, namely "that from the *circumstances* now in before stated the Deponent *apprehends & verily believes* that the said Rd. Trevithick was an agent or partner of or *in some other manner* connected with the said Edward Bull as an Engineer, and in constructing Steam Engines.

The biggest problem lay with trying to serve papers on Trevithick and his associate Stevens. The bailiffs soon found just how popular they were in the county when one of them arrived at a mine armed with an injunction. He was recognised by a group of miners who grabbed hold of him, tied a rope round his middle and suspended him over a shaft. The unhappy man, staring down into the blackness of what must have seemed a bottomless chasm was only too happy to agree to forget the whole thing and promise never to show his face near a Cornish mine again. The latter

promise was probably superfluous. James Watt Jnr suggested that
"some miner or other unsuspected person" might be talked into
doing the job, but no one volunteered. In the end the job of
keeping track of Trevithick and Bull and recording their activities,
would seem to have included a little industrial espionage.[13]

> I forgot to mention that both Bull & Trevithick were busily employed
> about the drawing of Poldice Engine – that he [Vivian] has found
> them so employed – *he does not say what the engine is* Mr. Watt showed
> me, when in Town a copy which Murdoch procured of the drawing of
> the Poldice Engine & said that these drawings appeared to be copied
> (with variations) from some engine of Mr. Watt's construction.

Poor Simon Vivian now bore the full brunt of Trevithick's anger,
and was threatened with having his head twisted off. Wilson was by
now used to this sort of talk and was fairly sanguine about it: "If
they should be as good as their word you will some way or other
make him amends, he is an excellent Smith, and would be service-
able at Soho, viz provided they leave him his head".[14] In the event,
Vivian did leave Cornwall with his family for a new home in
Birmingham, and the company were keen to use the threats against
him as part of their legal action, now that he was safely out of
harm's way. Not that James Watt, writing in comfort from Soho,
was inclined to take the threats that seriously in any case.[15]

> We think that Murdoch and all our friends should by no means avoid
> Bull & Trevithicks company. They *dare* do them no personal injury,
> and as to their insults, threats and abuse, they *may* become the
> subject of future affidavits. If anything has occurred or does occur so
> as to be useful upon the 29th. let Weston have it in a legal form.
> Are the threats & ill-language that has been used to yourself,
> Murdoch, Rogers, Mitchell and our other friends such, as if made
> matter for one or more affidavits, would go to prove the existence of
> the combination against us? – Do they amount to putting your
> person's in danger and are means employed to render you obnoxious
> to the County for having told the truth? If so give it them in
> Chancery; that at least will stop their mouths in future.

Although the parties fulminated against each other, uttering
blood curdling threats, it all looks a good deal more like public
posturing than actual incitement to violence. For their part,
Trevithick and Bull seem to have considered themselves more or

less invulnerable, if not actually invisible, and were sufficiently self assured to take themselves off to Birmingham en route to the Coalbrookdale iron works, to see what the opposition was up to. The opposition, for their part, could hardly believe their luck. Trevithick was, it seems, very annoyed at being recognised so far from home, but then how many Cornish giants were there likely to be taking an interest in steam engine manufacture in Birmingham? It was a double humiliation, for the bailiffs found the pair in a pub on the very day when there was a fireworks dispay at Soho to celebrate yet another legal victory over Hornblower. The two men, duly served with their writs, went off to dinner.[16]

> Bull took his dinner quietly, but Trevithick walked backwards and forwards in the house like a madman, and firmly resisted all temptation to dinner, until the smell of a hot pie overcame him – on which he set to, and did pretty handsomely but in such a manner as showed him not quite in mind. The rejoicing that was going forward at the very door, exhibited by fires and gunpowder work not a little contributed to his *happiness* while he stayed which was for a very short time indeed.

It must by now have been clear to Trevithick that the legal battle was lost, and that nothing more could be done with Bull's engine unless they were prepared to pay a premium to Boulton and Watt or wait for the end of the century when the patents expired and steam engine development would be open to all. There had already been strong hints in 1795 that he was tired of the struggle. A rumour was circulated that he was heading off to the East Indies to seek his fortune, an idea which Watt dismissed as no more than a ruse to get the bailiffs called off, but would not have been out of character for the impetuous young man. Nothing came of that, but in the middle of all the rancour and mud slinging, he actually applied for a job erecting engines under the auspices of Boulton and Watt. That must have come as something of a shock, and the proposal was certainly not greeted with any enthusiasm at Soho. They might, just possibly might have been prepared to enter into an agreement, but only if "he first makes his peace by a full and fair confession" of his old misdeeds and piracy. This did not seem very likely to occur, but in the summer of 1796 a most extraordinary letter arrived at Soho from a highly respectable mine captain, Thomas Gundry.[17]

> I have taken the liberty to trouble you with this by desire of Richd. Trevithick Jr. who have been for some time past employed by Edwd Bull in mechanism. He desires not to continue in opposition to you, and is ready to give up everything in this county and be under your direction. If you should employ him, you will certainly find him possessed of good abilitys in mechanics, natural as well as acquired, and is of an honest and peaceable disposition. He would be glad to serve you either in Cornwall or Soho. *The latter place in particular*. If this step is taken I think the opposition in Cornwall would to a great measure subside.

This was waving the peace flag indeed, though the recommendation of his peaceful disposition must have raised a few eyebrows. Watt replied that he would consider taking him on for a term of not less than three years at the maximum wage of a guinea a week. Watt was about as likely to welcome Trevithick into the fold as Trevithick was to sign on for a three-year engagement at a guinea a week. He would never go to Soho on such terms, and he would never work for Boulton and Watt in Cornwall under any terms at all. He could hardly expect a rousing welcome from the men he had been so roundly abusing for years. Wilson was able to get Murdoch's view of the matter first-hand in the September.[18]

> I found that his motives of wishing you to engage with Trevithick was an idea that it would take off his fathers rancour, and of course lessen the opposition against you in the Western part of the County, but that he had no thoughts of having any connection with him, as an assistant or otherways in this County.

Trevithick never even bothered to reply to Watt's offer, and so the whole charade came to an end. It was altogether a most curious affair, and the only rational explanation is that it really was just an elaborate game. Neither Trevithick, on the one hand, nor Boulton and Watt on the other, was ever going to admit to being in the wrong, but both must have been aware that the conflict was doing neither of them any good. The longer Boulton and Watt attacked the Cornish engineers, the more opinion in the county hardened against them. It cost a great deal of money, which would have been better spent on engineering development than on lawyers' fees. It would also have been far better to win opinion over, but the elder Trevithick who was still held in the highest esteem stood firmly against them. His long-standing antipathy was not likely to be eradicated as long as his son was being pursued all over Cornwall by bailiffs waving writs and injunctions. Young Trevithick also learned a lot from the experience. He had discovered just how open the field of invention and discovery really was, while at the same time it must have been clear to him by 1796 that the Bull engine was not the machine to topple the Watt engine from its dominant position. It was having a limited success, but, as time went by, flaws in the design were starting to appear: it was proving a good deal less sturdy and durable than the older beam engines. An ambitious young man did not want to spend his life tied to an invention that was not really capable of further development. He needed a way out, and it seems that he was sending signals to say that although he was not actually planning a surrender, he would welcome an honourable truce. He would pretend he wanted a job with Boulton and Watt and they would pretend to offer him one. His life was changing. It was time to move on.

CHAPTER FIVE

Strong Steam

The year 1796 may have seemed to be following the pattern set in the previous few years, but in fact it was to mark a significant turning-point in Trevithick's life. Relations between himself and Boulton and Watt see-sawed wildly. In part this was due to a change of personnel in Birmingham with the founders easing themselves out to make way for the next generation. James Watt Jnr was to prove an even more prickly character then his father.

Trevithick for his part was no longer in open rebellion but was agreeing to make premium payments on the engines he worked on, though he showed little enthusiasm for either paying in full or paying on a regular basis. At the same time, the suspicion lingered at Soho that he had not yet abandoned the trade of steam piracy. He was certainly not about to try too hard at this stage to ingratiate himself into the favours of Boulton and Watt. He had appeared as a witness in favour of Hornblower in the long-running case, which set him firmly in the Cornwall versus the rest camp, but it was an action that was to prove of immense benefit in the long term, for it was here that he first met Davies Gilbert. They were not obvious soul-mates: the engineer who had left school with little more than the three Rs, whose life was to be devoted to the world of mines and engineering, and the donnish former curate, who was to go on to hold the most prestigious scientific office in Britain, the Presidency of the Royal Society. Yet they seem to have taken to each other instantly, perhaps each recognising a shared delight in discovery and innovation. The relationship was not really one between equals and this had nothing to do with social status. Gilbert could not expect anything from Trevithick in the way of help in his own special fields of interest, and certainly not in advancing his career, whereas Trevithick had found a man who supplied something he would need very much over the years and which he totally lacked himself, scientific knowledge and expertise. Gilbert's advice was to prove its worth in the development of Trevithick's inventive genius. But the inventive phase of his life still lay a little way ahead: for the time being, the stormy relationship with Boulton and Watt remained the major preoccupation.

Anyone reading the Boulton and Watt correspondence covering this period could reasonably assume that there was a deep personal enmity between themselves and the Cornish engineers. This was obviously true of their professional relationships, but it does not necessarily follow that it had to extend to their personal lives. Even so, it still comes as a bit of a surprise to find that when James Watt Snr visited Camborne in the September of that year and dined with Murdoch, it was Trevithick who sat down at table with them. This was during one of the periods when it seemed that things were going well between the parties, but the warmth was short-lived and by early 1797 the icy blasts were blowing again. The news that Trevithick was planning to build an engine at United Mines was enough to set James Watt Jnr off on one of his tirades, in a letter that begins calmly enough, but where you can almost feel his blood pressure rising as it progresses.[1]

We have not felt one moment's hesitation as to the propriety of totally rejecting every idea of connecting ourselves with Trevithick and of withholding our consent for the erection of our Engines by him or anyone else upon the United Mines until all the Arrears are liquidated and we are assured that they will continue to pay in future. You will therefore send for Trevithick and inform him VERBALLY that his proposal is totally inadmissible and that no consideration of present emolument, were it ever so well secured, would induce us to permit *any* of our principles to be applied until we have received compleat indemnification for the past and security for the future. ...This is all you have to say from us to Trevithick. This repentance for past offences comes too late and his promises of future good conduct meet here with little credit. If his own conscience is insufficient to induce him to act with common honesty, we shall not bribe him so to do – Let him therefore take his swing.

The tone sounds harsh enough, but it was about to get harder.[2]

You will see by our last that we were fully aware of the sinister
Intentions of Trevithick; but whether his intentions be good or bad,
we have laid down for ourselves a line of conduct which cannot be
influenced by the behaviour of so paltry a rascal.

But if it seemed that the last thing in the world that they would
countenance was Trevithick building any engine anywhere at all, it
needed no more to mollify Watt than a suggestion that what was
actually being proposed was the erection of a Boulton and Watt
engine with all premiums to be paid in full. Watt, however,
remained suspicious.[3]

After the repeated proofs he had given of an inimical disposition
towards us, we must naturally receive with caution and distrust any
proposition coming from him unless seconded by persons of known
respectability and that until we are convinced of the sincerity of his
intentions, it would be absurd in us to enter into any negociation.
You may add that upon a satisfactory letter being written to us by
himself upon the subject, seconded by one from his father, offering
security for him, his application would probably meet with attention
from us. You may add that a letter from Mr. Kevill or any other of
our Cornish friends in his favour would have considerable influence
upon our determination.

His father penned his own simple note at the end of this rather
long-winded letter, which said all that was needed on the subject
without the verbiage: "If T. means fairly he should be fairly dealt
with, but you must be cautious what you say to him."

The two sides never could quite reach agreement: for every time
a real rapprochement appeared likely, there was a reverse as
Trevithick tried to pursue his own inclinations, while Boulton and
Watt did their best to keep tight control over everything that
happened in Cornwall. There may have been antagonism, but
there was also a grudging respect between the two sides – there was
even a hint that if Murdoch ever decided that he had had his fill of
the Cornish wars, Trevithick might be the man to take his place.
Equally, however, Boulton and Watt were not about to prejudice
their relationship with the highly competent and staunchly loyal
Murdoch by being seen to give any undue favours to Trevithick.
One new factor in the equation was a firm affirmation that, whatever had been in the past and whatever rumour might say in the
present, he was definitely not a partner of Edward Bull's. The

news was passed to Birmingham by one of the most respected businesses in the area, the Fox family of the Perran Foundry, among the most important engine builders in Cornwall.[4]

> A report having been circulated hereaway (and probably may have reached you) that Edwd Bull is a partner with Rd Trevithick in one or more steam engines that he is about to erect by your permission, we have had some conversation with R.T. on the subject who seems to be much hurt by a report which he asserts to be invidious and totally void of foundation – this we are disposed to believe.

Up to this point, everything we have heard about the disputes, quarrels and attitudes of the two parties has come from the Boulton and Watt correspondence, and nothing in Trevithick's own words. If anything from the early period had survived, we might expect it to be as fiery as the letters from James Watt Jnr. But when we do finally hear from the man himself, the letter is sober and businesslike, polite without being ingratiating and firm without being hectoring.[5]

> I Received your Letter last night stateing Mr. Boultons & Watts demand on my Engines, as to ding dong Engine saveings I have no objection to pay according to your Statement of £800 for a 63 Inch Cylinder. Ding Dong is 28 Inches which I believe gives a sum of abt £150 which sum I wo'd be bound to pay in monthly payment sho'd the Engine Continue to work Single which I believe will be but a very short time as every prepareation is already made for the purpose of working double. Now if its agreeable I will pay you the monthly sum above stated untill the Engine is turnd double which I expect will be in the coarse of two or three month and then enter in to bonds for the remainder of the time for double the saveings above stated –
>
> The terms for St Agniss engine I think is somewhat hard as there is a certainty that engine cannot be ready to work before the end of six or eight months and probably unseen obstacles may arise that may prevent her working much longer as the Resolutions of St Agniss Mines is not much to be depended on which wo'd be a great Hardship on my side sho'd it so happen. I have by no means any objection against agreeing after the same rate for that as I have for ding dong from the time she shall be set at work which I think is the properest time to agree.

It all sounds very sober and respectable. What had happened to the rebellious young firebrand who was all for throwing bailiffs down mines and tearing the heads off opponents? The young

Trevithick may have been impetuous but he was not a fool, and by 1796 he must have seen that, in the war with Boulton and Watt, the latter had all the big guns on their side. The following year was to see two major changes in his life. During his time with Bull he had a great deal to do with Harvey's of Hayle, who supplied most of the iron work and castings for the engines. The man he dealt with at the foundry was to become a close friend. William West's background was not unlike that of the elder Harvey, who had founded the firm. He had his own smithy at Helston, but was no ordinary blacksmith, having a considerable reputation as a clock-maker. He also had a considerable interest in the local mines, which was where his and Trevithick's paths first crossed. In 1784 West married Joanna Harvey and abandoned his own business to play a key role in the works at Hayle. Trevithick was a frequent visitor, when he could combine business with the pleasure of spending time with the Wests. This brought young Trevithick into the Harvey circle and more particularly introduced him to Joanna's younger sister Jane. There is no way of knowing when acquaintance with Jane turned to friendship, and then something stronger, and in any case the young man could do little about it. The Harveys were by now very important figures in the community, while the young engineer was still struggling to make a reputation for something other than an ability to get into fights and litigation. The Harveys were unlikely to look favourably on him as a suitor.

John Harvey was, in fact, a man who held very stern views on the subject of what was proper in a marriage. Jane's elder brother Henry has often been held up in contrast to Richard Trevithick. Where the one was considered a wildly unreliable character, the other was a pillar of the community, a sound businessman of impeccable respectability. But the young Henry also fell in love, with a housemaid, Grace Tonking. His father refused to give permission for the marriage to go ahead, so Henry set the girl up in a house on Foundry Hill, in Hayle. Over the years, the couple were to have five children, all of whom were acknowledged by Henry and given the name Harvey Tonking. When the old man died, the couple were at last free to marry, but by then the relationship was so well established and so widely known, that there no longer seemed any point. Henry Harvey may not have been the wholly conventional man he has always been painted, but he was certainly no hypocrite either.

Then, on 1 August 1797, Trevithick's father died, a man described by Gilbert as "the best informed and most skilful Captain in all the Western Mines". At his death, the adventurers turned to the son to carry on his work. Suddenly, the whole situation had changed. At twenty-six years of age, Richard Trevithick was no longer a quarrelsome young man of promise: he had been recognised as a leading engineer in his own right. He had acquired prestige and, just as importantly, a greatly increased income. Now he was able to propose to Jane Harvey and be accepted by her and the family. They did not wait long: the ceremony took place on 7 November the same year in the parish church of St Erth, a mile from Hayle.

Jane is described as being tall, fair skinned and brown haired and when she stood beside her 6 ft 2 in.-tall husband they must have made a striking couple. Neither was conventionally good-looking, and the portrait of Jane in middle age was certainly not painted to flatter. But the face that looks out is full of intelligence and character, and she would have need to draw on both over the turbulent years of her married life. It is a strong face, and she was to live long enough to survive into the age of photography and to be pictured with her sons. She was then in her nineties, but she still seems to be regarding the world with calm resolution. There is no detailed description of Jane at this time, but a friend, Richard Edmonds, described Trevithick in a very glowing reference.[6]

> He was unassuming, gentle, and pleasing in his manners; his conversation was interesting, instructive, and agreeable, and he possessed great facility in expressing himself clearly on all subjects ... His dress was plain and neat, and his general appearance such that a stranger passing him in the street would have taken him for some distinguished person.

Their first home was at Moreton House, Redruth, but they stayed there only nine months before moving to Camborne. The move would have given the young wife some inkling of what life with Richard might entail. Domestic affairs were always going to take second place to the much more interesting and exciting world of work. On leaving Redruth, he popped the house keys into an old coat pocket and at once forgot about them. Until he handed them over he was still technically a tenant, so he found himself paying a full year's rent and rates for a house he was no longer living in. The move reflected two changes in their lives. He had inherited his

father's work-load, which was largely based in Camborne, and she
was soon to give birth to their first child. Four of their six children
were to be born in Camborne: Richard in 1798, Anne in 1800,
Elizabeth in 1802 and, with a nod to the other half of the family,
John Harvey Trevithick in 1806. There is all too little known about
their home life, but from everything we hear it is clear that Jane
was a devoted and conscientious wife and mother who, as far as
she could, maintained stability and order in the home, even when
those commodities were notably absent in the life of her wayward
genius of a husband. He was one of those men who pursue their
dreams, devoting all their time and energy to some distant, grand
objective, blissfully unconcerned about their personal and material
surroundings. This can seem wholly admirable to an outside
observer and without such an attitude Trevithick would never have
made the great advances in engineering and technology that he
did. It must, however, often have been very irritating and at times
deeply distressing to the family who might share his enthusiasm
but not his indifference to poverty and such mundane matters as
paying the rent. Francis Trevithick, the fifth of the sons, born in
1812, put Jane's side of the story when writing the life of his father.

> Her husband was good-tempered, and never gave trouble in home
> affairs, satisfied with the most simple bed and board, and always
> busy with practical designs and experiments from early morning
> until bed-time. He sometimes gossipped with his family on the
> immense advantages to spring from his high-pressure engines, and
> the riches and honour that would be heaped on him and his chil-
> dren, but thought little or nothing of his wife's intimation that she
> hardly had the means of providing the daily necessaries of life.

Troublesome as it must have been, Jane Trevithick continued to
provide her husband with a secure, comfortable home background,
which spared him domestic worries, and left him free to let his
mind roam over a whole range of topics. It was now that his inventive genius began to blossom.

His first initiative did not involve a new invention, but represented a new adaptation of an old device. This time it was not a
change in the steam engines, but in the pumps that they operated.
The system generally in use involved bucket pumps working, in
effect, by sucking up water, which meant that the power for
pumping was supplied by lifting the rods in the shaft. Trevithick
turned to an invention that had first appeared in Britain a century

earlier, the plunger pump. He refined it and turned it into a very efficient machine and one perfectly adapted for use with the steam engine. In his version, the descending plunger pole forced water up through an H-piece into the pump column. Water was raised in a series of lifts, typically of around 30 fathoms each. This time the working stroke of the plunger came from gravity, while the steam engine was used to raise the plunger ready for the next stroke.

Trevithick's surviving accounts – not surprisingly less detailed, less ordered and less complete than his father's – contain an entry for 1797–8: "fixing a 7-inch pole-case with new lifts and wood wind-bore at Ding Dong". During that time he stayed at Madron, a couple of miles away from the mine, and those times were recalled for Francis Trevithick by a Mrs Dennis.[7]

> Her parents lived at Madron, near these mines and for two or three years Mr Trevithick came frequently to superintend the mine-work, staying at their house a few days or a week at a time. He was a great favourite, full of fun and good-humour, and a good story-teller. She had to be up at four in the morning to get Mr Trevithick's breakfast ready, and he never came to the house again until dark. In the middle of the day a person came from the mines to fetch his dinner; he was never particular what it was. Sometimes, when we were all sitting together talking, he would jump up, and before anyone had time to say a word, he was right away to the mine.

Jane Trevithick would most certainly have recognised this pattern of behaviour.

The plunger pump was a success and was widely adopted, though there was no financial benefit to Trevithick, other than for work he carried out himself. It did, however, lead him to think about variations on the theme. If a plunger could lift a column of water, then it naturally followed that a column of water could lift a piston. So, provided you had a good head of water, it would be possible to reverse the processes of the plunger pump to create a prime-mover, a water-pressure engine. Although this was not a new idea, it had scarcely been developed and it is unlikely that anything of the sort existed in Cornwall. As Trevithick got his ideas from practical experiment rather than from books and theory, it is likely that he in effect reinvented it. It was, after all, a logical extension from his own work. His first engine was built at Roskear, where there was a reliable source of water from a tributary of the Red River. The pole and its cylinder worked in very much the same way as a piston and cylinder in a single-acting steam engine. Water under pressure was admitted to the cylinder to raise the pole, then as the water was released the pole dropped under its own weight. This was the simplest form of the engine, but he was soon trying out a more sophisticated system at Wheal Druid.

In the new engine, water to the piston was controlled through two balanced piston valves, which allowed a reciprocal motion. To prevent jarring shocks to the engine, the valve pistons were made slightly smaller than the water passages, so that there was always a cushioning effect. Valve movement was controlled by an oscillating bob moving a sprocket wheel, over which chains passed to the linked pistons. The arrangement can clearly be seen in the diagram of his 1799 engine from an old encyclopedia. The water engine never found much use in Cornwall, partly because of a lack of suitable water sources, but it did get taken up in other parts of Britain. Perhaps the best known of the water-pressure engines was built for the Alport lead mines in Derbyshire, where it did sterling work for very many years. But while Trevithick was prepared to spend any amount of time perfecting his machine, he was not prepared to give the same amount of attention to getting paid for his work. It was a story that was to be repeated time and again, and rather too often for it always to have been the fault of the other party. Trevithick himself certainly did not see it that way as he told the whole sorry story to Davies Gilbert, while denouncing the Derbyshire owners as fools and scoundrels:[8]

the are the most ungreatfull clowns in the world. I have been 4 times at Derbyshire and sent them two men and once at Coalbrookdale for them, and paid my own expence and the mens. I sent them abt £60. I have been out for two years and before I cud get them to pay mee one farthen expence I was forced to threaten law, their excuse was that if the engine continued to work well a sufficient time to their satisfaction that then the wod pay my expences but as I had business in every part of England that the didnt expect that I shood ask any expences from them. I have traveled near two thousand miles on their account and been more than two months at the Drawings and engine at Different Times which I shall never receive one shilling for, if the find fault with the engine their wod be some reason for not paying, but the say its the best in the world.

He never got the reward he expected from the water-pressure engines, but he did have the satisfaction of seeing the plunger pumps win general acceptance throughout the mining districts of

Cornwall. It was very satisfactory proof that he could design and build machines that would work well and be put into service. It was time to move on to bolder schemes.

The end of the 1790s would also mark the end of the Boulton and Watt patent, and once that happened the way would be open for engineers to start building whatever engines they chose without having to face a costly legal battle they would almost certainly lose. Many men were preparing for that day. Boulton and Watt themselves were making plans to withdraw from the area that had given them so much trouble, selling their shares in the mines and calling their agents back to Birmingham. Richard Trevithick was also making plans and thinking of setting up experiments. One unfortunate result of the patent had been that anything that was being developed in the steam world had to conform to Watt's ideas, and that meant engines working at low pressure with separate condensers. If more power was needed, the answer was simple – all you had to do was build a bigger engine, and Boulton and Watt were to build some monsters over the years, culminating in a pumping engine at Herland in 1792 with a 64-in. (163 cm) diameter cylinder and a 9 ft (274 cm) stroke. Once Boulton and Watt had gone, however, Harveys built even bigger engines, and one can still marvel at the massive 90-in. (229 cm) engine they constructed at the Taylor's shaft for the East Pool and Agar mine. These were giants, made to last, and sturdy as Cornish granite. Such engines survived so long because they were ideal for their main work of pumping, as the rods oscillated with a steady rhythm to match the slow, regular movement of the great overhead beam. But Trevithick was thinking about other engines, where slow movement was not needed, nor even very desirable, and in particular of the whim engines used to wind men and materials up and down the shafts. Why not break Watt's cardinal rule by using "strong steam" at high pressure? It seems a very obvious solution to us today, but was by no means so clear two centuries ago when all the very best engines depended on the separate condenser for maximum efficiency.

The question that now exercised Trevithick was just how necessary a separate condenser really was. What if he were to use high-pressure steam expansively to drive the piston and simply let the exhaust steam escape into the open air? Common-sense suggested that it was not a good idea to expend a great deal of energy creating high-pressure steam simply to let it blow away in the wind. He took the problem to his new scientific acquaintance, Davies Gilbert.[9] "What" Trevithick wanted to know "would be the loss of power in working an Engine by the force of Steam raised to the Pressure of several Atmospheres, but instead of condensing to let the steam escape?" Gilbert knew the answer: that all that would be lost would be one atmosphere, regardless of steam pressure. In other words, the effect of the vacuum would be lost and nothing else, and that the loss could never exceed one atmosphere. And he added that this loss would be partly compensated for by the fact that an engine built on this principle would not require an air pump. Gilbert recalled that "I never saw a Man more delighted".

Trevithick set to work with immense enthusiasm, and the kitchen table was pressed into service as a laboratory bench as he began to think how he could devise a brand new type of whim engine. He was given active encouragement not just by Gilbert but by some very influential owners, of whom the most important was the newly created peer Lord de Dunstanville. This was the powerful mine-owning family, formerly the Bassets, who had employed his father and now they were among the first to see a high-pressure steam engine put to work. The scene was not the grand hall but the modest Trevithick kitchen, where everyone crowded in for the experiment. The model that was to be put on trial had been built by Trevithick's friend and now brother-in-law William West. Steam was provided by a boiler described as being like "a strong iron kettle" and the job of stoking was handed to the scientist in the party Davies Gilbert. When the high pressure had been achieved, the honour of turning the steam cock to set the whole thing in motion went to Lady de Dunstanville, and to everyone's delight the little engine sprang into life and the wheel turned.

The engines soon went into production and became known as "puffers" because of the steam that puffed out into the atmosphere with a roar and a whistle that it was said could be heard for miles. The first engine went into service at what seems to have been Trevithick's favourite spot for trials, Ding Dong, and over the next four years, at least fourteen engines are known to have been erected. Orders for the work appear regularly in his account books, and the book for 1800–01 quotes some actual figures.[10]

To receive for a Whim Engine for Mr. Millet 350 guineas

For Whe; Margaret	290	"
Do for House	20	"
	310	"
Ribelows	150	"

Whim engines were proving lucrative business, a fact not lost on Boulton and Watt. This time they were not ready to go to law, no point with the end of the patent so near. So they suggested something that they had resisted for years – a trial of one of their own engines against a Trevithick puffer. Early results were not favourable to the newcomer, but as they were conducted under the auspices of Boulton and Watt, no one was greatly convinced. Trevithick was not even greatly concerned. At this stage of his life, he was so busy trying to look after his interests up and down the country that he had scarcely enough time to look at the new engine built under his name at Dolcoath where, nominally at least, he was still Chief Engineer. However, hearing of a trial on his own ground, he hurried back to Dolcoath to take up the challenge. He went even further, backing his engine against the rival to the tune of £50, which suggests that he had now become a comparatively wealthy man, or was arrogantly reckless – probably both. An eye-witness and participant in the event told the story.[11] Benjamin Glanville who had taken up the wager was put in charge of the Boulton and Watt engine and Trevithick turned up to inspect his own engine, only to find that the piston was half an inch short, resulting in a considerable loss of power.

> A new brass piston was put in, and she beat Boulton and Watt all to nothing. I was landing the kibbals* for the puffer, because we tried Captain Trevithick's new kibbal and pincers made in our shop; we unloaded the kibbals, and sent them down again, almost without stopping the engine. The adventurers fixed upon a trial for three or four days; coals were weighed to each engine, and persons appointed to take account of the kibbals raised and coals burnt. Captain Trevithick's engine did the best; and, after the trial, a little pit was found with coal buried in it, that Glanville meant to use in the Boulton and Watt engine.

It was a triumph for Trevithick, in spite of the blatant attempt at cheating by the opposition, and his whim engines were soon familiar features on the Cornish landscape. The new engines looked very different from their predecessors. Boulton and Watt had already built whim engines of their own, which were essentially adaptations of the pumping engines. The massive overhead beam was rocked to-and-fro by a connecting rod from the piston in the steam cylinder, placed inside the three-storey engine house. The other end of the beam protruded

---

* "Kibbals" or "kibbles" were the ore containers.

outside the house. But in the whim engine, instead of being attached to pump rods it worked a cable drum by means of a sweep arm and crank. The cable then passed to the headstock above the nearby shaft. An engine of this basic type, although built much later in 1897 and by the local firm of Holman's, can be seen at East Pool. The Boulton and Watt engines worked by applying low-pressure steam, typically no more than 3 p.s.i., to one side of the piston, and by means of the separate condenser, providing a partial vacuum or "negative" pressure of, say, 12 p.s.i. on the opposite side. In this case the total working pressure would be 15 p.s.i. The only way more power could be obtained was by building bigger engines with bigger cylinders.

Trevithick's engines not only looked different, they were different. They worked with high-pressure steam, and that meant designing a new type of boiler to replace the old haystack boilers, little better than overgrown kettles sitting on a fire. The new design had to withstand pressures of around 50 p.s.i., and this was achieved by using a round boiler with an internal flue. A firebox was set in one end of the flue, and the hot gases passed through a U-bend to arrive at a chimney beside the firebox. A comparatively small cylinder was set into the boiler, and the exhaust steam, instead of being condensed, was released through a blast-pipe to the chimney. This had the effect of drawing the fire as each puff of steam made its noisy escape. The blast-pipe inevitably became very hot, but rather than seeing this as a problem, Trevithick turned it to his advantage. He placed a water pipe round the blast-pipe, which became a heat exchanger – the pipe was cooled and the water was warmed and could then be pumped back to the boiler. A model puffer of 1803–04 can be seen in London's Science Museum. But even as these new machines were being developed, Trevithick was working on new ideas.

There is another intriguing model in the Science Museum. It is clearly a puffer, but mounted on wheels. The drive through the crosshead from the piston no longer works some external machine, instead it drives the wheels of the engine itself through connecting rods. This is a machine that could move itself along. At first it might have seemed no more than an entertaining toy running around the kitchen floor, but Trevithick was planning for the future. He had realised that if he could make his puffers small enough, they could become portable engines, capable of who knew what? They could be driven to where they were needed, they could even go out on the roads and move people around. It was a concept that was to bring him lasting fame but, yet again, no fortune.

CHAPTER SIX

Steam on the Move

Goin' up Camborne Hill comin' down
Goin' up Camborne Hill comin' down
The 'osses stood still.
The wheels went around,
Goin' up Camborne Hill comin' down
Old Cornish Song

The movement from model to working puffer to moving model to road engine seems like a smooth and logical progression on the part of Trevithick. So it was, but the story is not quite as straightforward as it seems. Trevithick was not the first man to make a machine that could be driven down a road using the power of steam. That honour goes to a former officer in the Austro-Hungarian army, Nicolas Joseph Cugnot. He fought throughout the Seven Years War and when peace came in 1763 he retired to devote himself to scientific research, including questions of steam power. He soon saw that here was a possible answer to one of the problems of new warfare – moving artillery to where it was most needed. Until then, the work had required large teams of horses and skilled handlers. Cugnot felt a machine could make a far better job of it and he set out to build what was, in effect, the world's first steam tractor. The prototype appeared in 1769 and was followed a year later by an improved version, now preserved in Paris. This machine used high-pressure steam in much the way that Trevithick was to use it later, but it was an extraordinary, clumsy looking device. It was mounted on three wheels, with the drive being applied to the single wheel at the front. A massive copper boiler was set in a bracket in front of the wheel, supplying steam to cylinders mounted on either side of it. This same front wheel was also used for steering, which must have made the whole contraption all but unmanageable. There were two major problems which Cugnot failed to overcome. The first was that the boiler had no feed pump – there was certainly little enough room for any extras round that crowded front wheel. As a result the engine could only run for twenty minutes, then had to be given a twenty-minute pause to allow the metal to cool down before fresh water could be added: not very convenient in the middle of a battle! The second was the steering, which proved just as bad as appearances suggested it would. A probably apocryphal story describes how, on the trial run, it staggered down the road, collided with a brick wall and eventually overturned. At this point, the authorities decided enough was enough, stepped in and arrested the inventor before he could do any more damage. Development came to a halt, and no more was heard about the vehicle. But it had achieved a real result: it had moved under the power of steam with a load of around 4 tons at a brisk walking pace. No news of the experiment seems to have reached Britain, and if it did it is unlikely that either Trevithick or our next inventor heard anything of it.

We have already met William Murdoch, as one of Boulton and Watt's key men in Cornwall, but he was also destined to find fame as an inventor in his own right, following in his father's footsteps, or rather wheeltreads. John Murdoch designed an early form of bicycle, but not driven by foot pedals. Instead he used a pair of handles to operate a ratchet on the driving wheel. One reason we know about the device is that it came to the attention of Dr Samuel Johnson, who made what was regarded as one of his characteristically witty and telling remarks: "Then, Sir, what is gained is, the man has a choice whether he will move himself alone, or himself and the machine too." Which goes to show that even the cleverest men can make foolish remarks once they move outside their own fields of knowledge.

The story of Murdoch's experiments with a steam carriage has always been muddled, but from the point of view of our main story, two things need to be established as clearly as possible. Did Murdoch ever hold successful trials with a full-size steam carriage? How much, if anything, did Trevithick know of his work? Murdoch's most recent biographer, John Griffiths, has done a great deal to sort out the details of the story, but even at the end

some doubts remain.[1] The first mention of his interest in steam
carriages comes in a series of letters between Thomas Wilson and
James Watt begun in February 1784. Having discussed an earlier
plan for using small engines down mines – which Watt rejected out
of hand – Wilson went on to discuss Murdoch's stubbornness
when it came to his own ideas. He then raised the new topic.[2]

> He has mentioned to me a new scheme which you may be assured
> he is very intent upon, but which he is afraid of mentioning to you
> for fear of your laughing at him, it is no less than drawing carriages
> upon the road with steam engines ... I do not mention this from
> him, viz by his desire, but as it has taken such hold of him, I think it
> is right that you should be acquainted with it, and either consult
> with him, on the means he proposes to make it answer if you think it
> practicable, or endeavour to convince him of its impossibility, he
> says that what he proposes, is different from anything you ever
> thought of, and that he is positively certain of its answering and that
> there is a great deal of money to be made by it ...

At first it seems that Boulton and Watt were inclined to humour
Murdoch who, much as they appreciated his work on their behalf,
they regarded as unreasonably vain when it came to his own inventions. Convinced that the scheme would come to nothing, they
decided against taking any steps to stop his experiments, though
they dropped some very strong hints that they would prefer him to
concentrate on his work at the mines. However, they could not be
altogether certain that it would prove to be a failure. So, they took
steps to make sure that if it should happen to succeed, Murdoch
would not be able to take all the profits for himself. They clandes-
tinely prepared new clauses for their own patents to close any
loopholes through which he might squeeze to find space for a
patent of his own. Watt even sketched his own idea of a steam
carriage, which looked like a mobile garden shed, with a beam
engine inside, driving the axle through a sweep arm and crank. But
on the whole, they preferred to believe the plan would never work,
and as long as that seemed the likely outcome, he could amuse
himself with his experiments.

Murdoch, however, was soon well on the way to proving that his
scheme was practical and he built a working model, which is now
housed in the Birmingham Museum. Like Cugnot's artillery
tractor, this is a three-wheeled vehicle, but a good deal less clumsy.
A vertical cylinder is set inside the boiler, and the piston rod is

attached to a long overhead beam which provides the drive to a cranked axle. This time, the third wheel is unencumbered and is only designed for steering. In that land of piracy of ideas and inventions that was Cornwall in the 1780s, Murdoch very sensibly conducted his experiments after dark, and there are two stories of what happened on one such night. The account by a man called Buckle who had worked with Murdoch at Soho makes for a good tale.[3]

> At the time that Mr Murdoch was making his experients with his Locomotive Engine, he greatly alarmed the clergymen of the Parish of Redruth. One night, after returning from his duties at the mine, he wished to put to the test the power of his engine, and as railroads were then unknown, he had recourse to the walk leading to the church situated about a mile from the town. This was rather narrow, but kept rolled like a garden walk, and bounded on each side by high hedges. The night was dark, and he alone sallied out with his engine, lighted the fire or lamp under the boiler, and started the Locomotive with the Inventor in full chase after it. Shortly after he heard distant despair – like shouting; it was too dark to perceive objects, but he soon found that the cries for assistance proceeded from the worthy pastor, who, going into the town on business, was met in the lonely road by the fiery monster, who he subsequently declared he took to be the Evil One in propria persona.

Francis Trevithick, however, much preferred the version recounted by the rector's daughter. In this version, the tiny engine was moving along making "a fizzing sound" and zig-zagging down the path like "a lame duck". It was not terrifying, but comical, and something of a failure: it "disappeared after one brief outing on a dark night". One can see why he would prefer this version, since it gives his father clear precedence as sole inventor of the steam carriage, but there is nothing in the story to suggest that it was working badly. Fizzing, it might have been, but it was moving fast enough for Murdoch to have trouble keeping up, and it is hardly surprising that it was zig-zagging since there was no one to steer it.

That, as far as the Trevithick supporters were concerned, concluded the Murdoch story – one pathetic run on a dark night, and that at a time when their hero was still a boy. Even if he had known of Murdoch's work he was in no position to profit from it. But it was not the end of the story at all. Murdoch went on with his experiments, and it seems that he may have built as many as three models over the next few years, each larger than the last. The larger models were not constructed in secret inside the Murdoch home, but at the Budge Foundry. What is more there is a clear statement by Murdoch's son that the work continued into the 1790s and was known to both Trevithick and the man who was to become his partner, Andrew Vivian.[4]

> The model of the wheel carriage engine was made in the summer of 1792, and was then shown to many of the inhabitants of Redruth – about two years after Trevithick and A. Vivian called at my father's house in Redruth to consult him about removing an engine then on Hallamanin mine to Wheal Treasury Mine, where they wished the engine to work double. My father mentions this circumstance merely to bring to their recollection that on that day they asked him to shew them his model of the wheel carriage engine which worked with strong steam and no vacuum. This was immediately shewn to them in a working state.

This is a most revealing letter for it shows Murdoch advancing to the use of high-pressure steam, doing away with the condenser and breaking all the rules of the mighty Watt empire, and it may well have been some time before Trevithick began to think along similar lines. What we do not know, of course, is just how much Murdoch let out of the bag and just how long he gave the two young men to survey his invention. He was, however, clearly making immense progress. By 1795 he was ready to apply for a patent, and as he would have had a very good idea what his employers' reaction would be, he set off for London under the pretext of looking for skilled men to entice back to Cornwall. En route, he met Matthew Boulton and it must have soon become clear that Birmingham knew everything that had been going on. It was made equally clear that Boulton and Watt would oppose this patent as vigorously as they had Hornblower's. Murdoch knew very well that this was no mere threat, and he was faced with a dilemma. Boulton and Watt provided him with a good, secure income. Was he prepared to jeopardise this for the sake of an idea which would be subject to fierce legal challenge, and from which there was no guarantee that he would ever make a penny? One can make a pretty informed guess of what Trevithick's response would have been. One often reads criticism of Trevithick's recklessness and lack of understanding of the realities of the great world of finance. Murdoch took the "sensible" decision. He never went to a

full-scale trial of his carriage, and the honour of making the first
effective machine of this type passed him by. Not that Murdoch's
inventive genius was quenched. He went on to work in a field
where Watt had no interest or sense of rivalry. In 1792 he devised a
method of extracting gas from coal to light his home, and by 1798
he had introduced gas lighting to the Soho works. He had his own
triumph in 1802 when, to celebrate the Peace of Amiens, the
whole building was illuminated by gas.

That still does not answer the question of just how much
Trevithick knew about Murdoch's experiments. Apart from John
Murdoch's letter, there is a letter from Trevithick himself to
Davies Gilbert saying that Andrew Vivian had been making
enquiries about Murdoch's engine, but it is clear that they had no
notion of the principles on which he was working. They even got
confused with his other experiments and speculated whether he
might not be trying to use coal gas in some new engine, instead of
steam. In such a small community, where all the main participants
in the story lived close together and regularly met in their business
lives, it would have been impossible for Murdoch to keep his
experiments secret. But he would have been well able to keep the
details to himself. He was not a naive man, and he had dealt with
enough examples of piracy on behalf of his employers to be well
aware of the need for caution. It was only after Trevithick's own
successful trials had been made that rumours were put about by
Boulton and Watt, adding the steam carriage to their list of what
they claimed as piracies:[5] "they also say that driving a carriage was
their invention; that their agent, Murdoch, had made one in
Cornwall, and had shown it to Captain Andrew Vivian from which
I have been able to do what I have done."

He was extremely annoyed by the suggestion, not least because it
was well known that Watt had always attacked any use of high-
pressure steam, and had done everything he could to thwart
Murdoch's ambitions. Yet here were Boulton and Watt, of all
people, not standing up for the claims of William Murdoch, but
apparently claiming the invention as their own, with Murdoch
reduced to the role of mere agent. He had every right to be angry
at such a complete travesty of the truth. It has to be remembered
that this was not a statement made under oath to establish
Trevithick's claims for posterity, but an angry letter written to an
old friend about a piece of unpleasant hypocrisy on the part of an
old enemy. Trevithick may have been prepared to break bread with

the elder Watt, but he would have been happier breaking the head of his son.

It is always difficult to disentangle such complex stories, and especially so two centuries after the event. What one has to remember is that throughout the latter part of the 1790s there was huge excitement among all steam engineers at the prospect of soon being free to experiment as the hated Watt patent finally ran its course. Not only that, but all the most interesting experiments were confined within just one area – Cornwall. It would have been astonishing if only one man had been considering the possible uses of "strong steam", but posterity only remembers the successes and the more spectacular failures. We will never know how many were beavering away at their own plans for steam carriages, only to be disappointed. It has to be accepted that Trevithick knew Murdoch was working on the idea, but there is no reason to suppose that he was copying him, nor even any hard evidence that he knew what system Murdoch was planning. There is, however, a very clear line through Trevithick's own work. He had already made the crucial breakthrough with the stationary puffers; he had shrunk the giants of the early steam age and had opened up a whole new field of development. The nearest modern equivalent would be the revolution in computers when the vast machines filled with valves gave way to the personal computers and the microchip. He had built small engines, and had seen them wheeled to sites on horse-drawn carts – we even have a record of what it cost to move an engine, "ten shillings and sixpence". Although the words were written some years after his death, Trevithick would surely have agreed with the sentiments expressed by Thomas Aveling, one of the great developers of the traction engine, who carried on the work that Trevithick had begun:[6] "It is an insult to mechanical science, to see half a dozen horses drag along a steam engine, and the sight of six sailing vessels towing a steamer would certainly not be more ridiculous." Murdoch had spent years developing an idea, only to stop short when the end was seemingly in sight. It was Trevithick who was to make the steam carriage a reality, using ideas firmly rooted in his own earlier and proven successful designs. The days of models were ending: it was time for the real thing.

The work of making the engine involved many hands. The cylinder and boiler were cast at Harveys, assembly was entrusted to a local Camborne blacksmith, Jonathan Tyack, and some of the more complex and detailed work was carried out by Trevithick's

cousin and good friend Andrew Vivian, who had his own workshop
and lathe. Help was supplied by Arthur Woolf, probably not the
Arthur Woolf who was to go on to become a major developer of
the steam engine in his own right. It was a team of formidable
talents. Francis Trevithick saw at first-hand something of the problems his father faced. As an apprentice at Hayle in the 1830s he
looked over the workshop used by William West in making the
various models, and found "but a few small hand-lathes fixed on
wooden benches, a few drilling machines, and but one chuck-
lathe". He also took the opportunity to talk to the men who could
give first hand accounts of the building of the engine and its
momentous first outing. Quite the best was that of "old Stephen
Williams", and although much quoted over the years it is still
worth quoting again in full, for it really does convey the excitement
of the day.[7]

> I knew Captain Dick Trevithick very well; he and I were born in the
> same year. I was a cooper by trade, and when Captain Dick was
> making his first steam-carriage I used to go every day into John
> Tyack's blacksmiths' shop at the Weith, close by here, where they
> put her together.
>
> The castings were made down at Hayle, in Mr. Harvey's foundry.
> There was a deal of trouble in getting all the things to fit together.
> Most of the smiths' work was made in Tyack's shop.
>
> In the year 1801, upon Christmas-eve, coming on evening,
> Captain Dick got up steam, out in the high-road, just outside the
> shop at the Weith. When we get see'd that Captain Dick was agoing
> to turn on steam, we jumped up as many as could; may be seven or
> eight of us. 'Twas a stiffish hill going from the Weith up to
> Camborne Beacon, but she went off like a little bird.
>
> When she had gone about a quarter of a mile, there was a
> roughish piece of road covered with loose stones; she didn't go quite
> so fast, and as it was a flood of rain, and we were very squeezed
> together, I jumped off. She was going faster than I could walk, and
> went on up the hill about a quarter or half a mile farther, when they
> turned her and came back again to the shop.

This is all very lively, and gives the impression that everything
went as smoothly as could be, but looking at it again one is struck
by what an extraordinary day it was. This was the first trial of
something wholly new, yet it took place on a wet night, the vehicle
was made to go up quite a steep hill and even had to cope with a
poorly made surface. Yet not long before, the inventor had not

even been certain that a big machine turning its own wheels could get enough adhesion to move at all. For once, even Gilbert could not supply an adequate answer based on theory, but it was probably he who organised the beautifully simple experiment. He and Trevithick took an ordinary horse chaise out onto the road, and discovered that it could indeed be moved along simply by turning the wheels by hand. So that was that. What, sadly, neither Stephen Williams nor any of the other observers of the great event supplied was a description of the engine itself. Here the biographer is faced with a real dilemma. We know a good deal about the puffers and the models, but no accurate, contemporary drawings of the steam carriage seem to have survived. Francis Trevithick produced what he considered to be the likeliest arrangement to illustrate the *Life*, but although he drew on the memories of those who had seen the engine, we have no means of judging its accuracy. There is one very crude sketch, on a detached fragment of paper, dated "Cambourne 2nd December 1802".[8] It shows a four-wheeled vehicle, rather like a flat truck, with a steam cylinder set vertically over one set of wheels, and a huge boiler, like an overgrown kettle occupying the rest of the space. The top-hatted driver stands on a small platform behind the boiler. It can hardly be a realistic picture and, in any case, by that date the engine no longer existed. From the type of paper used it also seems to be a good deal later than the given date. But even if it is only a copy of an earlier drawing, it is still of great interest. It would make perfect sense if the anonymous artist had been given a description of the vehicle by a friend, and then produced this interpretation. It can all be brought down to a few essential features: square frame or chassis, boiler, vertical cylinder, four wheels and a separate platform for the driver. All that tallies with Francis Trevithick's more detailed reconstruction, and the latter is a good deal more plausible.

The great virtue of Trevithick's version is that it shows a clear development from the puffers. It does, however, leave a number of important questions unanswered: questions that had to be answered by the engineers responsible for building a working replica for the bicentenary celebrations. Two are fundamental: there is no form of chassis shown, and no method of steering. But if we look at this vehicle as one step in an evolving process that began with the puffer and ended with a steam locomotive, there are good grounds for thinking that the main features are right in general, if not necessarily in detail. At the heart of the vehicle is the return-flue boiler. The boiler contains water, through which a U-shaped tube passes. At one end of the tube is the firebox, the hot gases pass through the tube, heating the water and emerge at the chimney. As a result, unlike the system usually found in railway locomotives and traction engines, the fireman stands beside the chimney. The cylinder was set vertically into the boiler and the passage of steam controlled by a four-way cock. A crosshead above the piston carried connnecting rods passing on either side of the boiler to the drive wheels. In the first version, mechanically operated bellows, worked by the moving guides to the crosshead, provided the draught for the fire. This was not the only method used. The exhaust steam from the cylinder was passed down a pipe to the chimney, and when this was found to be efficient the bellows were no longer needed. One of the curiosities of the Trevithick story is that this excellent idea was later forgotten, only to be reinvented over a quarter of a century later, and most famously used by Robert Stephenson in his design for *Rocket*. Feed-water for the boiler was pumped from a reservoir on a platform behind the cylinder and was preheated by the exhaust steam. The same platform held the driver, who could check water levels by opening simple test cocks at the rear of the boiler. The safety-valve is shown in the drawing as a device similar to a steelyard, where the weight can be moved along the yard, which is graduated in steam-pressure readings rather than the usual weights. For the replica, a sturdy wooden chassis has been added and spur wheels from one of the drive wheels connects to a flywheel. The steerer has a platform or manstand at the chimney engine of the boiler. The actual steering is by a simple tiller device attached to the front axle. This was quite work enough for one man, and everything else, from operating the feed pump to firing the boiler, was the responsibilty of the driver who shared the manstand.

That covers most of the main features of the engine, but what exactly was it meant to be? Trevithick's name is remembered and celebrated as "The Father of the Railways", which colours one's thinking when trying to assess what was going on in 1801. But if we go back to the model that preceded the carriage, we find that it is fitted with a pair of screw-threaded legs that can be lowered to the ground to lift the driving wheels clear. The vehicle now becomes a stationary engine, just like any other puffer. Surely what he was doing at this stage was something even more extraordinary than beginning the railway age, though that followed on as a logical sequel. He was designing a small, versatile engine that was not only able to perform a whole range of different tasks but could be driven under its own power to wherever it was needed. He knew that the engine offered all sorts of possibilities, and the sight of so many enthusiasts clinging to the frame as it puffed up Camborne Hill must have reinforced the notion that road transport should definitely be added to the list. But that was only one use among many. So if one asks the questions: was this the first locomotive? The first traction engine? The first automobile? Or the first portable, all-purpose steam engine? – the answers are yes, yes, yes and yes.

The engine was destined to enjoy a very short life. Following the first successful run, Richard Trevithick and Andrew Vivian agreed to form a partnership to develop the engine, and they took it out on a short run to show it off to the Vivian family. The de Dunstanvilles had been present at the trials of the model and it seemed only right and proper that they should be among the first to see the real thing – and influential friends were always to be encouraged when starting an ambitious venture. Davies Gilbert joined the family for the expected viewing. On the morning of 28 December the carriage set off down the road to the de Dunstanville home at Tehidy, well over 2 miles from Camborne, with Trevithick and Vivian in charge. They never arrived. The story was told by Henry Vivian, Andrew's nephew, in a letter to his father.[9]

> They started to go to Tehidy House where Lord Dedunstanville lived, about two or three miles off. Captain Dick Trevithick took charge of the engine, and Captain Andrew was steering. They were going very well around the wall of Rosewarne; when they came to the gully (a kind of open water-course across the road) the steering handle was jerked out of Captain Andrew's hand, and over she turned.

Meanwhile Davies Gilbert, waiting for the engine, could only note in his diary that "the Carriage had broken down".[10] Sadly that was only a part of the story, and he added a fuller account in 1830.

> A very curious sequel followed this disappointment. The Travelling engine was replaced in a building and Trevithick and Vivian and the others determined on supporting their spirits by dining at the inn. They did so and forgot to extinguish the Fire that evaporated the water and then heating the Boiler red hot, communicated fire to the

wooden machinery and everything capable of burning was consumed.

So much time and effort, not to mention £70 worth of work was destroyed, yet Trevithick remained quite undeterred. Whatever faults of character have been attributed to him, they did have a useful tendency of cancelling each other out. A more cautious man would not have left the fire in, but then a more cautious man would never have built the engine in the first place. A more mercenary man would have taken better care of his property, but would have been devastated by the loss of it. For Trevithick it was scarcely a setback at all. He was already eager to move on to the next stage of development.

CHAPTER SEVEN

The Streets of London

These were exciting times for both Trevithick and Vivian, as the brand new concept of the high-pressure steam engine began to prove its worth. Here was a really versatile power unit, and they were only just beginning to explore its potential, constantly finding new applications. Trevithick was never noted for his business acumen, but Vivian was a man of good common sense. It would not have taken a great deal of persuasion to convince the engineering genius that if they were serious about developing the design for themselves, then the first essential was to get the protection of a patent to prevent its being exploited by others. If not exactly a case of poacher turned gamekeeper, it was certainly one of pirate turned patentee. So, armed with valuable introductions from both Davies Gilbert and Lord de Dunstanville, they set off for London in January 1802 to set the process in motion. They, or at any rate Vivian, were not so besotted with dreams of the future as to neglect profitable business in the present, so they stopped off at Bristol where they negotiated some engine orders.

On reaching London they wasted no time and at once began making use of the contact provided by their well-wishers in Cornwall, including a visit to one of Gilbert's most famous scientific friends, Humphry Davy.[1]

We waited on Mr. Sandys, who informed us that the caveat had been secured, and advised us to get the best information we could of persons who were well acquainted with patents and machines, of what title to give the machine, and what was the intended use of it. The next day waited on Mr. Davy with your kind letter, who with the greatest cheerfulness immediately waited on Count Rumford, to whom we had a letter of introduction from Mr. D. to wait on the Count on Friday morning. We found him a very pleasant man, and very conversant about fire-places and the action of steam for heating rooms, boiling water, dressing meat, &c; but did not appear to have studied much the action of steam on pistons, &c. The Count has given us a rough draft of a fire-place, which he think is best adapted for our carriage, and Trevithick is now making a complete drawing of it.

We are to wait on the Count when the drawing is completed, and he has promised to give us all the assistance in his power.

Rumford was a man with a considerable reputation, who had done original work on the specific heat of metals and the mechanical equivalent of heat, and had founded the Royal Institution in 1799. Whether his practical experience matched his theoretical knowledge is a different matter, and the firebox was to prove one of the most troublesome features of the new steam carriage when it was finally ready for testing. Probably more useful were the contacts who could help them through the official maze of patent applications. The letter continued with more details of the complexities involved.

Mr. Davy says that a Mr. Nicholson, he thinks, will be a proper person to assist us in taking out the patent, and we are to be introduced to him to-morrow, and then shall immediately proceed with the business. We shall not specify without your assistance, and all our friends say that if we meet with any difficulty nothing will be so necessary as your presence.

When we delivered Lord Dedunstanville's letter to Mr. Graham, he said he would give us every assistance in his power, gratis if wanted.

Mr. Pascoe Grenfell says he can find a way to the Attorney-General, if wanted.

It is strongly recommended to us to get a carriage made here and to exhibit it, which we also believe must be done.

By the end of February, Vivian was back in Cornwall and sending a chatty letter back to Trevithick who had stayed in London, busying himself with the specifications of the engines. It began with family matters.[2]

I arrived here last evening safe and sound, and missing my wife, was soon informed she was at your house, where I immediately repaired. Your wife and little Nancy are very well, but Richard is not quite well, having had a complaint which many children in the neighbourhood have been afflicted with; they are a little feverish when attacked, but it has soon worn off, as I expect your little son's will also; he is much better this morning and talked to me very cheerfully.

Mrs. Trevithick is in pretty good spirits, and requested I would not say a word to you of Richard's illness, as she expected it would soon be over; but as I know you are not a woman, have given you an exact state of the facts. All my family, thank God, I found in perfect health, and all beg their kind remembrances to you, as does everyone that I have met in the village.

"How do you do?" "How is Captain Dick?" with a shake by the hand, have been all this morning employed.

The letter shows the difference between the two men. Vivian appears educated and urbane, writing with easy fluency. Trevithick's letters are notable for their rather stilted style and wayward spelling. Letter-writing was not something he found easy, and seems to have been a necessary chore to be undertaken only when business demanded it. There is almost as much about Trevithick family life in this one letter of Vivian's as there is in all the surviving correspondence of the man himself. Vivian's letter then dealt briefly with mine business and gave a resume of a report on the Camborne engine in the Falmouth paper. It continued:

The same paper also mentions the increasive population of the parish of Camborne, *viz.* in one week nine women upraised, five pair of banns published on Sunday, and five more delivered to the clerk the Saturday following, eight children christened, and five weddings, *a rare week's work,* which have produced a few lines in verse, which I perused this morning; it describes the parson reprimanding the clerk, the sexton, and organist for getting drunk, and himself at the same time reeling against the altar-piece at the Communion table and breaking one of the commandments.

It is always pleasant to find that, even when two men are engaged in matters that will change the world, there is still time for humour and trivia. He added a postscript: "Mrs. T (your beloved wife) begs her love, and expects to hear from you often". It was an expectation very unlikely to be realised, as she was to discover over the years.

There was a certain amount of to-ing and fro-ing, as Vivian came back to London, while Trevithick went up to Coalbrookdale. Their first priority was to prepare the necessary specifications for the patents, based on the work already done and engines built and in service. Not that everything had gone entirely smoothly. The

destruction of the first road locomotive had been an indication of
the dangers of the new force they were dealing with, even if on this
occasion the accident was very much down to human carelessness,
with a little help from the refreshment at the inn. Most of the great
advances in technology that had created the Industrial Revolution
had been made by practical men, working almost intuitively and
testing their results by trial and error. With high-pressure steam
there was no room for error, but there was still no real attempt to
apply scientific theory in advance of manufacture. The one scientist who took an interest in such matters in Cornwall, Davies
Gilbert, went to look at a Trevithick engine adapted for grinding
corn at Marazion. He wrote this laconic entry in his diary, under-
stating what was clearly a very serious situation.[3]

> The boiler was of Cast Iron and its upper surface flat, the Fuel being
> applied within the Boiler in wrought iron Tubes. We stood near the
> boiler, if not upon it. When I came deliberately to calculate the
> Pressure exerted on the Flat surface of Iron, I drew the conclusion
> that perhaps my life had never been in such imminent danger.

There is no evidence of what advice Gilbert offered to Trevithick
on this occasion, but changes in boiler design soon appeared and
the version that was described in the patent application was very
different from the Marazion death trap. The obvious weakness was
the joint between the flat top and the main body of the boiler, but
the patent specification called for a "boiler made of a round figure,
to bear the expansive action of steam". This was a real improvement. The accompanying drawings show a familiar Trevithick
arrangement, with the cylinder set into the boiler and a large
flywheel to overcome the problem of dead centres. These occur
when steam pressure is equal on either side of the piston, so that
no movement is possible. One application is also shown, with the
engine driving a sugar mill. This was all good, sensible stuff, but
the real excitement lay elsewhere. The "puffers" were proving their
worth, but it was the road engine that had got everyone talking.
Trevithick was still a young man, just thirty years old and his first
taste of local fame had whetted his appetite for the greater glories
of the wider world. So, to the general specifications for engines, an
extra was added for a steam carriage. Everything was shown to
Gilbert who commented on the affair with his usual amused air of
detachment.[4]

The patent has very much occupied my attention as the partners are said to flatter themselves with the hopes of gaining little less than Messrs. Boulton and Watt and it would give me much pain to reflect that any disappointment of their hopes had arisen from my want of care, particularly as I shall only wait till they have gained half the sum attributed to Messrs. Boulton and Watt (£200,000) before I put in my claim to a steam carriage gratis as a reward for this labour.

He also gave the carriage a nickname – "Mr. Trevithick's Dragon".

In March, Vivian went on his own to London to make the final arrangements for securing the patent, which involved a good deal of paperwork and bureaucratic meetings, where Trevithick would probably have been more of a hindrance than a help. Vivian kept him fully informed of progress, and his breezy style makes it all seem almost pleasant.[5]

I arrived in town yesterday about three o'clock. I boxed Harry (that is, I went without dinner) that no time might be lost. This I should not have done, you may easily suppose, had the whole of the business been my own; but here you are concerned, which puts all inconveniences to myself out of the question. Of course I immediately repaired to Crane Court, where I was informed that the patent was to be sealed on Wednesday (tomorrow); and that they did not know whether the specification must be lodged on to-day, or a month from the sealing. They recommended me to Mr. Davy at the Rolls Chapel Office, for information where I immediately repaired, but could not find the gentleman. From there I shaped my course to Soho Square, and spent two or three hours with Mr. Nicholson; had the necessary alterations made in the rough copy of the specification.

At the Fantasmagoria Mary and Sarah Stamp and I got about eight o'clock, and returned about ten, well pleased. To-day I have been again at Crane Court, to the Rolls Chapel Office, and to the Patent Office at the Adelphi, and have got the whole business in a proper train.

Mr. Horton promised me to get the specification engrossed immediately. Mr. H. soon followed me to the Rolls Chapel Office, to request Mr. Davy to engross it, as he knew more of the business. I spent some time with the little gentleman, and have confirmed my opinion of him, that he is a very *clever little fellow*. He will do all in his power to get me out of town on Thursday evening; if so, you will see me on Saturday evening. ... To-morrow having no business of the patent until eight in the evening, when I must call at the Patent Office for the great knob of wax.

In fact, there was to be a slight delay, and Vivian finally put his signature to the documents and received the official "knob of wax" on Friday 26 March, 1802.[6]

The most striking features of the specifications are the drawings and explanatory notes for the steam carriage. This is very different indeed from the locomotive-traction engine type of design used for the Camborne machine. What we have now is a small engine being used to drive a carriage of the type commonly seen drawn by horses – or to use a phrase that was to come into use many years later, "a horseless carriage". The drawing itself is incomplete, but then all it claimed to show was an "improved steam-engine to give motion to wheel-carriages of every description". So the sketchy carriage floats in mid air, there is no fuel bunker, no water tank and most of the bearings seem to lack support. But at least the main features of the engine are clear.

Unlike the Camborne engine, the cylinder is horizontal, though still set into the boiler. The piston rod is forked to allow for the movement of the crank-shaft, which drives the rear wheels and a large flywheel. The rear wheels themselves are huge compared with those of the earlier engine, a design intended to ease the problems caused by driving over rough roads. Spur gears mesh with gears on the rear axle, and there is an indication that different gear ratios could be used. One very odd idea is put forward in the text that "heads of nails or bolts" might project from the wheel rim to give better adhesion, not an idea likely to find much favour with the road authorities! Quite why the idea was even considered is a mystery, since in the very next sentence there is a declaration that they are unlikely ever to be needed. The omission is even more curious. There is a mention of "bellows to excite the fire", which were not used when the carriage was built, but no mention of sending exhaust steam up the chimney, though we know that that was done. Had they patented the idea, they stood to reap rich rewards, for when steam blast was rediscovered later it was quickly adapted for all steam locomotives. They would have then been in the very happy position of receiving a premium on every locomotive built, for as long as the patent lasted. Much of the specification is vague about detail, either to keep a few little secrets hidden or because the inventors themselves were unsure what they were going to do in practice. For example, when it comes to describing varying gear ratios, it is very uncertain what was intended: "the power of the engine, with regard, to its convenient application to the carriage, may be varied, by changing the relative velocity of rotation of the wheels W, compared with that of the axis S, by shifting the gear or toothed wheels for others of different sizes properly adapted to each other in various ways, which will readily be adopted by any person of competent skill in machinery."

Details may have been left vague in places, but one thing at least was very clear, that here was something very new, and it was not long before it went into production. As before, the cast iron parts and wrought iron boiler were manufactured at Harvey's of Hayle under the supervision of William West, who was made a junior partner in the enterprise. When all was ready, West went down to London for the final assembly that was to take place at the coach-building works of William Felton at Leather Lane in Clerkenwell. Felton was a man of some distinction, author of a standard work on carriage design, and the body he built was a good deal larger than the one shown in the patent specification. It was a roomy affair, capable of holding eight inside passengers, two more than in the standard stage-coach. When the whole machine was finished there appears to have been one change made from the drawing in the specification, for there was now just one front wheel moved by a tiller instead of the two wheels on a moveable axle of the Camborne engine. Steering was always a problem, and the system used at Camborne could hardly have been called a great success as it was loss of control that had led to the accident and sad fate of that particular engine. In spite of the large drive wheels, approximately 8 ft (2.5 m) in diameter the ride was a rough one. There could be no springing on the rear axle, since it would have been impossible to keep the gears meshed if there was any movement of the crank-shaft relative to the axle. Certainly one of the first passengers was unimpressed.[7]

> Captain Joseph Vivian recollects that about 1803, his father, then a captain of a vessel, on his return from London told them that he and his nephew, John Vivian, had been invited to take a bit of a drive with Captain Trevithick and Captain Andrew Vivian on their steam-carriage: they went along pretty well through a good many streets, and were invited again for the next day; but Captain Vivian thought he was more likely to suffer shipwreck on the steam-carriage than on board his vessel, and did not go a second time.

John Vivian gave a much fuller account of his travels on the carriage:[8]

One or two trips were made in Tottenham Court Road, and in Euston Square. One day they started about four o'clock in the morning, and went along Tottenham Court Road, and the New Road, or City Road: there was a canal by the side of the road at one place, for he was thinking how deep it was if they should run into it. They kept going on for four or five miles, and sometimes at the rate of eight or nine miles an hour. I was steering, and Captain Trevithick and some one else were attending to the engine. Captain Dick came alongside of me and said, "She is going all right". "Yes", said I, "I think we had better go on to Cornwall". She was going along five or six miles an hour, and Captain Dick called out, "Put the helm down, John!" and before I could tell what was up, Captain Dick's foot was upon the steering-wheel handle, and we were tearing down six or seven yards of railing from a garden wall. A person put his head from a window, and called out, "What the devil are you doing there! What the devil is that thing!"

They got her back to the coach factory. A great cause of difficulty was the fire-bars shaking loose, and letting the fire fall through into the ash-pan.

The waste steam was turned into the chimney, and puffed out with the smoke at each stroke of the engine. When the steam was up, she went capitally well, but when the fire-bars dropped, and the fire got out of order, she did not go well.

At this stage, Trevithick might well have regretted taking the advice of Count Rumford on the design of fireboxes. A special trial was laid on in Oxford Street, which was cleared of horses and carriages for the occasion. The shops were closed, but all the upper windows were crowded with spectators, who waved and cheered as the Trevithick Dragon puffed its way through London. An eye-witness to that event, a Mrs Humblestone, described the huge enthusiasm of the crowd, but that enthusiasm did not extend to any potential investors and no one placed an order for the new wonder machine. It was a huge disappointment to Trevithick and Vivian who had invested so much time and money in the venture. In the end, the best they could do was sell off the power unit for use in a hoop rolling mill, where it continued to work well for many years but, sadly for posterity, was not preserved. So what went wrong? Why was no one prepared to take up the idea?

For a start, the twin problems of rough riding and poor steering had not been solved – and were not to be solved for many years, long after other engineers had made their own attempts to interest the world at large in steam carriages. Experience with a full-size replica recently built by Tom Brogden of Macclesfield, only served to confirm the difficulties. It is only possible to provide the drive to one wheel or the other, never both at once, because of the lack of any form of differential gear. The result is a considerable amount of torsion, and a tendency to twist the frame. It does, however, make it possible to have one gear ratio on one drive wheel and a different ratio on the other. It ran well at up to 8 mph on the flat, though its climbing abilities left a great deal to be desired. Inevitably, the patent drawings left a lot of questions unanswered, and solutions had to be found for such fundamentals as sequencing the valves. These problems were easily solved, using simple means, and we now know that the carriage worked quite well, but was by no means perfect. What was on offer was a machine that was, in effect, doing the same job as the familiar horse carriages, but with considerably less comfort for the users. Had the roads been better it might have turned out differently, but the road authorities had no interest in steam. In fact they were vociferous opponents of steam carriages throughout the nineteenth century, seeing not so much an improvement in transport as an increase in road repair bills. The startling novelty of the idea, which appealed so much to the cavalier spirit of Trevithick, made the carriage seem unattractive to the more conservative financiers, not to mention the public at large. There was a general dismay at the whole prospect of this new, ungainly, noisy, smoking beast being let loose on the streets.

Katherine Plymley was a clever and astute Shropshire lady and no enemy to innovation – she had been most impressed by Thomas Telford and his pioneering ideas in civil engineering – but she showed no enthusiasm at all when told of road locomotives on a visit to Cornwall.[9]

> A man of the name of Trevithic [sic] has lately invented a machine to go without horses – it moves by steam; and goes with extreme velocity – the danger seems to be of the water being exhausted & of course the machine taking fire – this however may certainly be easily guarded against – it goes equally well up & down hill as upon the level – it was first tried between Camborne and Truro – it is I am told a very ugly & large vehicle and would be very frightful to a horse.

This appears to be the first, though by no means the last, appearance of the argument that steam engines of all kinds should be banned because they frightened the horses. If such a broad-minded person as Katherine Plymley was so unenthusiastic about the idea of steam carriages, there was little hope of finding ready acceptance elsewhere.

Trevithick abandoned steam road carriages for ever, but happily business was booming in other areas, with his engines performing a variety of tasks from boring cannon to pumping water. And he was pushing ahead with experiments to use steam at ever-higher pressures, extending the boundaries of technology at an almost frightening rate. The following letter, written from Coalbrookdale in August 1802, shows just how far things had moved.[10] The point that one has to remember is that just two years previously steam pressure was limited to around 10 p.s.i., or "lb. to the inch" as Trevithick referred to pressure.

> Shod have writ you some time sence, but not haveing made sufficient tryal of the engine, have referd it untill its in my power to give you an agreeable information of its progress. The boiler is 4 ft Diam; the Cylinder 7 in Diam, 3 feet Stroake. The water-piston 10 In, drawing and forceing 35 1/2 feet perpendr, equal beam. I first set it off with abt 50 lb. on the Inch pressure against the steam-valve, without its Load, before the pumps was ready, and have sence workd it several times with the pumps, for the inspection of the engineers abt this nibeourhood. The steam will get up to 80 lb. or 90 lb. to the inch in abt one hour after the fire is lighted; the engine will sett off when the steam is abt 60 lb. to the inch, abt 30 Stroakes per mt, with its load. Their being a great deal of friction on such small engine and the steam continues to rise the whole of the time its worked; it go at from 60 lb. to 145 lb. to the inch in fair working, 40 Stroakes pr mt; it became so unmanageable as the steam encreased, that I was obligd to stop and put a cock in the mouth of the Dischardging pipe, and leve only a hole open of 1/4 by 3/8 of an inch for the steam to make its escape in to the water. The engine will work 40 Stroakes pr mt with a pressure of 145 lb. to the inch against the steam valve, and keep it constaintily sweming with 300 wt. of Coals every four hours. I have now a valve makeing to put on the top of the pumps, to lode with a Steelyard, to try how many pounds to the inch it will do to real duty when the steam on the clack is 145 lb. to the Inch. I cannot put on any moore pumps as they are very lofty already. The packing stands the heat and pressure without the least ingurey whatever.

This is an extraordinary account of just how far he was prepared to push the limits with what sounds like a very basic test rig, with very few, if any, safety measures in place. It certainly impressed the engineers who saw it, as Trevithick proudly wrote, later in the same letter.

> They are constantly calling on mee, for the all say the wod never beleve it unless the see it, and no persone here will take his nebiours word even if he swears to it, for the all say its an imposiabelity, and never will believe it unless the see it.

And at the very end of this letter, as if it had not described wonders enough, comes this intriguing postscript: "The Dale Co have begun a carrage at their own cost for the real-roads and is forceing it with all expedition."

This is the very first reference anywhere to the idea of running a steam locomotive on rails, and all we have is a scribbled note at the end of a long letter! Early biographers of Trevithick suggested that although the experiment was begun, it was never concluded, because the manufacturers were too nervous to pursue such a revolutionary idea. But the man in charge at the time was William Reynolds, one of the boldest industrialists of the age, who had himself already toyed with the idea of building a steam locomotive. His nephew, W.A. Reynolds, gave this convincing account of what happened, though it should be noted that it was written down long after the event.[11]

> There was a beautifully-executed wooden model of this locomotive in my Uncle William Reynolds's possession, which was given me by his widow, the late Mrs. Reynolds of Severn House after his death. I was then a boy fond of making model engines of my own, and I broke up this priceless relic to convert it to my own base purpose, an act which I now repent as if it had been a sin.
>
> The Coalbrookdale engine is, I believe, the first locomotive engine on record intended to be used on a railroad. The boiler of it is now to be seen in use as a water tank at the Lloyd's Crawstone Pit and the fire tubes and a few other portions of it are now in the yard at the Madeley Wood Works. I never knew how it came to be disused and broken up.

A visitor to Coalbrookdale in 1884 made this observation in a pamphlet: "An old cylinder is also cherished as a valuable relic. It originally belonged to Trevithick's first locomotive".[12] The description and dimensions fit well with a drawing dated 1803 of a "tram engine" with a 4¾ in. cylinder and a 3 ft stroke. For a long time, his drawing was thought to relate to the famous Penydarren

engine of 1804, but it now seems far more likely that it is indeed
the earlier Coalbrookdale locomotive. If this engine really was built
and did run in 1803, it seems quite extraordinary that no mention
of it ever appears in any surviving correspondence, which seems to
leave a question mark hovering over the whole story. There may,
however, be an explanation for the silence in an event of the same
year by the Thames in Greenwich. On 8 September there was a
catastrophic boiler explosion. Trevithick rushed to the scene, and
wrote a full account of what had happened. He began by describing the massive boiler as being round, 6 ft in diameter with cast
iron walls more than an inch thick. Yet he found a fragment which
he estimated as weighing 500 lbs, buried 1 ft deep in the ground
over 100 yards away from the site of the explosion. Not surprisingly in such a terrible explosion, three men were killed and a
fourth seriously injured. It seemed to be just the disaster that the
opponents of strong steam had prophesied. It did not, however,
take long for Trevithick to find out what had really happened.[13]

> It appears that the boy that had the care of the engine was gon to catch
> eales in the foundeation of the building, and left the care of it to one of
> the Labourers; this labourer saw the engine working much faster than
> usual, stop'd it without takeing off a spanner which fastned down the
> steam lever, and a short time after being Idle it burst.

Trevithick ended the letter glumly. "I beleive that Mr. B & Watt is
abt to do mee every engurey in their power for the have done their
outemost to repoart the exploseion both in the newspapers and
private letters very different to what it really is".

All this happened right in the middle of the Coalbrookdale
experiments. Trevithick had satisfied himself that the explosion
was caused by carelessness and not by any intrinsic fault in the
engine or boiler. Nevertheless, he took extra precautions with later
boilers, adding a second safety-valve and a crude form of fusible
plug. But the harm had been done. All the old doubts about strong
steam had been raised again and potential customers began to shy
away. This was not the time to publicise experiments on even
higher pressures, nor was it a good time to announce that he had
plans to set high-pressure boilers on rails and run them past streets
and houses. On balance, it seems probable that a locomotive was
run on rails at Coalbrookdale, though we can never know how
successful it was. The same is certainly not true of the next railway
experiment.

Trevithick's birthplace photographed in 1871, surrounded by the workings of South Crofty Mine. *(Royal Institution of Cornwall)*

Dolcoath copper mine in 1831. Richard Trevithick senior was a mine captain here when Richard was born in 1771. *(Royal Institution of Cornwall)*

Penponds, the house where Trevithick spent his early years.
(copyright and publication rights reserved Cornwall Record Office)

A portrait miniature of Trevithick as a young man. *(NRPPER/Science and Society Picture Library)*

Davies Gilbert, Trevithick's friend and scientific mentor in a portrait by Thomas Phillips of 1833. *(by permission of the President and Council of the Royal Society)*

Matthew Boulton's Soho Works c. 1780. From here, he and James Watt planned the conquest of Cornwall by steam. *(Birmingham City Archives)*

The remains of Ding Dong Mine photographed early in the 20th century, the site of Trevithick and Bull's engine experiments. *(Simon Cook)*

(right) Trevithick's Cornish boiler: the return flue had the firebox on the right and connected to the chimney on the left. *(SCMPOW Science and Society Picture Library)*

(below) Murdoch's model for a road carriage. *(Birmingham Museums and Art Gallery)*

A Trevithick mystery: representation of a road carriage based on the Camborne engine, but with a boiler which seems to have a spiral flue from the firebox. *(Royal Institution of Cornwall)*

Full scale working replica of Trevithick and Vivian's London carriage built by Tom Brogden. *(Tom Brogden)*

The Penydarren tramway still in use in 1862 with a southbound train hauled by two horses waiting in a turn out. Construction goes on overhead on the Taff Vale Railway viaduct. (*John Minnis*)

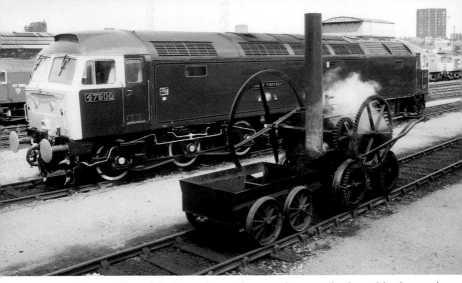

The working replica of the Penydarren locomotive overshadowed by its modern successor at Cardiff in 1987. *(National Museums and Galleries of Wales, Department of Industry)*

Trevithick's drawing for the Gateshead engine of 1804. *(NRMRLO Science and Society Picture Library)*

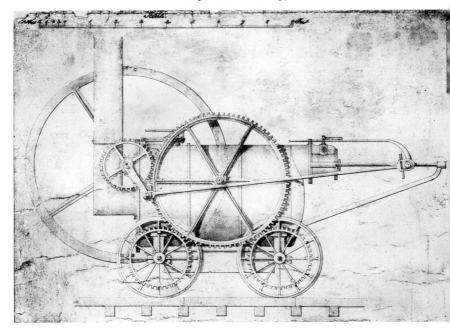

CHAPTER EIGHT

Penydarren and After

In that action-packed year of 1803, Trevithick received a letter from Samuel Homfray of the Penydarren iron works at Merthyr Tydfil, requesting him to pay a visit in order to discuss the installation of his high-pressure engines. This was one of the new, rapidly-developing areas in South Wales, that were so characteristic of the Industrial Revolution. There were four great iron works that had been established in and around Merthyr, starting with Dowlais in 1759, followed by Plymouth 1763, Cyfarthfa 1765 and Penydarren itself in 1784. All were highly successful, innovative and fiercely competitive, though they could co-operate when it was in their mutual interest to do so. One area where this was essential was in transport. By the 1790s canal mania was at its peak in Britain, and it looked sadly anachronistic to see the product of four modern iron works being sent down to the port at Cardiff by pack-horse and lumbering cart. In 1790 the iron masters had successfully promoted an act of Parliament for the construction of a canal from Merthyr into Cardiff, and in February 1794 the Glamorganshire Canal was officially opened.

The canal was not just successful, it was too successful. With forty-nine locks in just 24 miles of waterway, congestion soon reached chronic proportions, and the worst section of all was at the upper end of the canal, between Merthyr and the wharf at Abercynon. The co-operative spirit that had built the canals quickly evaporated and Richard Crawshay of Cyfarthfa, who had the controlling interest, was soon demanding preferential treatment for his boats. This was, not surprisingly, resented by the other partners. They found, however, that there was a significant clause in the act which allowed proprietors within 4 miles of the main canal to "make collateral cuts or railways". No doubt the intention was that any of the companies could make a short branch from their works to the nearest point on the canal, but that was not what it actually said. The four manufacturers laid out their "collateral railway" so that it bypassed the whole section down to Abercynon, a run of some 9½ miles. This episode did nothing to improve relations between Homfray and Crawshay, but it no doubt sharpened the former's enthusiasm for any scheme that might give him an edge over his rival.

The construction of the line was typical of tramways of the period. It was built with a gentle 1 in 145 gradient down to the canal, which made life easier for the horses that were taking the loaded trucks or trams downhill, but only had the empties to haul back up the slope. Because it was built for horse haulage, the space between the rails had to be kept clear for their hooves, so instead of the familiar transverse sleepers of modern railways, the rails were fixed into square stone blocks. A hole in the centre of each block was plugged with wood into which the rail was spiked. One can still see lines of these old blocks along the former track bed beside the River Taff. The rails themselves were a mere 3 ft (1 m) long and were set apart to give a gauge of 4 ft 4 in. (1.32 m). They were L-shaped in cross-section, so that the plain wheels of the trams were kept in place by the vertical flange. For Trevithick such a smooth, regular track must have seemed the answer to a prayer, after having to cope with the bumpy roads that had bedevilled his trials with the earlier steam carriages.

This was not the only factor that appealed to Trevithick about the situation he had found at Penydarren. He had initially been invited to build engines for use at the works, but here was a chance to show just what his machines could do. Versatility was all, and this seemed the perfect opportunity to demonstrate it. He could build an engine that would help in the manufacture of the pig iron that was the main output of the works, and that same engine could then be coupled to the trams to take the same iron on the first leg of its journey to the customer. It was an engine that need never be idle. Two centuries after the event, we think of Trevithick at Penydarren as starting the railway age, because we know just how important the railways were to become. But if we had been looking at the situation at the beginning of the nineteenth century, things would have looked very different. The canal system was still being developed as the most modern, most efficient method of moving goods, and the tramway's role was simply to feed goods down to this national network. They were built in a somewhat haphazard manner to a variety of different gauges, because there was never any intention to link them together. This also suited Trevithick's ideas. He was not looking at a national transport revolution as such, but was thinking in terms of supplying multi-purpose engines that would suit the individual needs and demands of the customer. Some of the engines he hoped to supply would be used for transport, but not necessarily all. But before he could put these new ideas into practice, he needed a customer who would welcome the challenge of the new. In Samuel Homfray he had found just the man. It is even possible that Homfray had locomotives in mind when he invited Trevithick to meet him, having already heard of either the road carriages or possibly even the Coalbrookdale engine. In any case, he does not seem to have needed much convincing, and soon the two men were laying their plans.

The scheme inevitably came to the attention of Richard Crawshay, who, probably on the grounds that anything Homfray favoured he was against, declared that the whole thing was impossible: smooth wheels on smooth rails would simply spin uselessly. Argument soon led to a formal challenge and a very considerable wager. Each man handed 500 guineas to a third party, Richard Hill of the Plymouth works, who was to act as stakeholder and referee in the trial. In order for Homfray to win the bet, Trevithick had to build a locomotive that would haul 10 tons of iron from Merthyr Tydfil to Abercynon and return with the empty trams. This was what a single horse would expect to achieve, with the load spread between five trams.

The engine was constructed at Homfray's works, and was very similar to the Coalbrookdale engine, containing many of the features already tested in the road engines. There was a return flue of wrought iron set in a cast-iron boiler, so that the firebox was set next to the chimney. An $8\frac{1}{4}$ in. diameter cylinder with a 54 in. stroke was set into the boiler immediately above the flue. The piston rod connected to a crosshead, reaching right across the engine, and from here the drive was taken through gears to the two wheels on the left-hand side and to a large flywheel. The presence of the latter, as before, was to overcome the dead centre problem, and is a clear indication that it was also intended for use as a stationary engine. Several things are not shown: was there a feed water heater? What system, if any, was used for braking? And how did anyone manage to fire the engine without having his head knocked off as the crosshead crashed to-and-fro like some overgrown trombone slide? Some of the answers can be provided, in general terms, from the later descriptions of runs. On one of these, for example, the return journey with the empty trams was held up, and Homfray gave an explanation: "this was owing to the little forcing pump not being quite right to feed the Boyler & he was obligd to wait & fill with cold water".[1] That strongly suggests that the boiler feed pump would normally provide a hot water supply, but gives no practical details. As one would expect with a prototype, there were features that could have been improved for greater efficiency. The fact that the drive was only being applied to one side of the engine meant that the effective tractive weight was only half the locomotive weight, and there was a constant tendency to push the wheels against one side of the flanged rail. This was not stupidity on Trevithick's part. What was lost in efficiency of the locomotive was gained in efficiency when the engine was used as a stationary power-source, when the drive was taken just from the one side. But the great question of the day was, would it work at all, and on the answer to that hinged not only a 500 guinea wager, but the possibility of the development of a wholly new form of transport. The answer was relayed by Trevithick to his scientific mentor, Davies Gilbert, in a series of increasingly excited and enthusiastic letters.[2]

> Last saturday we lighted the fire in the Tram Waggon and workd it without the wheels to try the engine, and monday we put it on the Tram Road. It workd very well and ran up hill and down with great ease, and very managable. we have plenty of steam and power. I expect to work it again tomorrow Mr. Homfray and the Gentleman I mentioned in my last will be home tomorrow. The bet will not be determed untill the middle of next Week at which time I shod be very happy to see you.

In the next letter, written five days later, he described more successful experiments and stressed the multi-purpose aspect of the locomotive.

> The Tram Waggon have been at work several times. It works exceeding well, and is much more managable than horses. We have not try'd to draw but ten tons at a time yet, but I dought not but we cou'd draw forty tons at a time very well for ten tons stands no

chance at all with it. We have not been but two miles on the road
and back again, and shall not go farther untill Mr. Homfray comes
home. He is to dine home to-day and the engine will go down to
meet him. The engineer from Government is with him. The engine,
with water encluded, is abt five tons. It runs up the Tram road of
two Inch in a Yard 40 stroakes pr mint with the empty waggons.
The engine moves forth 9 feet every stroak. The publick is much
taken up with it. The bet of 500 Hundd Guineas will be desided abt
the end of this Week, and your pressence wod give mee moor satis-
factn than you can consive, and I dought not but you will be fully
satisfyde for the toil of the journey by a sight of the engine. The
steam that disscharged from the engine is turned up the chimney abt
3 feet above the fire, and when the engine is working 40 St pr mt,
4½ ft Stroake, Cylinder 8¼ In Diam, not the smallest particle of
steam appears out of the top of the chimny, tho' the Chimny is but 8
feet above where the steam is delivred into it, neither is any steam at
a distance nor the smallest particle of water to be found. I think its
made a fixd air from the heat of the Chimny. The fire burns much
better when the steam goes up the Chimney than what it do when
the engine is Idle. I intend to make a smaller engine for the road, as
this has much moore power than is wanted here. This engine is to
work a hammer. Their will be a great number of experiments tryd by
this engineer from London respecting these engines, as that is his
sole business here and that is my reason for so much wishing your
here. He intends to try the strength of the boiler by a forceing pump,
and have sent down orders to get long steam guages and forceing
pumps ready for that purpose against he arrives. We shall continue
our journey on the road today with the engine untill we meet Mr.
Homfray and the London engineer and intend to take out the horses
out of the coach and fasten it to the engine and draw them home.

This is a letter packed with intriguing snippets. It looks forward to
an event which would have represented the first passenger coach to
be drawn by a railway locomotive, though it presumably would have
run between the tracks not on them – it would be too much to expect
to have a coach at just the right gauge. It makes clear that, at this
time, the engine was seen primarily as a stationary engine, which had
been adapted for the occasion of the wager, and that Trevithick was
already laying plans for a new locomotive, which would not necessarily be expected to do any other type of work. It clearly shows that
he saw the advantage of steam blast-pipe exhaust, and the whole
letter oozes confidence. The "London Engineer" was Simon
Goodrich of the Navy Board, and Homfray wrote to him, giving an
equally enthusiastic account of the work to date.[3]

I have the satisfaction to inform you the Tram Road Engine goes off very well – we have made a Journey on our Tram Road 9½ miles in length – it took 10 Tons long wts of Iron & about 60 or 70 people riding on the Trams which added 4 or 5 tons more to the wt – it goes very easy 4 miles an hour, & is as tractable as a Horse, will *back* its load, & move it forward as little (& slow) at a time as you please – with this Engine we can make the different tryals – & I am now preparing a pump to lift water, a Barrell to wind a Ball up & down – with any other matters I may think you will like to see it do – & move it about from place to place.

Trevithick wrote his own accounts of the trials to Gilbert. Even though there was a mishap on one run, he can be forgiven a certain amount of self-satisfaction. The following letter appears to be describing the same run as that in Homfray's letter, but in this version there is the added information that was certainly not intended for London eyes that the return journey had been delayed by a slight accident. One of the bolts holding the axle to the boiler had come loose, letting all the water out. It took the rest of the day to get the engine back to Penydarren. However, the run was still judged a success.[4]

The Gentleman that bet five Hundd Guineas against it rid the whole of the journey with us and is satisfyde that he have lost the bet. We shall continue to work on the road, and shall take forty tons the next journey. The publick untill now call'd mee a schemeing fellow but now their tone is much alterd.

Although everything was going well as far as the wager was concerned, there were more serious matters for Trevithick to worry about. A favourable report from Goodrich could make all the difference to the acceptance of the new engine. He was planning what promised to be a most impressive demonstration of his engine's power and versatility.[5]

We have 28 feet of 18 Inch pumps fixd for the engine to lift water as those engeneeres particulearly requested that they might have a given weight lifted, so as to be able to calculate the real duty don by a bushell of coal. Its the waggon engine that is to lift this water, then go from the pump itself and work a hammer, and then to wind coals and lastly to go the journey on the road with Iron. We shall have all the work ready for them by the end of the week. They intend staying here abt 7 or 8 days, and as the report that they will make on their return will be the standing or the condeming those engines, its my reason for so ancxiously requesting your presence.

The results were to be compared, as far as duty was concerned, with Boulton and Watt's results, and Trevithick urged Gilbert to supply accurate figures for the latter's engines to ensure fair play. His anxiety at such a crucial moment is obvious, as he ended with an even more fervent appeal to Gilbert.

> Perhaps there may never be such an opportunity when your assistance in those experements will be of so great a benefit to mee as at this time, therefore I hope you will forgive me for again Requesting your attendance on a business that may be of such consiquence to me.

Just as everything seemed set for the demonstration, there was an unexpected and, as it turned out, most unfortunate delay. Homfray was involved in an accident when his gig was overturned, resulting in injuries to his face, a sprained ankle and a dislocated elbow. As the main backer of the whole project was now bedridden, there was nothing for it but to cancel the demonstration, at least for the time being. Trevithick at once wrote to Gilbert, explaining that his presence was no longer urgently required, but at the same time asking him if he knew of any influential men who might be interested in the project, and assuring him that they would be made very welcome at Penydarren and given every opportunity to see the engine at work. The letter arrived too late, for Gilbert had already left for South Wales, and he arrived at Penydarren on 12 March. There is no record of what he thought at the time, but recollecting the events in 1839, his report has a very gloomy tone that stands in marked contrast to the optimism of the two enthusiasts, Homfray and Trevithick. He makes a particular point of noting extensive damage to the cast-iron tram rails, that cracked under the weight of the engine. The experiment, he concluded, "was considered as a failure". But the runs did continue after Gilbert's visit, for there was still a wager to settle. Hill was proving to be an exacting referee.[6]

> The Tram engine have carryd two Loads of 10 tons of iron to the shipping place since you left this place, but Mr. Hill says that he will not pay the bet, becase there were some of the tram plates that was in the tunnel removed so as to get the road in the middle of the arch. The first objection he started was that one man shod go with the engine

without any assistance, which I performd myself without help – and now his objection is that the road is not in the same place as when the bet was made. I expect Mr. Homfray will be forced to take steps that will force him to pay ... The Travleing engine is now working a hammer.

There is no record of any visit from Goodrich. The subsequent history of the engine seemed lost, and as other engineers, especially those of north-east England, began to build locomotives of their own, there was a growing tendency to denigrate Trevithick's efforts. It was written off as at best, an interesting if crude experiment, and, at worst, a total failure. However, William Menelaus, who had been works manager at Dowlais took the trouble to hunt down one of the men involved, who had worked with Trevithick in setting up the engine.

It was he who had the sketch that we now think of as showing the Coalbrookdale engine, and this is his first-hand version of events.[7]

When the engine was finished she was used for bringing down metal from the furnaces to the old forge. She worked very well; but frequently from her weight broke the tram-plates, and also the hooks between the trams. After working for some time in this way, she took a journey of iron from Penydarren down the Basin Road, upon which road she was intended to work. On the journey she broke a great many of the tram-plates; and before reaching the Basin she ran off the road, and was brought back to Penydarren by horses. The engine was never used as a locomotive after this; she was used as a stationary engine, and worked in this way several years.

The world did not beat a path to Trevithick's door, but there was one order for a locomotive from Christopher Blackett of Wylam Colliery on Tyneside. The engine itself was built at the Whinfield iron works at Gateshead. This was to lead to a great deal of controversy in the nineteenth century, when strenuous efforts were made to prove that this was not only built quite independently of Trevithick, but actually earlier, making it the first railway locomotive. John Turnbull, then aged eighty, was able to recall those days when he had been an apprentice at Whinfield's.[8]

It was all made at his master's. The engineer was John Steel, who was regularly employed at the works, "and a very clever fellow". When she was finished, a temporary way was laid down in the works, "to let the quality see her run". There were several gentlemen present, and she ran backwards and forwards quite well. Mr. Blackett, however, did not take her; – "there was some disagreemency between him and the master, and she never left the works, but was used in the foundry as a fixed engine, to blow the iron down".

What those claimants did not mention was that John Steel had arrived at Gateshead direct from Merthyr Tydfil, where he had worked on the Penydarren engine and had been sent from Wales specifically to oversee the work being carried out in Northumberland. It was obviously a good deal cheaper to send plans and a competent overseer to Northumberland than it was to ship a finished engine round the coast. The design is almost the same as its predecessor, except that the cylinder was now set at the opposite end from the chimney, so that the fireman was in less danger of decapitation.

The failure was again nothing to do with the engine itself. It did not take Blackett very long to realise that the machine was far too heavy for the wooden rails laid at his colliery. That was the first problem he dealt with, arranging for all the tracks to be relaid with metal rails. And if any further proof was needed that Blackett was not dissatisfied either with the engine or its designer, once the work was completed in 1808 he wrote to Trevithick to ask him if he was prepared to build an engine for his brand new rail system. Had the letter arrived even a year earlier, railway history might well have been rewritten, but by now Trevithick had moved on. He had reluctantly decided that the railway locomotive had no future until the rail problem was finally solved, and he had no more confidence in Blackett's newly laid iron tramway than he had in the old wooden one. His reply simply stated the blunt facts that he had "discontinued the business, was engaged with other pursuits, and could render no assistance".[9]

That year, Trevithick had, in fact, made one last attempt to interest the public at large, and the politically and economically powerful men of London in particular, in the steam locomotive. He could, had the proprietors agreed to risk their new rails, have run a Penydarren type of trial on the Surrey Iron Railway that had opened in 1803 and was built from the Thames to Croydon in the same manner and to the same gauge as the Welsh tramways. But this time he was going for something new. He abandoned any idea of building a multi-purpose engine and concentrated on the locomotive aspects.

Fig 2: *Davies Gilbert's own ticket for riding Catch-me-who-can. It notes that he also rode on the Penydarren engine.*

Freed from the constraints of having to run machinery as well as haul a train, he could move to a much simpler design. The single cylinder was now set vertically in the boiler, providing a direct drive to the rear wheels. It was built at the Hazeldine iron works under the supervision of John Urpeth Rastrick.

The one aspect of the Penydarren experiment that seemed to have attracted most attention from the public had been the wager. Trevithick was never a man to waste a good idea, so when the new machine was ready, announcements began to appear in the press of a new challenge. The engine was to be taken to Newmarket races in the October, where it would take on any "mare, horse or gelding". If he could not sell his locomotive on the basis of the work it could perform, perhaps he could get buyers on the basis of it being the fastest form of transport in the world. Whether this was ever meant as a real challenge or was simply a publicity gimmick, it certainly had the desired effect. The press was soon full of stories: "The novelty, singularity and powerful application against time and speed has created admiration in the minds of every scientific man".[10]

In the meantime, Trevithick capitalised on the excitement by putting the engine on public display. The spot he chose was, ironically, very close to the site of what was to become the terminus of Robert Stephenson's great railway from Birmingham: Euston Station. He laid out a circular track and surrounded it by a high wooden fence. In an attempt to solve the problem of cracked rails, he replaced the stone blocks of the old tramway with wooden sleepers. There were the inevitable problems that one might expect with a temporary track.[11]

> Abt 4 or 5 days since I tryd the engine which workd exceeding well, but the ground was very soft, and the engine, abt 8 tons, which sunk the timber under the rails and broake a great number of them, since which I have taken up the whole of the timber and Iron and have laid Balk of from 12 to 14 In Square, down in the ground, and have nearley all the road laid again, which now appair to be very firm, as we prove every part as we lay down, by running the engine over it by hand. I hope that it will all be compleat by the end of this week.

The engine was coupled to an open carriage and the public were invited to come and view at a shilling a go and take a ride. Among those who came to take up the offer was Davies Gilbert's sister, Mrs Guilmard, who had suggested the name for the engine – "Catch-me-who-can". It was a jolly name, designed to attract customers, but smacked more of the fun fair than a serious attempt to advance public transport. Trevithick needed the paying customers to meet the expenses of the demonstration, and he had to hope that the fun fair aspect would not deter the serious visitors and potential customers. The best and most reliable account we have of the working of the engine was given in a letter to the *Mechanics Magazine* in 1847 by the highly respected engineer, John Isaac Hawkins.[12]

> ... he placed a locomotive engine, weighing about 10 tons, on that railway, on which I rode, with my watch in hand, at the rate of 12

miles an hour; that Mr Trevithick then gave his opinion that it would go 20 miles an hour, or more, on a straight railway; that the engine was exhibited at one shilling admittance, including a ride for the few who were not too timid; that it ran for some weeks, when a rail broke and occasioned the engine to fly off in a tangent and over-turn, the ground being very soft at the time.

Mr Trevithick having expended all his means in erecting the works and inclosure, and the shillings not having come in fast enough to pay current expenses, the engine was not set again on the rail.

It was another bitter disappointment – not enough shillings, no orders. Not that the engine went to scrap, for it was destined for a more glamorous future than the rest of Trevithick's locomotives: it was installed in a fine old barge that had originally been used by the Lord Mayor of London. Disillusioned, Trevithick turned away from the steam locomotive, and not even Blackett's offer could now tempt him back. The decision has earned Trevithick much criticism over the years, none harsher than in what is traditionally a generous form of writing, his obituary in the *Civil Engineers' and Architects' Journal* of 1833.

Trevithick began better than Stephenson; he had friends in Cornwall and London, and he ought not to have left Stephenson to work out the locomotive engine and the railway. Trevithick was always unhappy and unlucky; always beginning something new, and never ending what he had in hand. The world ever went wrong with him, he said; but in truth he always went wrong with the world. The world would have done enough for him, had he chosen to make a right use of any one thing. He found a partner for his high-pressure engine; he built a locomotive; he had orders for others; he sent one to Wylam, which like most things in which he had a hand was so wretchedly made that it was put to other uses.

So many writers have repeated these charges over the years, that this is an appropriate place to pause and assess his role in railway history. It is quite obvious from all we know of the trials that the main problem lay with the track, not with the engines themselves. This makes the cutting remarks about the Gateshead engine both cruel and wildly far from the mark. The early engines had all been designed to fulfil more than one purpose. Far from being badly made, they proved perfectly capable of running on rails, and when the rails proved inadequate, of working machinery. Trevithick was not a metallurgist nor an iron founder. It was not up to him to design a new form of rail, to make the transition from cast-iron plate to rolled edge rails. Should others, notably Homfray who had a major share in the locomotive enterprise, have taken up the challenge? Perhaps, but there was no obvious incentive to do so. The Penydarren experiment had shown that the engine could perform the work done by a single horse on the tramway. But we know from old photographs that the trams were not normally pulled by single horses, but by teams of three or even four. So the maximum load that could be moved by steam was little different from that managed by the horses regularly in use, nor could it move appreciably faster. It is unlikely that the cost of one railway locomotive would be less than that of four horses. As with the road carriage, there was no great incentive to change from a method of transport that had been well proven down the years to an untried and potentially very expensive novelty. It was all very well for others to talk of future developments, but men such as Homfray had to weigh the considerable expense of experimenting with new ways of making rails and then re-laying over 9 miles of track, which had only just been put down, for what seemed at best a dubious advantage.

That does not mean that because Trevithick abandoned locomotive development his work was wasted, and that, when the world did return to steam railways, the engineers started all over again from scratch. Work restarted only when economic conditions changed. In 1812, the Napoleonic Wars had raised the price of fodder to unprecedented heights. The advantages of steam power, particularly at a colliery, where fuel was all but free, suddenly became a matter of considerable interest. Middleton Colliery, near Leeds, was linked to the Aire and Calder Navigation by a tramway, which served as a feeder just as the Penydarren tramway had fed the Glamorganshire Canal. The manager, John Blenkinsop, collaborated with a local engineer, Matthew Murray to turn it into a steam railway. The track problem was still unresolved, but thanks to Trevithick's work, it was at least clearly understood: a heavy engine cracked the rails. Simply building a lighter engine was no answer, for it would not necessarily provide enough power. What Blenkinsop and Murray were looking for was a way of increasing the traction without increasing the weight of the engine. This they did by building a third toothed rail beside the track, which would engage with a cog on the locomotive, the first rack and pinion railway. It was opened in June 1812 with two locomotives, and the debt to Trevithick was acknowledged in indisputable and tangible form: a royalty of £30 was paid on each engine. It was, of course, typical of Trevithick's luck, or lack of foresight, that he had, by then, sold his share in the patent. And there is one more direct link to be made. Many people came to see the new railway. Among them was Grand Duke Nicholas of Russia, who was so impressed by what he saw that as Czar Nicholas he ordered the construction of Russia's first railway – and there was a young colliery engineer from Northumberland, George Stephenson. It was Trevithick who began it all, and his influence was felt right through the first years of railway development.

But even if Trevithick had not been the great originator that he was, the criticism would still have little validity. As we have seen, he was not thinking of the railway locomotive as part of some vast transport system that would spread throughout the country and ultimately over the whole world. He saw it in terms of the world he knew, as a means of taking goods to an existing, still developing web of waterways, that was still regarded as one of the wonders of the age. When the Penydarren locomotive first ran, the great iron aqueduct of Pont Cysyllte had only recently opened, and work had just begun on the Caledonian Canal which would allow ships to cross Scotland from coast to coast. These events attracted far more public interest than the steam locomotive. And one always has to remember that his great enthusiasm was not just for the world of transport, broad as that was, but for the whole realm of steam in its seemingly infinite diversity. He took a very rational decision. Over a period of eight years, he had devoted a huge amount of time and a good deal of his own money to an attempt to develop the steam locomotive, first on the roads then on the railways. And the world, it seemed, did not want to know. He had scant reward to show for all his efforts. Very well, if the world was not yet ready for steam locomotives, then he would turn to other, more commercial developments.

We can look back, as the acidic obituarist did, and see what had happened to railways by 1835, but Trevithick had to take his decision in 1808. That gentleman might have remembered that Stephenson's first locomotive only appeared in 1814, ten years after Penydarren. Trevithick was not in a strong enough financial position to wait patiently for the rest of the world to catch up, for a new technology in iron and steel that made durable rails available and for a new demand for alternative transport. He took what history might choose to think of as a wrong decision, but one, which in the circumstances of the time, looks wholly rational. He moved on.

CHAPTER NINE

The Versatile Engine

The story of locomotive development from the first table-top model, through the road carriage to the "Catch-me-who-can" has been dealt with in the last three chapters as a continuous narrative, which made for coherence, but tends to give the impression that this was Trevithick's sole preoccupation during those years. Although this would certainly have been enough to satisfy most men, he was, in fact, busy on a whole variety of projects throughout the early years of the nineteenth century. He must sometimes have felt he was dealing with a steam-age hydra, for as soon as he had finished with one application of high-pressure steam, two more seemed to spring up in its place. Another man might have selected one aspect of the engine, concentrated on developing that and then settled down to enjoy a comfortable and profitable life. That was never Trevithick's way. It was simply not in his nature to turn away from a challenge, and if any new use occurred to him then he simply could not rest until he had at least looked into it. It was not the recommended way to accumulate a fortune. He was certainly not averse to making money, and he was constantly talking to friends about the wealth that would one day be his. It was just that, in practice, he could never really settle down to making it his first priority: the cash in the bank would never have the same appeal as a new idea waiting to be explored. He could fool himself into believing that he was chasing the new idea because it offered even greater prospects for money making than anything he had ever tried before, but the truth is that he would have pursued the new idea even if he had known in advance that, as all too often proved to be the case, it would end up showing no profit whatsoever, or might even make a loss. This did not make life easy for his family who lived in a state of perpetual insecurity, uncertain whether they were to end as nabobs or paupers. But it was good news for the world of technology: ideas flowed, some of which he was to develop himself, while some were to be taken up by others. In this one decade he came up with enough radical ideas to fill the lives of most men, even without considering the transport developments which have ensured that his name lives on.

It is easy to forget that when Trevithick and Vivian took out their patent, it was for both stationary and locomotive engines, and while the latter seemed to offer the more exciting possibilities, it was the former that brought in the orders. At Penydarren itself, whatever problems he may have had with the tramway locomotive, he found no difficulties at all with the engine that had brought him to South Wales in the first place and which was to work in the rolling mill. There were two stages in the rolling process. Wrought iron from the "puddling furnace" emerged as a spongy ball, with traces of liquid slag trapped in the tiny holes. These were removed by hammering to produce what was known as a "puddled bar". The bar was then reheated and passed through grooved rollers to provide a round- or square-sectioned iron bar. It seems that Trevithick's engines were used in both processes, powering both the hammers and the rollers. In this letter he gleefully recounts the performance of his engine, comparing it with two Boulton and Watts (Boltons) at Dowlais (Dolas).[1]

The engine will rolle 150 Tons of Iron a Week with 18 Tons of coals and the two engines of Boltons at Dolas burns 40 Tons to rolle 160 Tons; the are a 24 Inch and a 27 In. Double. That at Penydarran is 18½ Inch 6ft. Stroke, works abt. 18 St. pr minute; it requires the steam abt. 45 pounds to the Inch above the atmosphire. I workd it expancive first and found that when working the hammer which was a moore regulear load then rolling with steam high enough to work 12 St. pr. Mt. with the cock open all the stroak. Then I shutt it of at half the stroake which reduced the number of stroakes to 10½ pr. Mt. and the steam and lode the same in both but I did not continue to work it expancive becase the work in rolling is very uneven and the workmen wod stop the engine when working expancive, but when the Cylinder was full of steam the Rollers culd not stop it, and as coals is not an object here, Mr Homfray wishd the engine might be workd to its full power.

Apart from anything else, the letter shows very clearly that Trevithick already had a very complete understanding of the advantages of working expansively and varying the cut-off point for steam admission into the cylinder. In an engine, once the steam valve is closed, steam continues expanding in the cylinder until the exhaust valve opens. By altering the point when the valve is closed, the engineer can control the power output. Once the locomotive experiments were over, he was free to attend to other business. Never a man to delegate, he set off on an exhaustive and exhausting round of visits to Coalbrookdale and the industrial centres of the north-west. It helps to put locomotive development in perspective if one realises that at this time, two engines had been set down to run on rails, but in the following letter, he speaks of well over forty stationary engines either at work or under construction.[2] Already manufacture was keeping the Coalbrookdale works so busy that they had been joined by Hazeldine of Bridgnorth, who by then had seven engines in hand. The very long letter provides details of a variety of engines in use in all kinds of industries, in foundries, coal mines, leather dressing and milling; of pumping engines and rotatative engines. And all the time he was looking for new applications, and showing that he was an early exponent of what we would call "lateral thinking". He met some "Spanish merchants" at a Liverpool foundry who wanted to order two engines for South America. There was considerable interest in a steam powered sugar mill – already mentioned in the patent specification – but there was a major snag. West Indian plantations suffered from severe water shortages; where there was not enough water to drink, no one was going to look kindly on a proposal that involved using this precious resource to fill a boiler for an engine. Trevithick promptly improvised a solution, ingeniously utilising the process itself.

I found that ten Mules wod Rolle as much cane in an hour as wod produce 250 Gallns of the Cane juce and that juce will produce one pound of sugar from one Gallon of juce which the boile untill the Water is all avaperated and the sugar produced. I told them that the engine boiler might be feed with this juce and have a cock in the bottom of the boiler constantly runing and by takeing a great or small stream from it the might make the juce as rich as the liked. In this process, as the juce wod be so far on towards sugar, and the fire that worked the engine wod cost nothing becase it wod have taken the same quantity of fuel under the sugar pans to evaporate the water as it wod in the engine boiler, and the steam from the engine might be turned round the outeside of the furnace to destill the rum. As the destillerys do not require but a slow heat, I think the steam wod answer a good purpose round the out side of the pan. If this method wod answer, the cost of working the engine wod be nothing at all even the engine wod be there working with out fire or Water. The spainyards told me that if this plan wod answer, that the wod take a thousand engines for south america and the spanish west Inidias.

He also reported more encouraging news from South Wales, where they had started using a mixture of graphite and water instead of grease as a lubricant for the piston, and as a result "the cylinder is as bright as a looking glass". Trevithick was confident that he would soon do even better.

> I have not the smallest dought but that I can make a piston with out any freiction or any packing whatever, that need not to have the Cylinder Cover taken up one in 7 years, and its a very simple plan. It will be perfictually tight; its by restoreing an equal liberum on both sides the piston.

Even this impressive list of work in hand, future work planned and ideas to be investigated does not cover all the projects which occupied him at this time. And this was the source of many of his problems. Today it is commonplace to hear criticisms of companies that fail to plough enough of their profits back into research and development. Trevithick seemed quite happy to put *all* his profits into new projects. His wife later recalled how, on the rare occasions when he did sit at home, he would chat about the fortunes they were all going to enjoy one day quite soon, while remaining wholly unaware that the family scarcely had enough to keep going on a day-to-day basis. He simply did not notice such things himself. He was quite content provided he had enough food, no matter how plain, and a bed to lie in, no matter how uncomfortable – and assumed that others shared his tastes and believed in his dreams. Jane Trevithick, it seems, accepted her lot with equanimity, and seldom tried to deflect his mind to deal with such mundane matters as household bills.

The high-pressure engine was proving a great success, and more and more were coming into use, but the three partners in the patent – Trevithick, Vivian and West – were not seeing any very great return on their investment. When they had started out, they had talked of emulating Boulton and Watt, but the Birmingham partnership thrived because their circumstances were totally different. James Watt had joined a highly profitable concern and helped transform it into one of the great manufacturing empires of the age. They made certain engine parts at their own works, and these were always the most intricate parts – those which commanded the highest profit margins. They had the premium from all the engines in use, and, as we have seen, they had the resources to go to law if it was not paid. The Cornish trio were very differently placed. They had no manufacturing base of their own, though at Coalbrookdale and Bridgnorth they had the services of the most successful and enterprising iron works in the land. This ensured good workmanship, but as customers placed their orders through the Trevithick group, it was their responsibility to see that all was well. It was an arrangement that brought them only expenses, not profits. Any gains had to come through the premiums. Their customers were widely scattered, and they lacked the organisation to keep their interests under control. When disputes over payments did arise, they were more likely to provide fees for lawyers than cash for the partners. Andrew Vivian's accounts for the first two years of the partnership show premium payments of £1250, which is a very good beginning, but the next column shows expenses running at £1097-0-4. That left Trevithick and Vivian, the major shareholders, with just over £60 each and half that for West. It was scant reward, and matters were not about to get any better.

The Cornishmen should have known, if anyone did, that it was one thing to get a patent, but quite another to enforce it. There was no shortage of users who were ready to dispute terms. There was a lawsuit threatened by a man named Dixon, who was challenging the legitimacy of the patent, while another, a Mr Davy, seems actually to have persuaded the authorities that he was the injured party, and that Trevithick was trying to extract money under false pretences. As a result, the unhappy engineer was marched off to gaol, though he was very speedily released. None of this helped any of those concerned, but it fell particularly hard on Vivian, where personal tragedy was added to severe financial problems.[3]

> I have yours of the 18th instant, for which I am much obliged. It found me in a most melancholy situation. I returned from London here on Tuesday evening, between five and six o'clock, and found my poor Andrew much weaker than when I left him. He rejoiced to see me, but soon told me that we were soon to part to meet no more

on earth; and after taking the most affectionate leave of all, he said he had given up the world, and all that was therein, and resigned himself to will of that God who gave him life. About three or four o'clock the next morning the Almighty was pleased to take him. The dear boy was perfectly in his senses, and appeared to leave the world without pain. This has been a sad stroke to me, and have scarcely been able to write a letter since. My poor wife is still very unwell, and so is the infant child.

Had I not been so much in want of money at this present time, would not part with my share in the patent for the sum you have offered it at; but my circumstances at present oblige me to do what, in other circumstance, I would not.

If there is any risk at all in going to law with Dixon, why not avoid it? It is certainly very easy to make a friend of him, as the non-existence of the patent can be but of little consequence to him.

My finances at present oblige me to empower you to make another offer to Sir William Curtis; that is, my share as it now stands, for 4000*l*., and to receive the other thousand if you succeed against Dixon. But should it not come to a trial, the last-mentioned thousand to be paid at the expiration of one year.

At least he had never lost faith in the venture, even if he had been forced to sell his shares. The figures quoted meant that the patent was then valued at £10,000. No one, it seems, quite believed in the hundreds of thousands that were being suggested just a couple of years earlier. Sir William Curtis's name appears again in the Trevithick story, but not in this context, and it seems that the new investors were a Mr Bill and Samuel Homfray. Trevithick was scarcely better placed than Vivian, and he sold a part of his share as well, so that at the end of the transaction, Homfray emerged with a controlling interest and half the shares. West continued to hold on to his more modest portion.

The partnership of Trevithick and Vivian has inevitably been likened to that of Boulton and Watt, with Vivian cast in the role of the steady man of business and Trevithick the temperamental genius. Earlier in the book (page 15) there was mention of the fact that Henry Vivian, writing of his father in 1845, noted that he was something of a calculating genius, able to work out engine duties in his head. He then went on to describe Trevithick as having the livelier mind but less exactitude, and added that "They did well together, but badly when separated".[4] It has to be said that whatever Vivian's arithmetical abilities might have been, the partnership never did fare well and was never run on very business-like lines. It is certainly true that Vivian's subsequent career was also far from successful. He was later to enter another partnership, variously known as The United Mining Company and Blewett, Harvey and Vivian and Co. This, too, faltered and Vivian was reduced to some fairly desperate measures to try and keep his different ventures going. He was also purser for four mines, and he found himself caught up in the seemingly never-ending war between the Harveys and the Copperhouse Foundry. Both parties imported coal for the mines, and the latter tried to take advantage of a temporary financial problem at Harvey's. They undercut them by slashing the price of coal to absurdly uneconomic levels in an attempt to drive them out of business and Vivian was one of those who could not resist the temptation of saving badly needed cash. The trouble was that he was in a partnership involving Harvey, and he could hardly have expected this to be well received. Worse still, although Harvey's were temporarily strapped for cash, they had still been allowing Vivian goods on credit. By 1812, Henry Harvey had had quite enough of the United Mining affair and when the partnership was dissolved he came out the winner in the courts. He wrote to Vivian in a sternly formal letter.[5]

> Having previous to my Appointment as Manager and Receiver of the Partnership Effects at Hayle Foundry, entered into Recognaizance for faithfully discharging that office & collecting the Partnership debts, I have to request you will without delay Settle with me the amount of the debt due from you in your private capacity, and also the several sums due from you as Purser of Binner Downs, Wheal Strawberry, Wheal Trenoweth, and the United Hills. I request your immediate answer to this letter.

It does seem that Andrew Vivian was not quite the perfect man of business after all.

There is one amusing little story connected to this affair. Although Harvey was annoyed by Vivian's actions, it was Blewett who Harvey regarded as the true villain. In what might have been taken as a gesture of reconciliation, Blewett sent a silver teapot to Betsy Harvey, which Henry decided to take as a blatant attempt at bribery. He hurled the offending object into the fireplace. Trevithick happened to be visiting at the time, and he had no such qualms. Announcing that it would do nicely for Jane, he wrapped it in his handkerchief and took it off home.

West, the practical man, who had taken on the task of erecting the prototypes, proved the steadiest of them all. He held on to his share, even though there was very little hope of ever seeing anything much in the way of profit, and got on with his own life, making a new and successful career for himself as a maker of precision chronometers. Little was heard of him until 1815, when it seems Trevithick, cannoning around as usual, decided that, for some reason he was unable to make clear, West owed him money. West was having none of that, and firmly declared that he had no intention of paying, and if Trevithick insisted then he was quite ready to go to arbitration. His opinion of his former partner had sunk immeasurably, and he wrote with much bitterness that "it must distress my mind to think of paying for your blunders". And in a telling phrase, he compared Trevithick's habit of using any money that did come in to finance new ventures to "the caterpillars on the island of St Helena, eating up the product of industrious labour".[6]

So a partnership begun with such high hopes, ended in mutual recriminations and acrimony. Could anything have been done to save it, to turn it into a sound, profitable business? Common-sense suggests that once the patents had been obtained and the first orders secured, there should have been a period of consolidation. The successful engines should have been scrutinised, and where necessary improved, with the improvements covered by new patents. It would also have been wise to identify which of the various types of concerns that were using the engines were likely to prove the best customers and concentrate on supplying their needs and those of others like them – iron works, collieries and so on. It was not the time for dashing around starting new projects. Offering such advice to Trevithick was a bit like suggesting to an alcoholic that it would be a good idea not to have a drink, just after he had sat down at the bar – very good counsel, but very unlikely to be heeded.

Davies Gilbert was well-aware of his protegé's shortcomings. When he was asked to provide a reference for Trevithick, he replied that as he had never employed him that was not possible, but he gave this very fair and tactful assessment.[7]

But having amused myself by investigations on mechanical subjects I cultivated his acquaintance as a sensible enterprising young man – that I have found him in an eminent degree. I believe the whole neighbourhood unanimously consider him as a strictly honest man, and no other fault is imputed to him than that, common to most

Geniuses, of sacrificing in some instances routine employment and certain gain to prospects of fame or great wealth.

There were few, if any, men better placed to assess Trevithick's character, for Gilbert never lost his faith in him, and was always ready with help and advice, for which he neither asked nor received public acclaim. Throughout his life he acted as scientific adviser, steadying influence and good, helpful friend. That assessment was written in 1805, when Gilbert had already had ample opportunity to observe Trevithick's tendency to run off in new directions at even the hint of a good idea. To be fair, one of the first examples can be put down to patriotic fervour, but it perfectly illustrated Trevithick's tendency to dash ahead of the field.

When the dubious Peace of Amiens came to an end in 1803, Britain was back at war with a France now firmly under the control of Napoleon. The British, who had welcomed the peace with wild celebrations just a year earlier, were typically unprepared when it ended. Napoleon, by contrast, had used the time to regroup his forces and was now poised to invade the British Isles. Only the fleet stood between Bonaparte and conquest, and local militias were hastily raised. Trevithick at once became one of the de Dunstanville corps of volunteers, though not one, it seems, who was disposed to rush to arms at the first alarm. There is a charming story of the Trevithicks being woken by a drum beating through the streets of Camborne one night.[8]

> Trevithick awoke his wife, and asked what all the noise could be about. "Oh! I suppose the French must be come; had you not better put on your red coat and go out?" "Well, but, Jane," suggested the volunteer, "you go first and just look out at the window, to see what it is!"

There were, however, more serious demands on his talents. It was, after all rather more sensible to make use of his inventive genius and engineering skills than to set him on guard duty with a musket. The French invasion fleet had mustered at Boulogne and a government delegation approached Trevithick, at Gilbert's suggestion, to ask him if he considered it feasible to use a steam-powered vessel to tow fire ships into the heart of the enemy fleet. He promptly agreed that the idea was excellent, but typically did not stop at just giving an opinion. He announced that he actually had two steam cylinders available right there and then, and all he needed was the word, and he would start at once to construct the tugs. His enthusiasm led him even further than that.[9]

> If you think you could get Goverment to get it putt in to execution, I wod readley go with the engines and risque the enterprize. I shod think that its posiable to make these engines to drive ships in to the middle of the fleet, and then for them to blow up. However, I shall leve all this buisness to your judgement, but if you give mee encoragement respecting the posiability of carrying it in to force, I am ready to send off these two engines on speculiation. I beleive if you do not bring this buisness forward, some other person will, and it wod not please mee to see another person take this scheme out of our hands. Be silent abt it home, for I shod not like my family to know that I wod engage in such undertakeing.

One can quite see that Jane might not share his enthusiasm for going off on a suicide mission. Things soon began to move forwards. He was invited to discuss his ideas with the Marquis of Stafford, who in turn gave him an introduction to Lord Melville at the Admiralty. There he was to discover, as others had done before and would do after, everything ground to a halt. He met what Brunel was to describe later as "the withering influence" of Navy officialdom – "They have an extraordinary supply of cold water and capacious and heavy extinguishers". Trevithick was not the man to show patience when confronted by the slow grindings of bureaucratic machinery.[10]

> I was at the admeraltrie office and was order'd to wait a few days before the culd say to mee what the wanted. I call 5 or 6 days foll'ing and never received a satisfactorey answere, only to still wait longer. But I left them without knowing what the wanted of mee for I was tired waiteing, and was wanted much at Coalbrookedale at the time. When the send for mee again, the shall say what the want before I will again obey the call.

He may have got bored waiting for the Admiralty to reach a decision, but that did not mean his own enthusiasm for the project had been dampened. So, typically, without waiting for anyone to tell him what to do or what was required, he set out to build a steam vessel on his own. It happened that a 10 in. steam cylinder was then available at Coalbrookdale. There is a little confusion here as Trevithick described it as being loaded onto a 60 or 70 ton barge, ready for shipment to a cotton mill at Macclesfield. The barge could not reach Macclesfield by canal, so one can only assume that it was being sent off down the Severn for transhipment. A rough-and-ready contraption was assembled from machinery and bits and pieces available at the works. The engine drove a crank-shaft set across the barge, with improvised paddle wheels at either end. Trevithick described them as being like undershot water wheels, and they were constructed out of flywheels, each with six boards stuck around the rim to act as paddles. These were quite small, just 26 by 14 in. (66 × 36 cm.), but they moved the vessel along at a very respectable speed, which he estimated at 7 mph.

His was by no means the first paddle steamer to take to the water, nor even the first in Britain – there was a French trial on the Seine in 1775 and William Symington's vessel puffed across a Scottish loch in 1788. But it is very unlikely that Trevithick had heard of either of these, though word might have reached him of Symington's later steam tug, the *Charlotte Dundas*, that was given a successful trial in 1802. But even if he knew of the experiments, he would have been unlikely to have had much of an idea about the mechanical arrangements, which were in any case quite different from those that he used. He had simply grasped the essentials almost intuitively and produced a brilliant piece of improvised design. Nothing more was heard about the steamer, and the fortunes of war resulted in the rapid movement of the invasion army to a different front. The vague interest in steam soon dissipated itself through the Admiralty corridors until scarcely a wisp was to be found. But it had turned Trevithick's thoughts in a new direction: he was beginning to contemplate the use of steam on water as well as on land. And once an idea had engaged his attention, it would only be a matter of time before he began to act.

The first decade of the new century was a time of great frustration for Trevithick. He was well-aware that he had done something entirely new and very important, nothing less than creating a major revolution in the use of steam power. Yet he was met with indifference and denied his rights on every hand. His letters have a constant refrain of how impressed someone or other was with his newest engine, how much better it was than anything that had ever been seen before. It looks less like boasting, and rather more like an attempt to convince himself that his ideas really were as good as he thought them, an attempt to boost his rather battered self-esteem. When he had worked in Cornwall he had been among his own kind and enjoyed a reputation second to none, but he was not content with mere local fame. So he had come to London to establish a reputation that would spread through the whole land. London had not appeared very impressed by Trevithick, but the engineer had seen enough of the capital to convince him that this was where he needed to make his mark. He was determined to stay and force the powerful and influential to take note.

He had made a simple but significant mistake: he had taken London on its own assessment. He saw political and financial power centred there, and had assumed that everything else flowed from that. But one lesson he could have learned from the eighteenth century was that scarcely any of the developments that had brought about the great sweeping changes of the Industrial Revolution had their origins there. Nor was there much sympathy in the capital for the men who were making the changes. What may have seemed a desirable route forward to the patrician scientist Davies Gilbert, was not necessarily appropriate for a young Cornish engineer. He had, in a way, been fortunate in the Gilbert connection, which had given him introductions to leading scientists such as Humphry Davy, but that did not mean that he had won Davy's wholehearted support. The eminent scientist was inclined to consider Trevithick as little more than the mechanic who had a necessary role in turning academic theory into useful practice. Davy made his views on the matter plain in a letter to Gilbert.[11]

> Whenever speculation leads to practical discovery, it ought to be well remembered & generally known. One of the most common arguments against the Philosophical exercise of the understanding is "Qui bono". It is an absurd & a common place argument; but much used: so that every fact against it ought to be carefully registered. Trevithick's engine will not be forgotten, but it ought to be known & remembered that your reasoning & mathematical enquiries led to the discovery.

It was just this attitude that was later to lead to a famous and furious dispute, when Davy utterly rejected George Stephenson's entirely valid claim to have independently invented the miners' safety lamp. To Davy, the idea was "false" and "absurd", simply because Stephenson was no scientist. Such a man could not have done, on the basis of practical experience, what he had done by careful laboratory research. There was a good deal of that thinking in his attitude to Trevithick. Nevertheless, it was in London that Trevithick determined to do great things and establish his reputation for posterity.

CHAPTER TEN

Time on the Thames

When Trevithick had first come to London to show off his steam carriage he had arrived at a time when the real focus of interest was on the River Thames, not on city streets. The old system that had existed for centuries, where vessels lay at anchor in the tideway to be served by lighters, was finally being replaced. The river was being dredged and London was getting its first wet dock complex, where ships could stay alongside the quay at all states of the tide, with water levels controlled through lock gates and sluices. The City Canal was being cut through the Isle of Dogs, close to the sites where work was going ahead on the East India Docks and the even grander West India Docks, with one dock for import and another for export. All this work involved a considerable amount of river improvement, and it was inconceivable that steam power should not be involved in this great flurry of civil-engineering activity. The earliest date given for Trevithick's involvement comes in an account written over half a century after the event, when Captain John Vivian recalled not just his ride on a steam carriage, but also a visit to the new docks area. There he claims that he "saw Trevithick breaking the rock at the East India Dock entrance to the Thames at Blackwall, using a water-wheel worked by the tide, and also a small high-pressure engine for driving or turning large chisels and borers, and other contrivances for breaking and clearing away the rock to increase the depth of water".[1]

This report is more than a little misleading in suggesting that Trevithick was directly involved with the rock-breaking machinery. The rock in question, the Blackwall Rock, was a stone outcrop, roughly 100 metres by 50 metres in area and less than a metre below the surface at spring tides. It represented a serious threat to shipping using the new docks. A special act of Parliament was passed in July 1803 authorising a loan of £100,000 for the work of clearing the massive rock. Early attempts at blasting it away failed, and early the next year the distinguished civil engineer William Jessop was called in to tackle the problem. He devised the rock-breaking machinery, with a steel chisel attached to a cast-iron ram, like a conventional pile driver. Once sufficient rock was broken away, a cylinder was to be sunk from which miners could work outwards, with the interior pumped dry. The machinery was built at the Butterley Iron Works, in which Jessop was a partner. So where does Trevithick fit into the story? There are two possibilities. The first is that he supplied the high-pressure engine mentioned by Vivian to drive Jessop's machines. In a letter quoted in part in the last chapter,[2] he referred to work that he had in hand in September 1804.

> The engine for the West India docks was neglected in my abstance from the Dale but I expect it will be ready to send of in ten days. In abt 3 weeks from this time I shall be in London to set it up; it will please you much for its a verry neat and compleat job and I have no dought but it will answer every purpose exceeding well.

The reference to the West India Docks is easily explained. Jessop's main occupation at that time was as Chief Engineer for the West India work, so any order he placed would have come from his office there. So, it could well be that Jessop was preparing machinery for work on the rock, and Trevithick's reference to "every purpose" suggests that this new engine was being used for a variety of tasks and working different machines. John Vivian's dates, however, do not tally, for the chisel and borers were not set to work until 1804. There was, however, other work going on in the area, notably dredging, and here Trevithick's involvement is a good deal clearer. Perhaps it was this side of the work which Vivian recalled and which he had confused with the actual breaking of Blackwall Rock. To try and clarify this aspect of the story also creates a few problems, and we have to look back to the early years of steam dredging.

Trevithick was not the first to apply steam power to dredging. That honour went to Boulton and Watt in 1796, but theirs was a crude device. It was a ladle dredger, which was no more than a series of scoops worked by winches and controlled by long handles. The Boulton and Watt machine had just four ladles and was used in Sunderland Harbour. A much more useful device, as far as the application of steam was concerned, was the bucket-chain dredger, in which, as the name suggests, buckets were attached to a continuous chain worked, either by men on a treadmill, or by a horse whim. The famous civil engineer John Rennie recommended using steam to replace animal power for a similar dredger in Hull Docks in 1802, but before it was set to work he was pipped at the post by the American, Oliver Evans, who worked what must be called the first successful modern dredger in Philadelphia. It seems an obvious use of steam power, but there were problems to overcome. With the old animal-powered dredger, if one of the buckets hit an unyielding object, such as a large stone, the animal might heave away for a bit trying to shift it, and then give up. If a steam-powered dredger hit an obstacle, the bucket would stop, but not the engine, and considerable damage could be caused unless a suitable safety mechanism was installed. The solution used in the early dredgers was to build in a weak link, which would fracture but could be easily repaired.

It is easy to see why Trevithick would be interested. Here was something new, which always appealed to him, and a compact but powerful engine was just the thing for putting on a boat and taking out on the river. It was a conjunction that had already occurred to Samuel Bentham, who in 1796 had been appointed to the very important post of Inspector-General for the naval dockyards. Although born into a wealthy family, his life had never been idle. He had gone through a full apprenticeship as a shipwright, and had travelled widely in Europe to see what other countries were doing about ship-building, docks and harbours. He was, unlike the Admiralty Board, an enthusiastic innovator and by 1803 he was himself considering inviting Trevithick to install a high-pressure engine in a chain dredger. This would have been a most valuable contract, but sadly the Greenwich boiler explosion (see page 86) led to everything being cancelled. It was, however, another encouraging sign for Trevithick, and even if the navy was not prepared to chance his invention, there were others working on the Thames who were.

The next piece of evidence about Trevithick's role in these matters comes from a Mr Bendy, who had actually worked with him on the Thames dredgers. Francis Trevithick stayed with the Bendy family when collecting material for the biography of his father. He heard a great deal of anecdotal evidence, including dark tales of sabotage. This is not too surprising since, as with so many industries at that time, the introduction of steam threatened older forms of working. Bendy was quite specific, however, about the dredger, made for use by the company which was already busy on the Thames works, Hughes, Bough and Mills.[3]

It was fixed in the year 1803, and was altered by Mr. Deverill (the patentee of the double engine) in the year 1805. The cylinder was 14½ inches in diameter, the stroke 4 feet, the chain-ladder 28 or 30 feet. The largest quantity of stone and gravel lifted in one tide was 180 tons. The reason for using the word stone is from its being part of Blackwall rock. The engine was cast at Hazeldine's at Bridgenorth but finished at Mr. Rowley's factory in London, by some men from Cornwall, and a part of the machinery by Jackson, a Scotch millwright. The working time between tides was from six to eight hours, in from 14 to 18 feet of water at the entrance of the East India Dock. The expense of the engine and machinery, a little more than 2000*l*. I should think the time she worked was about ten or eleven years.

This, then, is certainly not the engine mentioned in Trevithick's letter, since that was being built at Coalbrookdale. What is still not at all clear is whether Trevithick was responsible for the whole of the dredger design or just the power unit. The one thing that is at least established is that by 1804 he had two high-pressure engines at work in and around the dock construction sites. But that only represented a part of the work being carried out on the river at that time. Trinity House, the body best-known for controlling light-houses, also had a long-standing agreement for undertaking dredging on the tidal river, and now the Trevithick story gets a little less murky. One of the ways in which Trinity House made money was by dredging up material and then, instead of simply dumping it on shore, selling it on as ship's ballast. The profit margins on ballasting were small to minute, so any cost-saving was especially welcome. All the work, up to that time, had been done by hand. The ballast was loaded into lighters, and once a vessel was full it was taken away to be unloaded into vessels at anchor on the tideway. The men who did the work, the ballast heavers, were clamouring for more money, which Trinity House were disinclined to pay. So they advertised for alternative ideas.

Trevithick clearly thought this was no problem at all. It was almost an article of religious faith with him to believe that anything that could be done by hand could be done better and cheaper by machine, preferably powered by steam. For the past three or four years, he had been preoccupied with promoting the steam locomotive, but as that seemed to be leading nowhere, he was quite prepared to look at alternative plans. He had, by the end of 1804, seen enough of steam dredging to feel supremely confident that it was an area ripe for development, and he had some useful contacts who could further his cause. He already knew one of the most influential men in the city, the Lord Mayor, Sir William Curtis, who had shown an interest in taking up Vivian's share of their joint patent. The contract being offered was for supplying 500,000 tons of ballast a year at sixpence a ton, which would bring in a very useful gross income of £12,500 a year. As always he presented himself to the world as full of confidence: the contract was his for the asking, and the whole thing could be done with no difficulty whatsoever.[4]

> I am to do nothing but wind up the chain for 6d pr Ton which is now don by men. The never lift it above 25 feet high. A man will now get up 10 Ton for 7s. My engine at Dolcoath have lifted above one hundd Tons that height with one bushell of Coals. I have two engines all ready finishd for the purpose and shall be in town in abt 15 Days for to sett them at Work.

Stating that he intended to do it and that he saw no problems in doing it was, alas, not quite enough to persuade Trinity House to hand over a valuable contract, no questions asked. They had no particular reason to take his word for it, even if he had been involved in constructing a dredger then at work on the river – and we do not know the degree of his involvement. His proposals were passed to John Rennie, who really did know about dredging, and Trevithick was ordered to come up with specific, detailed proposals, rather than vague suggestions. In May 1806 he submitted a report with an outline of how he proposed to organise the work.[5]

> I am of opinion that by adopting Machinery to be worked by steam to raise the Ballast, and employing the craft merely for its conveyance to the Shipping; thereby dividing the business into Two distinct branches; a great improvement may be made, and a very

considerable saving in the expences will accrue; as the number of Men and Craft employed, and the consequent Wear and Tear of Materials wod be greatly diminished.

Two days later he made a personal appearance and was questioned about his ideas, which to his chagrin were declared not to be sufficiently worked out. He had to go away and revise the proposal; and even then, instead of getting an unconditional contract, he was told that he should start work so that his methods could be assessed in practice. When everything was shown to work, and only then, would he be awarded the full contract. Persuading Trinity House had proved far more difficult than he had ever imagined: he was about to find that the same was true of dredging. He discovered that what worked well at Dolcoath with a stationary engine firmly fixed to the ground and lifting material up from a hole, was not necessarily equally successful when the engine was mounted on a bobbing boat, subject to tides and currents, hauling unknown material from an unseen riverbed.

He soon had three dredgers at work, two working near the entrances to the East and West India Docks and one at Woolwich. There were two 10 horsepower engines, one set in a former gun brig, the *Blazer* the other on a barge, and a 20 horsepower engine on a former bomb-ship. Trevithick himself gave details of them when tendering for work at Falmouth harbour in 1813, when he suggested that all three were successful. It has to be said, that this was not a wholly-accurate description of what was going on along the Thames. The old bomb-ship at Woolwich had the easiest task, being required to do no more than scrape up mud from the riverbed. The *Blazer* proved very troublesome and we now know that this was the dredger that had gone to Hughes, Bough and Mills, who were less than happy, as Hughes' assistant at the time recalled.[6]

The Blazer dredging engine was deficient in some parts of its machinery as it could not perform what it was intended to do. They then wished me to go on board the Blazer and examine it, but I strongly objected, saying I did not like to interfere with any other person's business. Mr Hughes then told me that if I would not go on board, and see what was wrong, the vessel must be put into Perry and Well's Dock, for it was a very great expense to keep her on the river with two sets of men, without doing scarcely any work at all.

Mr Hughes then showed me a calculation of the expense of the Blazer dredging engine and pressed me very much to go on board and make the necessary alteration, and I then complied with his request. The Blazer was after that employed to assist in finishing the contract at the East India Moorings and afterwards to raise gravel near Westminster Bridge, and various other places in the river & docks.

The unknown writer of this piece was presumably the Mr Deverill mentioned by Bendy, who might also be the equally mysterious Mr Deveral who is recorded as suggesting the idea of a steam hammer at about the same time.

Meanwhile the ballasting work was also going badly. After testing his dredger at Barking, Trevithick moved it to Limehouse and asked for lighters to be sent down for filling. Trinity House, however, were beginning to lose patience. Performance was still far short of what had been promised, and they were in no mood to enter into contracts for any further work. When they asked him exactly when his machine would do the work that he had specified, he replied that he had unfortunately discovered that what he really needed was a much more powerful engine. This was not a problem, and he would be more than happy to install such an engine, when he was sure everything would work perfectly. However, it would cost him £5000, and sadly he would have to ask for the price of ballast to be raised by threepence a ton. As Trevithick was supposed to be applying steam to cut costs, he was either wildly optimistic or sadly naive if he thought they were now going to agree to a whopping great fifty per cent increase. He was not delivering ballast at the promised tonnage nor at the agreed cost, and one can hardly blame Trinity House for calling a halt.

This was not one of the more glorious episodes in Trevithick's life. Normally when he had work that excited him in hand, he was busily telling everyone about it. The lack of correspondence in this case suggests that he was not giving the dredging business the attention it obviously needed. The steam carriages and locomotives were failures only in the sense that they did not attract paying customers. The dredgers failed because they did not work well enough, a very different matter. Neglect may have been only a part of the story. Trevithick may have been one of the greatest, arguably the greatest, mechanical engineers of his day, but he was not familiar with the vagaries of rivers and moving water. It was here that a man like Jessop had the edge, for he had spent almost his whole life building canals, improving river navigations and draining wetlands. He was to carry on using steam dredgers to good effect, notably in his work with Thomas Telford in building the Caledonian Canal. Nevertheless, Trevithick's dredger engine was considered sufficiently important to be recorded in an encyclopedia, which provides one of the fullest accounts we have of the state of technology at the beginning of the nineteenth century.[7] There is an illustration of the engine, which is a clear derivative of the standard puffers. But even here there is a slight mystery, for it is described as being a 6 horsepower engine, and Trevithick himself intimated that the smallest dredging engine he built was 10 horsepower. The drawing is dated 1803, and there is a second drawing showing it in place in the dredger. It does certainly seem to confirm that a Trevithick engine had been installed in a dredger at an early date, for no one can doubt that this is a puffer, even though Trevithick himself is not named. It does nothing, however, to settle the question of when he first started to design a dredger of his own, nor indeed is there anything to show that he ever did so at all. It is perhaps worth repeating what he wrote to Gilbert at the beginning of the ballast saga, that he was "to do nothing but wind up the chain".

Francis Trevithick, eager as ever to promote his father's cause, claimed that John Rennie saw the Trevithick dredger and only then went off to Hull to build one of his own. We can now safely take that suggestion and put it away on the shelf and admit that, in this area of technology at least, he made no very significant contribution, other than to provide an appropriate, compact power source as he had done in other industries and other situations. In any case, by 1808 it was clear that any enthusiasm he had ever had for dredging had vanished. He was not prepared to pursue the matter any further and he sold the whole of his ballast business off, presumably to Hughes, Bough and Mills. He had not, of course, abandoned his locomotive plans and he was still meeting the demand for high-pressure engines, but he would not have been the Trevithick we know if he had not also been quite ready to set off on a new tack, heading in some previously undreamed-of direction. He had not enjoyed much good fortune floating about on the Thames: now he was about to plunge far beneath it. His new project was to be nothing less than a Thames tunnel. It seems extraordinary that a man who for years had concentrated all his

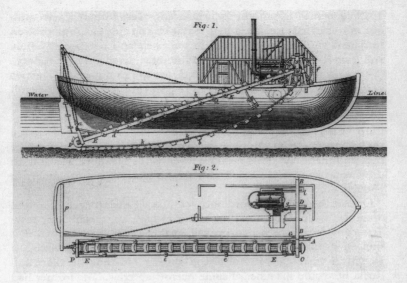

Fig: 1.

Water Line.

Fig: 2.

Fig 3: *The steam dredger, with an easily recognisable high-pressure "puffer" providing the power.*

effort on inventing machines should now be seriously considering what looks like a wholly different career as a civil engineer. But, at this stage, the project offered a problem with which he was very familiar from his time as a mining engineer in Cornwall. What was under construction was not a full-size tunnel, but a driftway. This was to do two things: it would prove the ground for the main tunnel, and when construction of that got under way it could be used as a drain. To a miner it was just another long adit. That certainly seemed to be Trevithick's view of it. He was well used to burrowing deep underground, with vast quantities of earth and rock overhead, and it probably seemed to make little difference if there was also water on top of that. If he had taken the trouble to enquire why he had been called in he might have been a little less sanguine.

The first requirement before anything could be done was to get an Act of Parliament. This was passed in 1805 which allowed work to start and authorised the newly formed Thames Archway Company to raise £140,000 in £100 shares and to borrow a further £60,000 if needed. One of the most enthusiastic supporters of the scheme was another Cornish engineer, Robert Vazie, who not only carried out the initial tentative test borings, but showed sufficient confidence to buy shares himself and persuaded family and friends to do the same. He was the obvious man to take charge of the engineering works. The tunnel was to run under the Thames at Limehouse Reach, where the river goes through a great U-bend, and the site chosen was quite close to that of the present Rotherhithe road tunnel. Vazie's plan was the obvious, straightforward one which any mining engineer would have adopted: sink a shaft somewhere on the river bank to a depth well below the river bed, and then send out a heading towards the far shore. He sent off to Cornwall for experienced miners and work began in earnest in 1806.

One of the most extraordinary features of the story is the blind optimism with which everyone seems to have approached the task. The canal age, which had peaked in the 1790s, had shown, if it showed nothing else, the total unpredictability of tunnelling. If Trevithick had chatted to Jessop during his time at Blackwall Rock, he would have heard some harrowing tales. The former had just overseen the completion of Blisworth tunnel on the Grand Junction – now the Grand Union – Canal. Work had begun on this 3482-metre long tunnel in a similar mood of high optimism in 1793. When work started it was assumed that the whole canal would be completed within the allowed budget of £500,000, but the company had to go back to Parliament time and again for authorisation to raise extra capital, and by the end the costs had almost trebled. And Blisworth tunnel was finally opened in 1805, twelve years after work started. Vazie's tunnelling efforts fared even worse than Jessop's. The first year's budget was spent and all there was to show for it was an incomplete shaft on the south bank at Rotherhithe. He had not yet even begun to make a move towards the river itself, 100 metres away.

It was very unsatisfactory, and there seemed to be only three realistic options: continue putting faith in the appointed engineer; sack him and bring in someone else; or call in expert advice. The company managed the remarkable feat of doing all three. They kept Vazie on, and they asked the opinion of not one but two expert engineers, John Rennie and William Chapman, which was no help at all because they simply disagreed with each other. And they called in a new man, not to replace Vazie, but to work with him on an equal footing. The new man was, of course, Trevithick, who had Gilbert to thank for the recommendation. As always, he claimed to see the job as little more than routine. Given that the sinking of the shaft had revealed some very disturbing features, in particular a large area of quicksand, this seems unjustifiably optimistic. But it was Trevithick's way to assume all would be well until it proved otherwise, and then deal with any problems that arose.[8]

> Last monday I closed with the Tunnel gents. I have agreed with them to give them advice and conduct the Driveing the level through to the opposite side, as was proposed when you attended the commette; to receive £500 when the Drift is half way through, and £500 more when its holed on the opposite side. I have wrote to Cornwall for more men for them. Its intended to put 3 men in each core six hours' course. I think this will be making a thousand pounds very easey, and withoute any risque of a loss on my side, and as I must be allways near the spot to attend to the engines on the river, an hour's attendance every day on the tunnel will be of little or no inconvenience to me. hope 9 months will compleat it. From the recommendation you gave me, they are in great hopes that the job will now be accomplishd; and as far as Capn Hodge and my self culd judg from the ground in the bottom of the pit, theres no dought of compleating it speedily.

Within a week he was at work, driving the driftway out from the foot of the shaft, and, at first, everything seemed to be going just as he had predicted.[9]

> The level is 5ft high, 3 ft wide at the bottom, and 2ft 6In Wide at the top within the timber. The first week we drove 22 feet. This week I hope we shall drive and timber 10 fathoms. As soon as the railway is laid I hope to make good 12 fathoms a week. The disstance we have to drive is abt 188 fathoms [344 m] the ground is sand and gravel and stands exceeding well, except its when we hole into leareys and holeing to such houses of water makes the sand very quick. We have discovered three of these holes which contained about twenty square yards. Its very strange that such spaces shod be in sand at this Deypth. When we cutt in to the places we are obliged to timber it up close untill the sand is drayned of the water, otherways it wod run back and fill the drift and shaft. I cannot see any obstickle likley to prevent us from carrying this level across the river in six month as the Engine throws down a sufficient quantity of air, and the railway underground will inable us to bring back the stuff, so as to keep the

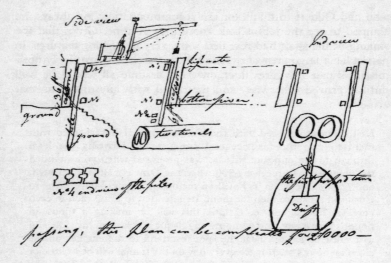

Fig 4: *Trevithick's sketches for his Thames tunnel proposal. The drawing on the left shows the caisson sunk down to the riverbed. Piles are being driven by steam inside the caisson to allow the bed to be excavated, and the double-bored tunnel is shown. The drawing on the right shows caissons, piles, tunnel and a drain down to the old drift. The line of the original tunnel is indicated surrounding the drift. A typically optimistic note announces that it can all be done for £10,000.*

level quite clear, and the last fathom will be as speedily drove as the first.

As the work proceeded out under the river, Trevithick was able to persuade the company to provide a more powerful pumping engine as a precaution against flooding. He might still be talking up the job, expressing supreme confidence, but when it came to practical matters of safety he became altogether more cautious. His reports remained upbeat, but he was aware, as any experienced miner would be, of the very real threat of inundation. How far the good progress was due to Vazie and how much depended on Trevithick's arrival on the scene there is no means of telling, but when things started to go wrong the directors were quick to apportion the blame. Vazie on his own had not done well, Vazie and Trevithick had done better: if things went wrong, and there were unnecessary delays, it was perhaps time to try Trevithick on his own. By October 1807, the drift had advanced 394 ft (120 m) and it must have come as a bitter blow to Vazie who had devoted four years of his life and invested his own money in the project to see the whole thing taken out of his hands and passed over to his part-time associate. In retrospect, one can see that it would have been far better to have made the clean break back in August, for now there were bound to be suspicions among Vazie's supporters that Trevithick had been plotting all along to take his place.

With Trevithick in sole charge, however, the decision seemed to be vindicated, for work now went on twice as fast as before. Then, at the end of November, instead of sand and gravel they were faced with solid rock. With the drift uncomfortably near the riverbed, there was no question of blasting it away, so the only thing to do was to break it up by hand, with chisels and wedges. This was the first sign that they were not going to find uniform conditions all the way across to the far bank. Worse was to come. The tunnellers ran into a patch of sandy clay which, ominously, was mixed with oyster shells, suggesting that they were too near the riverbed for comfort. They edged forward with a good deal of caution and then reached quicksand, which collapsed allowing a gooey, wet mass to flow into the drift. It was a very uncomfortable time and extra care had to be taken in shoring up the drift, and the advance became ever slower. Then on 26 January 1808, when they had reached 1028 feet (313 m) from the shaft, the roof itself began to break up and river water flooded in.

They managed to stop up the hole, and soon the drift was pumped dry again. Meanwhile Trevithick had problems of his own to face. The Vazie faction had continued to try and undermine his position. One of the shareholders had been attacking Trevithick for being over cautious, in refusing to open up the drift to the full width of the tunnel once they had arrived at the middle of the river. Trevithick who was already fighting against appalling conditions in the drift was scathing. "This gent was never in a mine in his life, neither do he know any thing about it. He called a general meeting to discharge me, but he was taken no notice of".[10] In fact, the meeting went in the opposite direction, and the board ended up offering him £1250 to see the whole project through to completion.

It was now all too clear to Trevithick that he was not going to make "easy money" out of the project, and that, on the contrary, even if everything now went well, he would still be occupied here for some time to come. He sent for his family to join him. It was not just the prospect of spending a long time on the tunnel that influenced him, but it must have seemed that his future lay in London. It was here that great projects were going forward, not in the remote far-west of England, many days' journey from the capital. Jane was not at all keen to give up her country home for a house in London, and her brother Henry Harvey urged her to stay in Cornwall. He had no very strong faith in his brother-in-law's money-making schemes. Harvey's idea of building a fortune was to establish a solid base and slowly build up from there, as his family had done with great success at Hayle. He definitely did not approve of dashing all over the country, pursuing one new idea after the other.

Just how much Jane knew of London life is uncertain, but it is unlikely that she would have got a very accurate picture from her husband. Certainly, if he had given even a hint of the squalor of life beside London's river she would never have left Cornwall. Some parts of London had been improved in the eighteenth century. The noxious River Fleet, scarcely better than an open sewer, had been covered over, but nothing had changed its character. Anything and everything was tipped in, to re-emerge into the light as the little river joined the broad Thames. Upstream of Rotherhithe, where Trevithick had settled, were the vile-smelling slaughter houses of Whitechapel and a rich variety of noisome tanneries lined the river-bank. In theory, everything was scoured out twice a day by the tides. In practice, the normal appearance of the river was a stream the colour of molasses, but smelling a lot less sweet, and each low tide left a gleaming, stinking scum clinging to the banks. This was what faced Jane when she arrived with the four children, Richard, Anne, Elizabeth and John, all under the age of ten.

Her disillusionment with her new surroundings was compounded by discovering her most recent letters unopened in her husband's pocket. All he could say in his own defence was that he could not bear to read them in case her pleas persuaded him to let her stay in Camborne. While it might have been flattering to be told how much she was wanted, nothing could reconcile her to the squalor of her new London home. Typically, Trevithick had chosen it because it was near the shaft, showing as little thought for his family's comfort as he regularly showed for his own. Now Jane was adamant. She would stay in London, but not in Rotherhithe. Soon they were all off again, to a much more pleasant situation in Limehouse. Here she met the French wife of an old friend of theirs from Cornwall, and the two women were able to meet regularly to compare notes on the miseries of life in exile.

Jane had scarcely had time to unpack before disaster struck at the drift. On 26 January 1809 the roof collapsed and water flooded in. There was a desperate scramble to escape down the narrow drift with the water rising round the men. Trevithick himself was in the drift at the time, and typically he waited to make sure everybody was safe before he floundered out, his head just above the water level, scarcely able to breathe. He lost his shoes and his hat, and, caked with slime and clay, he marched off home to Jane, otherwise unharmed. Whatever criticisms could be made of Trevithick's character, no one could ever question his qualities of courage and endurance. Nor could anyone accuse him of failing to rise to a challenge. After what must have been a nightmarish experience, he went straight back to the drift to examine the damage and begin the work of drainage. It was just one of those problems waiting to be solved.[11]

> Last week the water broake down on us from the river, through a quick sand, and fill'd the whole of the level and shaft in 10 minutes, but I have stop'd it compleatly tight and the miners at work again. We are beyond low water Mark on the north side with the drift; and if we have no farther delays we shall hole up to the surface in 10 or 12 days.

He ended the letter on a characteristically optimistic note: "I have no dought of accomplishing my job." The directors had a meeting on site and must have been considerably taken aback to find that rather than being asked to puzzle over what should happen next, they were presented with a highly ingenious solution. Trevithick proposed sinking a caisson down to the riverbed to surround the site of the collapse, after which clay would be poured in to plug the hole. A second shaft would be sunk to remove the spoil. The navigation authorities might not have been too keen on establishing a large caisson right in the middle of the tideway, but that was of no concern to Trevithick. The real opposition came predictably from the Vazie faction, demanding Trevithick's resignation for what they described as incompetence in allowing the accident to happen in the first place. The discontent that had been seething for months now broke out in earnest and there was a good deal of plain speaking. The report of the directors' meeting in April 1808 spelled out in the clearest terms that there had been a minority at work attempting to impede progress "and darken Mr. Trevithick's reputation".[12] The directors stood firm.

> as no act of Mr Trevithick's incompetency was ever shown, though many were falsely alleged, and as the directors never observed any instance either of neglect or want of skill in him, but that on every occasion where his knowledge, his intelligence, and experience in his profession were questioned and examined by competent persons, his talents appeared very superior to the common level, the confidence which the directors reposed in him was not shaken.

But in spite of this unequivocal statement, they still felt bound to offer a sop to the vocal opposition. They agreed to call in two experienced mine engineers from north-east England, who had had no previous connection with Trevithick, to inspect and report on the works. The result was a complete vindication of Trevithick, so that he could reasonably have expected to get back to work without further interference. But once doubts have been raised, they are not easily dispelled. The proprietors were no longer prepared to let the engineer have his own way, without covering themselves by seeking second opinions. The situation was becoming increasingly absurd. They wanted clear statements from experts, but there were no experts on tunnelling under rivers, because no one had ever done it before. Trevithick did his best to ignore the politicking and went on with what he was best at, using experience and imagination to think of a solution to an increasingly difficult problem.

His next suggestion was entirely novel and very daring. He could no longer see any point in continuing the drift, for there was nothing new to be learned from it – the worst had already been revealed. It was time to start the tunnel proper. He proposed sinking a large caisson down to the riverbed. Inside this he would drive piles and excavate to a depth equal to that of the tunnel floor. Inside this space, which would be kept dry by pumps, a fifty-foot-long section of tunnel would be constructed out of brick. When it was complete and waterproof, the piles would be removed, the caisson lifted and moved along ready for work to start on the next section. At each move a hole would be drilled up from the drift to act as a drain. The tunnel was to have a double bore and each bore would be wide enough for a roadway and footpath. In August, the directors shied away from this revolutionary proposal. Trevithick responded by coming up with an even more innovative plan. This time he proposed doing away with the brickwork, using cast-iron sections instead. It is perhaps worth noting that when a tunnel was finally opened under the Thames at Rotherhithe, a century later in 1908, it was entirely lined with cast-iron. Whether a technique that succeeded using the technology of precision casting and fine machining that was available in 1908 would have worked in 1808 is a different story.

Everyone seemed to want to call in experts, so Trevithick decided it was time he had one of his own, and asked Goodrich for an opinion on his proposals. He agreed with Trevithick that there was no point in continuing with the driftway or in trying to enlarge it by driving through still more quicksands. He declared that the new ideas, however, seemed very practical. The directors were no longer prepared to take anyone's word for anything, so still more experts were called in, this time in the form of high-ranking officers in the Royal Engineers. Things were getting out of control, with no one able to take any decisions about anything. Confusion became absolute in March 1809, when the directors threw the whole question of how to build the tunnel out to public competition. The now terminally nervous board who had been quite unable to decide what to do about one idea put forward by their own engineer, in whom they had declared full confidence, were now faced with fifty-four different plans from people they knew nothing about. The next step was inevitable. They called in yet more experts. One was William Jessop, the other the mathematician Charles Hutton, who was best known for his work on mapping and, rather bizarrely in the circumstances, a text book, not on tunnels, but on bridges. At least they put the board out of their misery. They came up with a definite and unequivocal reply: it was not possible to build a tunnel under the Thames. The days of dithering were over; the Archway Company ceased to exist, and with it Trevithick's involvement with tunnelling.

This was not quite the end of the story. One of the proprietors, I.W. Tate never lost faith. When he heard of a new device, a tunnelling shield, patented by Marc Brunel, he revived the whole idea. By 1824, Marc Brunel had begun work on a new tunnel, downstream of the old driftway, at Wapping. Brunel was to find life no easier than Trevithick had done, but at least he lived to see the work completed with a grand official opening in 1843.

The Thames tunnel was a failure, but a most valiant one.

Trevithick was quite literally advancing into the unknown, uncertain each day what he would meet, good ground, solid rock or treacherous, shifting quicksand. Flooding was a constant risk and became a terrifying reality. The surprise is not that he failed, but that he achieved so much. His resolution was admirable, especially when viewed against the background of a concerted campaign against himself. He demonstrated his great abilities in improvising solutions to the most difficult problems, and with his proposal for prefabricated sections he came up with a proposal of staggering originality. Brunel, even with the advantages of a better technology, found the task as demanding as Trevithick had done. He, too, was to see the whole works drowned out, had to face agonising delays, and only just lived long enough to see the work completed. In retrospect we can see that Trevithick did not have the resources in 1808 to see the work through to completion, but it was certainly not obvious then. He did far more than anyone could reasonably have expected, even if what he achieved fell far short of what he promised and fervently desired.

Trevithick was never a man to brood over failure. Tunnelling over, he promptly turned back to older preoccupations, and it was now that he was able to devote time to working on his locomotive, "Catch-me-who-can". The early London years had been full of hopes, but had ended in disappointments. He was undeterred. He had not yet finished with London: it was simply that the time had arrived for yet more new plans and new ideas.

CHAPTER ELEVEN

End of a Dream

One result of Trevithick's experiences during the first years of his life in London was that he had learned first-hand just how inefficient many of the long-established work practices were. One reason that he had been so confident of success in the ballasting business had been his observation of the way it was being managed under the old system. The ballasting boat left the Pool of London at high tide and reached the dredging site at half ebb. Working flat out, the five men on board could load 45 to 50 tons before the next half tide, when the water became too deep for them to continue. They then moved away to unload at the waiting ship. A full ballasting crew was on board the whole time, and were paid for the whole time, but only worked for part of it. To Trevithick it made no sense. It also seemed to him to make no sense that, even after steam dredging had been introduced, and the lighter was filled by steam power, it was still unloaded by manpower. He certainly did not consider it beyond his ingenuity to increase the use of the steam engine, and if it could be used for ballast, then why not for any other cargo as well? He had plenty of time to develop his ideas after the failure of the Archway Company, but he was now desperately short of cash. One way he chose to raise finance was to follow Andrew Vivian's example and sell off his share in the high-pressure engine patent. He had already started disposing of his lucrative mine shares to help pay for earlier projects, so it seemed a natural step to take, but it could hardly be described as sound financial thinking. In effect, Trevithick had used his inventive genius to acquire a patent for high-pressure engines, which were proving their worth and beginning to bring him some revenue – and with

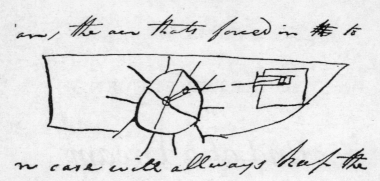

Fig 5: *Trevithick's sketch for a paddle-steamer from a letter of 1806. It shows the simple drive, but not the air pump.*

better management could be expected to bring in a good deal more. Now he was getting rid of his rights at just the time when he should have been enjoying the rewards. He was sacrificing real present gains for the sake of uncertain prospects. It was a bad habit that he would never be able to cure.

Two ideas were coming together in Trevithick's mind: cargo moving and cargo loading and unloading. New docks were being built, but most of the shipping in Britain's busiest port was still moored out in the middle of the river, where it was served by a variety of lighters and barges. So, the first thing he began to consider was how to get the cargo moved between ship and wharf. We have already seen that he had conducted experiments with a somewhat crude paddle-steamer at Coalbrookdale. On that occasion he had only tried the vessel on still water, but someone must have heard of his experiments and enquired if he could supply an engine to drive a 100-ton clipper. This was something quite outside his experience, and although he had plenty of ideas, he looked for reassurance and advice, as he always did on such occasions, to Davies Gilbert.[1] The problem that worried him was what would happen in rough water, when the paddle wheel might be swamped by waves and lose its efficiency. His idea was ingenious, but unnecessarily complex. He planned to use a horizontal engine, mounted below decks, driving an internal wheel in the hold.

This Wheel is to work in an Iron case, air-tight; the axle to work in a stuffing box, and a pump to force air into this case to keep down the

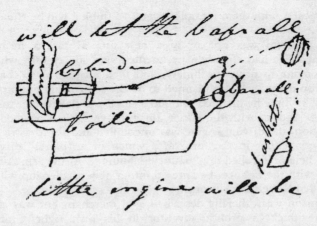

Fig 6: *Trevithick's original sketch for the nautical labourer, first drawn in 1804. It shows the horizontal cylinder mounted above the boiler, the chimney, the barrel (barrall) and a basket of coal.*

water from flooding the wheel, so that onely the flotes on the extremity of the wheel shall be in water, and then onely extend abt 15 Inches below the keel of the ship ... The air thats forced in to this wrought Iron case will allways keep the water down in this case to the level of the bottom of the ship, and a space will be left on each side the wheel, so that the air will never be dissplaced by the working of the wheel.

Nothing seems to have come of this particular proposal, but he kept the idea in his mind when he turned his attention to cargo handling. His first ideas seem to have centred on the notion of having some sort of steam engine at work in the newly built wet docks, but that was quickly ruled out. A moveable engine had actually been ordered for the West India Docks in 1804, but was never used. The authorities would not allow fires to be lit within the dock complex, because of the risks in an enclosed area crowded with wooden ships and surrounded by all kinds of flammable goods stored on the open quays. This was considered so important a matter that the Act of Parliament for the docks had a clause forbidding fire-lighting, and that included fires in boilers. He had, however, heard of steam in use elsewhere, and made a note about "a small engine makeing at Staffordshire, for the London Coal ships to carry with them for unlodeing ... I think it will be equal to 6 men".[2]

The problem was not really a new one as far as he was concerned. He had already experimented very successfully with a puffer engine to drive machinery, and then adapted it so that it could also drive itself. He planned to do the same again out on the water. This time he planned to build a small paddle-steamer to act as a tug. And, as with the puffer, once the vessel had reached its destination, the driving engine was uncoupled and set to work the machinery, either in the form of a winch or a "barrel" driving endless belts. He called it a "nautical labourer". At the same time, to help with the finance, he entered into a new partnership with a man called Robert Dickinson.

Dickinson was officially described as a merchant but was also, like Trevithick, a prolific inventor in his own right. Francis Trevithick's and later biographies have cast Dickinson in the role of arch villain, a view that Trevithick himself voiced, but only after things started to go seriously wrong. The suggestion has also been made that Dickinson latched on to Trevithick only in order to exploit his ideas. But he would appear to have had no need to steal other people's inventions, as he took out twenty patents of his own over the years. That represents a considerable investment in time and money, and shows considerable faith in his own abilities. The really interesting question is why Trevithick chose this particular partner in the first place. What he needed at this time was a sober man of good business judgement, working from a sound financial base. But Trevithick was not the least attracted to such men: he much preferred those who would be instantly enthused by his ideas and would leap into action – men, in other words, very like himself. What he did not need was any ideas for new inventions, but it was the inventive mind that most appealed to him. So, instead of a solid financier he finished up with a fellow inventor. It was not a partnership to inspire confidence. The likelihood is that Dickinson was not really a scoundrel at all, but a reasonably honest man who just happened to have as good a business sense as his new partner, but a rather better-developed sense of self preservation – and that was a recipe for disaster.

In 1808 they took out a joint patent for the nautical labourer. The paddle-steamer was designed in just the way he had suggested in his letter to Gilbert in 1806. He envisaged the new vessel as working like a tug in the first instance, towing barges out to the vessels at anchor, but he was not entirely confident about its power. When working against a strong tide or current, he proposed that the barges carried long poles or "setts" which could be pushed down into the river bed. Once the setts were firmly in place, the barges were secured to them and the tug would puff on ahead for the full length of the tow-line and drop anchor. The setts were then lifted, and the barges winched in. The process could be repeated as often as necessary. Once the barges had come alongside the ship, the tug would revert to its other function, and the engine would operate the winch to move the cargo. The official document ends with a very Trevithickian statement, which glosses over all potential difficulties, gives no real details on how the machine would work, but manages to suggest almost infinite versatility for the invention.[3]

> Where towing of vessels and discharging of vessels may not both be wanted, the apparatus may be relieved of part of its load, and of part of the expense of construction, that is to say, where only towing may be wanted the machinery need not be loaded with those parts which apply to the discharging of vessels; and, on the other hand, where towing is not wanted, but only discharging and unloading, the parts that apply to towing may be dispensed with.

However good the idea may have been in theory, and it is doubtful if the notion of pumping in air above the wheel would have survived a practical experiment, there were two wholly intractable problems that prevented it ever being put into practice. The first was the law that prevented steam engines being used in the docks. This applied to steam vessels as well as land-based engines. Possibly, had the will been there, a concerted effort might have brought a change in the law, but the will was lacking. In itself this was not a crippling restriction. There was still plenty of work to be had out on the open river, among the massed shipping in the Pool of London; but the second obstacle was probably beyond the power of anyone to remove. The all-powerful Society of Coal Whippers, representing the port labourers, blacked the new machine and threatened to drown its inventors. Even the Cornish giant who had cheerfully braved floods in the tunnel took that seriously, and for a time actually had an escort as he went about his business. Over the years, the dock labourers were to prove the most conservative and intransigent work force in the land and the most jealous guardian of ancient rights and agreements. Once their opposition had been declared, the nautical labourer was doomed.

Trevithick had, of course, other new ideas and plans instantly available. The next proposal seems to have come to him almost by chance from a small beginning. Francis Trevithick heard the story from his elder brother, Richard, who described an incident that happened when he first arrived in London as a ten-year-old.[4]

> my father, on coming into the house on a Sunday morning, desired me to fetch a wineglass, and taking me by the hand, walked to the old yard near the Tunnel works. There was an old steam-engine boiler in the yard; my father filled the glass with water from the boiler gauge-cock, and asked me to tell him if it was good water. We used to speak of this as the origin of the iron tanks.

One would like to think that the father made the experiment first on himself, before trying it on his son. In any case, what he had discovered was that fresh water kept in an iron tank was not contaminated. From this small beginning, it required a leap of the imagination to reach the next stage. Up to then, liquid cargo had been universally stored in wooden casks, which were necessarily built as circular barrels to make them watertight. From this point of view they were excellent, but when they were packed together in a ship's hold a great deal of space was wasted. Trevithick realised that it was perfectly possible to make square iron tanks that would be waterproof and waste no space whatsoever, as they could be packed closely side by side. It seems a very obvious idea, but it was undoubtedly new and Trevithick and Dickinson made it the subject of their next patent, taken out in October 1809. They published a pamphlet in February the following year which is particularly interesting, for it shows that they had already seen other uses for the tanks, which were later to be developed and widely used.

> With respect to the Royal Navy, the patentees presume to think that the adoption of iron stowage would be advantageous in a more than common degree. If ships of war were provided with metal tanks for containing their beer, water, provisions, and stores, would not the necessity for ballast be in part done away?

Trevithick was so used to hurling ideas around that he may not even have realised just how important this almost throw-away remark was. Iron tanks to store water were to become standard in years to come, and of immense value in ensuring good fresh water supplies. And using water tanks for ballasting, pumping seawater in when extra weight was needed and pumping it out when cargo was loaded, made for great flexibility and accuracy in trimming a vessel. It was also a good deal less troublesome than loading and unloading stone or pig-iron bars.

This time, at least, there was nothing to stop the partners putting their ideas into practice, and they established a site for manufacturing iron tanks. Trevithick must have been delighted at finally getting one of his inventions into production – poor Jane was a good deal less pleased. Her husband's immediate idea was to have everything under his own eyes, so manufacturing began right next to their new home in Limehouse. Anyone who has ever visited a boiler works or shipyard will know the colossal din that results from hammering and riveting hollow iron containers. Once work got under way, she must have started to regard Rotherhithe with something like nostalgia.

Trevithick's first idea was to try and interest the Admiralty in his idea, but ran up against the all too predictable wall of apathy. This was immensely irritating, as they were potentially major customers, but there were plenty of merchantmen who might be more readily convinced that the words "new" and "bad" were not necessarily interchangeable. He was, in any case, constantly thinking up new ways of using iron containers. An iron box filled with air will float, so he came up with the notion that is now in general use throughout the world, hollow metal buoys.

His next idea was even more exciting. If you sink a box full of water below the surface, and then pump out the water, it will bob up again. If you have big boxes and enough of them and attach them to a sunken ship, then when they rise, the ship will rise with them: you are in the salvage business. That experiment was tried at Margate. Now Trevithick met another fine old British institution – the demarcation dispute. One man, for example, had been given the job of fastening the boxes to the ship's sides. He was, he declared, quite willing to fasten the bolts, but drilling the holes they would have to go through was nothing to do with him at all. When a man was found who would drill holes, he refused to fasten any bolts. In spite of all these frustrating problems, the sunken vessel was successfully raised to the surface. One can well imagine, however, that, by then, a man like Trevithick would not be in the best of moods and would not be keen to hear any fresh arguments. The next part of the story was told to

Francis Trevithick by his mother. Once the vessel was raised, Trevithick declared his job was done: the ship owners disputed this, and said it had to be brought back to dock. Trevithick said he was ready to do this, but wanted extra payment for towing it; the owners said they would pay no more. Obstinacy led to exasperation, and in a fit of temper, Trevithick ordered the men to cut the tanks free. He lost his fee, the ship was back on the seabed, and no one had gained a thing. Trevithick's career as a salvage expert was, it seemed, at an end. But the experience was not wasted, and he was to put it to profitable use a few years later.

It was not just the Trevithick temper that threatened the profitability of the whole business. He had brought trusted men in to look after the day-to-day running of the concern; John Steel, of Penydarren and Gateshead, and two Cornishmen, Samuel Hambly and Samuel Rowe. They were all good workmen, but they had no experience of running a business. Dickinson was becoming increasingly exasperated. Jane Trevithick had, not unreasonably, refused to allow him to use her home as an office. There are also indications, from later correspondence, that whatever her husband might think, she neither liked nor trusted him. He was dismayed by the chaos that reigned in the yard. An undated letter lists a catalogue of problems, most of which he attributed to Steel.[5]

I have only just received the letter sent you by Cockshott's attorney so long ago as the 6th, and which you had detained till the 11th, although it states that the expenses *are going on, &c.* This is most unaccountable.

Steel has never yet furnished me with Thomas and Rudge's account, made out as I desired a week ago. This is a conduct not to be allowed.

I have a letter before me just received from John Steel, Horseferry, for 90*l.* for barge hire. These with the acceptances I am under, and the sums I have paid already, make me begin to look about me, and for once to express myself dissatisfied generally.

It is but of little use I know, and for me to attempt to take any part in the management were ridiculous; and even Mrs. T. has flatly objected even to my sons being in the house; so that on the whole, to know anything about it, I must give myself wholly up to it.

I am much dissatisfied with the neglect of Steel as to the keeping accounts, as well as other things; seeing that half his time, I shall say *nine-tenths,* he does little or nothing. It were easy for him to have *made* a temporary set of books for the present, and to have entered every transaction, had it been only for my satisfaction.

The way we are going on I shall tire of, finding sums of money, and *nothing done*

The list continues with details of work not being carried out on time, and, very worryingly, the necessary paperwork for chasing up new orders was being neglected. We hear so little of Dickinson's point of view that it is worth looking at this letter in a little more detail. It is very clear that he is providing a good deal, if not all, of the finance. Francis Trevithick comments that Steel and the others objected to his meddling in engineering affairs, but the whole of the letter is a tirade against ineffficiency and lack of management, not about the practical side of manufacturing at all. If this really represented the true state of affairs at the works, then it was obviously necessary for one or other of the partners to spend time there in sorting matters out.

Instead, what emerges is an all too familiar story. When they should have been consolidating what they had, Trevithick and Dickinson were actually busy pushing ahead in new directions; putting in applications for a bewildering array of new patents. Some were simple improvements to existing devices, such as a special crane attachment for the nautical labourer, but there was also a set of revolutionary ideas for the use of iron, from an iron floating dock to an iron ship with telescopic iron spars. It was as if they were trying to map out the future of the shipbuilding industry for the rest of the century. Many of the ideas were excellent in themselves, but far beyond any resources they could muster. How far they could have been developed at the time we shall never know for in May 1810, for the first time in his life, the giant was felled, laid low by a life-threatening illness. Francis Trevithick described it as "typhus and gastric fever", leading to "loss of intellect and brain fever". Dickinson sent along his doctor and the Trevithicks called in theirs, and the two experts promptly disagreed – so a third was called in to provide yet another opinion. In the end it seems to have been the man's own constitutional toughness that pulled him through, in spite of the best efforts of medical science to finish him off. It must have been incredibly difficult for Jane, not knowing who to believe nor which of the recommended treatments to follow, a dilemma not helped by an anonymous letter warning her that the treatment she was following would surely kill her husband. The only sensible advice, and the advice she most wanted to hear, came from her brother. He might not always approve of

Trevithick, but he was stalwart in any family emergency.[6]

> Our hearing by every other post from Mr. Blewett, of Trevithick's
> rapid recovery, and also by Dr. Rosewarne last Saturday that the
> fever had quite left him, gave us great satisfaction; but we are much
> concerned for your situation.
>
> In your letter of the 25th ult. you seem to be much alarmed from
> Trevithick's weakness, but I think you cannot expect otherwise than
> that he will be very weak for some time, after so dreadful an attack.
> Do not be alarmed, I hope he will do very well; you must not say
> anything to him about his business that is likely to hurry his mind,
> until he gets better. If Mr. Dickinson receives money, he must be
> accountable for it. I beg that you will not hesitate asking Mr.
> Blewett for what you want. It gives us great happiness to hear that
> you enjoy health in this great trial. If you think it necessary and you
> wish it, I will come to you, but I sincerely hope that your next will
> bring a more favourable account; I know Mr. Blewett will be very
> happy to do anything for you in his power, and I wish you would ask
> his advice in any business that you think is not proper for Trevithick
> to be told of until he gets better.
>
> I hope you find Mr. Steel honest: in that case it is not in Mr.
> Dickinson's power to cheat you.
>
> Do let me know how Trevithick's affairs stand, and what his
> prospects are. If he is not likely to do well where you are, do you
> think he would consent to return to Cornwall – if not to settle, for a
> little while? His native air might be a means of getting him about.
> Both my sisters join with me in love to you and family.

Blewett was still Harvey's partner at that time (see page 107), an
arrangement which was not to last much longer than that between
Trevithick and Dickinson. Just how far the latter relationship had
deteriorated can be gauged from Harvey's letter, though sadly we
have no direct evidence of what exactly was going on during
Trevithick's illness. We do, however, know the outcome.
Trevithick had agreed, or been persuaded, to return to Cornwall.
It seems somehow typical of the family that what was intended as a
quiet homecoming for an invalid and his eleven-year-old son,
Richard, turned into quite an adventure. They set off on the
Falmouth Packet with a gun-brig for escort, for the country was still
at war with France. A three-day voyage took them to Dover where
they anchored. The voyage did wonders for the invalid. He had
been carried on board, but now he went ashore and took his first
short walk since he had been taken ill. They had scarcely left Dover

before a French warship appeared and the chase was on. The British skipper had the advantage of knowing home waters and was able to navigate the difficult passage near the shore and give the enemy the slip. Six days after leaving London, they were in Falmouth. According to Francis Trevithick, his father then took his boy by the hand and walked home. If they really did walk sixteen miles it was a truly miraculous recovery. It was a sad home-coming, for Trevithick's mother had died two months earlier, and no one had been able to tell the sick man of his loss.

Trevithick was home and rapidly recovering his health: the same could not be said of his business. In his absence it had been tottering along and in February 1811 crashed completely. The partners were declared bankrupt and ordered to present themselves before the Commissioners of Bankruptcy. Trevithick revealed that the partner-ship had debts of £4000 and that he himself had been forced to mortgage his property and borrow from friends. He had just shaken off the miseries of London for recuperation in the country, and now he had not only been forced to return in ignominious circumstances, but was about to face fresh indignities. He was far from home, without his family for comfort and lacking the resources to meet the demands that rained down on him. All his possessions were seized, and with no home and no money, he was forced into a "sponging-house", from which, if the worst happened, the next step was the debtors' prison. This was his blackest hour, but when it came to the settlement, the creditors received 16 shillings [80p] in the pound, a good deal more than they might have expected. Eventually, he was discharged of his bankruptcy or rather, as he was keen to point out, the partnership's bankruptcy. His disillusionment with his former partner was absolute. "I never was in debt to any person: not one shilling of debt was proved against me under the commission, nothing more than the private debts of my swindling partner".[7]

The dreams of fame and fortune in London had died. He had survived near drowning, a desperately dangerous illness and bank-ruptcy. His youth was behind him and he was already moving into his middle years. It would have been easy to succumb, to settle for a more modest, stable life as a mining engineer in Cornwall, happy with a loving family, regular work and a good, steady income. That he could never do: it would have been an admission of defeat. Old ideas, old plans had failed. Very well, it was time for new ideas and new plans.

CHAPTER TWELVE

Renewal in Cornwall

Now that the London adventure was over, Trevithick's family life was every bit as much in need of restoration as was his business life. He had spent a long time away from his wife and children and then, when they had finally joined him, it had proved a far from happy experience by any standards. The bailiffs had been and taken everything of value, and some things of no monetary value, including his letters and working models, whose loss means as much to historians as it must have meant to Trevithick himself. He needed some time to recover from his illness, but he was all too aware that there was also a very pressing need to find money just to keep going from day to day. And soon there were to be new expenses to meet. Shortly after their return to Penponds, Jane became pregnant and in 1812 she gave birth to a third son, Francis, who in later life was to become his father's biographer. There was to be one more child, Frederick Henry, born in 1816. Whatever tribulations the family might have gone through, and whatever problems lay ahead, the children do not seem to have suffered and all lived to a decent old age. The time had definitely come for Trevithick to make some money from his inventions, rather than merely spending it on them. He had the means at hand, and over the next few years he managed successfully to expand on the established basis of high-pressure engines, while constantly looking for new applications. But he was equally ready to look at any opening that offered a profit, and in doing so made new contacts, rather more useful than the tenuous links he had forged in London.

One man he met soon after his return was Sir Christopher

Hawkins. A considerable landowner, he had a fine Georgian mansion at Trewithen, between Truro and St Austell, still visited for its magnificent gardens. His wealth and influence helped him to get elected Member of Parliament for St Ives, where he was responsible for a number of public works, including a Free School for the children of the poor. He was also concerned with increasing the prosperity of his constituency. John Smeaton, the great civil engineer, had been responsible for the construction of the harbour, which was completed in 1770. Today we think of the town as a quaintly picturesque holiday resort, but in the nineteenth century it was a major fishing port, handling up to 50,000 hogsheads of pilchards a year. The hogshead is a rather vague measure that could be anything from 450 to 600 litres, but either way that is a lot of pilchards, so that the town was "most abominably tainted with the effluvia of the fish cellars".[1] Hawkins felt that with better facilities, trade could be increased even further, and he supported a plan for building a breakwater, to provide added protection to the harbour. The man he called in to investigate was Trevithick, which is a little odd as this was one area where he had no previous experience.

He carried out a rough, initial survey and there is evidence that by now he had learned one valuable lesson. He put cash in hand before future prospects, even if he still dreamed of grander things. He wrote to Hawkins about the project.[2] "I was employed a few days at St Ives, by the subscribers to the breakwater. I would be very much obliged to you to say if I must call on Mr Halse for payment". But he also made it clear that, given half a chance, he would be off experimenting again.

> If I had money I would immediately construct an engine in a ship, at my own expense, much rather than be assisted by any other person, but the misfortune I lately met with left me without a shilling; therefore I am obliged to attend to other business for a maintenance of my family, instead of attending to purposes of twenty times the value.

Sir Christopher Hawkins may have declined to take up the hint dropped by Trevithick that there was a fortune to be made from paddle steamers, but he was to play an important part in later events. In the meantime, Trevithick was returning to the area where he had enjoyed the most conspicuous successes in the past, the local copper mines. His main interests lay in converting existing engines for use at higher pressures and supplying brand new engines of his own design that would work expansively. This was all very good, but in order to produce steam at the appropriate pressure, he needed to improve on the old style of boilers.

He had been thinking about the problem for some time, ever since he had begun work on the first puffers. Providing steam for a small, portable engine was one thing, but raising enough to power a big beam engine was quite another matter. He developed his new boiler design as early as 1806, coincidentally at exactly the same time that an American inventor, Oliver Evans, was coming up with a very similar solution. They would not have known of each other's work, but Evans can claim the honour of being the first to see his design put to use. He was able to produce steam at the very high pressure of 120 p.s.i., but sadly for him, American technology was not yet far enough advanced to make much use of his invention. Trevithick seems to have first put his ideas into practice at Dolcoath in 1812. The first generation of boilers for steam engines, the old waggon and haystack boilers, were little more than large iron vessels full of water, with a separate fire underneath. Not very efficient in the first place, they became less so with use, as deposits from an often dirty water supply settled on the bottom of the vessels, forming an insulating layer. His new boiler was very different, not just an improvement on an old design, but a radically different concept. The boiler itself was cylindrical, and the grate was set in the end of a tube running the whole length of the cylinder. On reaching the far-end of the tube, the hot gases from the fire divided to pass back under the cylinder through brick flues and were then reunited to pass under the boiler to the chimney.

The first trials took place either at the end of 1811 or early in 1812. The prototypes were made of wrought iron plates, but these were rather crude and the joints had to be made watertight by caulking. They proved to be very leaky and there was an unfortunate tendency for the caulking to catch fire. Better machining would eventually solve these problems. It all went well enough for Trevithick to promote his invention at once. He placed this advert, dated 27 May 1812 in the *Cornwall Gazette*, and invited orders to be placed with William West at the Hayle Foundry.[3]

HIGH PRESSURE STEAM BOILERS, with the fireplace in the midst of the water. The same may be applied to any Engines working on Messrs. Bolton and Watts' plan, in a short time after such Boilers are made; where the savings are worth attention, as being far above the old mode of working. A specimen of the same may be seen at Dolcoath Mine, where the Agents had full power from the Patentees to make trial of these Boilers, under certain restrictions of premium to be paid, if the savings should prove satisfactory. The plan at Dolcoath is three Boilers, (2 of 5 feet and one of 6 feet diameter, about 20 feet long) working a 63 inch double Engine, 11 strokes per minute about 200 fathoms deep. The above Boilers were fixed by William West; of whom instructions and drawings may be had on application.

Trevithick was now eager to seize an opportunity which would allow him to develop this new line of improving existing engines into a profitable business. He visited a mine at St Agnes where things were in a sorry state as he described to Sir Christopher Hawkins.[4]

Several of the Advrs. had given up their shares rather than put in a new engine and the remainder of them very sunk. I told them that I could fork the waters with the present engine and draw instead of 40 gallons of water to a stroke 47 fathom deep which she did last month draw 85 gallons per stroke 60 fathoms deep by altering the engine in the same principle that I have made Dolocath great engine and several more now altering.

He calculated that for an outlay of £1000 he could drain the whole mine and halve the coal bill, but he lacked capital.

I have not money sufficient to carry it in to execution as I must lay out a large sum on making the engine in the Gwithan mine and unless I can be assisted with £500 I shall not be able to undertake the job. If you think it worth your notice to manage this undertaking by lending me the above sum for 6 months I will pay you interest for it and before drawing any part of it from you would get materials for that purpose that shall amount to above the sum and also give you an order for the Advrs to repay you the whole sum before receive any part myself.

Hawkins showed no interest, whether from a lack of enthusiam for mining investment in general or from an all-too-understandable reluctance to trust Trevithick's assurances of guaranteed profits. However, at the other mine mentioned in the letter, at Gwithian, things were going forward in a most encouraging manner. This was Wheal Prosper, and there is a very full account of it, supplied by

Richard Hosking, who worked on erecting it.[5] This was not an adaptation of an existing engine, but one built to a brand new design by Trevithick at Hayle. The first interesting features relate to the boiler, which was similar to Dolcoath but with one minor modification. "Cylindrical Boiler, 24ft long from 5ft 6in to 6ft diameter, with fire Tube in the usual way, except a little flattened on the upper side, so as to give more steam room in the Boiler". Flattening of the flues was eventually discontinued, when it was found to be a source of weakness as pressures increased. The engine itself was a 24 in. beam engine with a 6 ft stroke, but quite unlike earlier engines. It was a single acting, condensing engine working expansively, as Hosking made clear. "The Engine worked more expansively than any other Engine I have seen, except Taylors at United Mines. Should say cut off at 1/9, or even less". This was an inverted engine, with the main beam underneath the cylinder instead of above it as in the conventional arrangement. In the power stroke, steam was allowed into the top of the cylinder at a pressure which Hosking estimated at around 40 p.s.i. It was then shut off and allowed to expand in the cylinder, forcing the piston down and lifting the pump rods at the far end of the beam. The exhaust steam was condensed, creating a partial vacuum for the next stroke. The passage of steam was controlled through a three-way cock – opening the steam passage, closing the passage and opening the exhaust.

Trevithick was not the only engineer working in Cornwall to advance steam technology. Arthur Woolf had, like Trevithick, left the area, but had returned to try his own new ideas. He designed a boiler with an array of cast-iron tubes, but it proved most unsatisfactory as the tubes tended to crack in the heat. He also resurrected the idea, first put forward by the Hornblowers, of building compound engines, and in this he was a good deal more successful. But it was Trevithick's work that showed the way forward. The new style of boiler was soon so generally accepted that it became known simply as "the Cornish boiler". Even steam enthusiasts can rarely be heard enthusing about boilers, which lack the romance of a grand, powerful engine, but without the one the other is just so much scrap metal. As for the engine itself, that too was to have lasting importance, as the first true, distinctive Cornish engine.

Just how good were the new inventions? Fortunately, from 1811 onwards we have a measure of engine efficiency. In that year, Joel

Lean was appointed official Registrar and Reporter of Duty, given the task of making independent assessments of the work done by engines in Cornwall and publishing the results in Lean's *Engine Reporter*. The very first report of August 1811 gave figures for eight engines, ranging in size from 36 to 68 in. (91 to 173 cm), with duty from 9.3 million to 22.3 million. These engines, all bigger than Trevithick's at Wheal Prosper, showed an average of 15.7 million. When Wheal Prosper itself was first reported in 1813 it was recorded at 26.7 million, an extraordinary result for what was a first experiment with a new design.

It really did look as if Trevithick's wild days were over, and that he was settled on a straight, firm road to prosperity. With ever-stronger links being forged with Henry Harvey, there was the basis for a sound partnership with a man who could be relied on to keep a good grip of the finances. If things had gone smoothly, and if they could have survived the likely personality clashes, both men could have looked forward to handsome profits. It was not to be, and on this occasion at least, no blame could be laid at Trevithick's door. It was the dissolution of the Blewett, Harvey and Vivian partnership that brought progress to an abrupt end. A court injunction stopped all work at the Hayle Foundry for a period of three months, after which Harvey was fully occupied sorting out the various claims, a process that lasted right through until January 1816, when Harvey & Co re-emerged as one of the greatest builders of steam engines in the land. But the opportunity for partnership had gone; the continuity was broken. Trevithick was still to have work executed at Hayle, but he was already forming new alliances, particularly with John Urpeth Rastrick, who was now a partner in the Bridgnorth Foundry.

Rastrick was a man of considerable talents. Although at this stage in his career he was wholly involved with the work of the foundry, he was already taking a considerable interest in the workings and details of the steam engines themselves, a fact that he preferred to keep to himself. His notes on steam, giving detailed dimensions, were all in code. It was not a difficult code to break. In amongst a set of meaningless cyphers, put in merely to cause confusion, there were nine conventional letters of the alphabet representing numerals. These were the important measurements. He learned a lot from Trevithick, and was to become a highly-respected designer of railway locomotives, some of which went to the very first American railways. On top of this he became, like the

Stephensons, equally involved in the civil engineering side of railway development. We are lucky in having one long letter of 1812[6] which is worth quoting at length, for it provides a chance to see what an outside observer made of the two Cornish rivals, Woolf and Trevithick, and also shows Rastrick to be a man of decided opinion, and as ready as Trevithick to seize any opportunity on offer.

The letter describes a journey that began with a long ride on horseback from Shropshire down to South Wales where he looked over the local iron works. After that, he and his horse took the packet across the Bristol Channel to Ilfracombe and continued the ride into Cornwall, where he had introductions to "the principal Miners". At Camborne, he found Trevithick away from home, but he met Woolf who took him along to see his own new engine at Marazion. Rastrick was not impressed: "I never had any good Oppinion of Woolfe's Engines, for the Complication was in my mind sufficient to condemn them". The next day he met Trevithick.

> I spent several days with him and he went with me to see several People who gave me orders – I mentioned to him that I was going to see the Breakwater at Plymouth, he thereupon agreed to accompany me: I went to see an Engine put up by Trevithick, which works with less coal than any Engine I know of. It is a single Power Engine with an Air Pump and Condensor, only two nozzle valves, but the principal Advantage it has is by working with a Steam of high elastic Power and shutting off the Steam at one-third the Stroke, it expands for the other two-thirds of the Stroke, is then so far lowered in Power as not to exceed the Power of the atmosphere and of course becomes verry easily condensed.
>
> If an Engine is properly calculated, well-executed, and put together, on this Plan I am persuaded it will consume less Coal than any Engine whatever as it can be made so extremely simple.
>
>   Trevithick and I set out and rode along the Southern Coast of Cornwall to Plymouth. I delivered your letter to Mr. Mitchell who conducted us thro the Dock Yard, but I was by no means so well pleased with it as I was with Portsmouth. We now went to Oreston Quay to see the Manner in which the Business was conducted there of getting and Shipping the Stone – we found the Principal Quay was rendered quite useless as it had sunk according to the information we had recieved about 20 feet not perpendicular but by inclining in such a Way that should they continue to build on it, the Foundation will probably be uppermost as it seems to turn thus.

They were building on it when we were there altho it is evident that no vessel can come alongside of it since the Mud or Soil is hove up in such a way as not to allow a sufficient depth of Water. The Method in which they get the Stones and convey them to the Quays; the Construction of the Vessells the way of Loading and discharging is in my oppinion, the *verry verry worst* that could be thought of by the greatest Bungler that ever was.

He continued with a description of the stone loading vessels, and then ended his account of the visit to Plymouth:

There are a variety of Ways which occurred to Trevithick and me and which might enable the Contractors to get money by their Contract provided they were allowed to addopt the Method that could be proposed, as it is I am told the Contractors are loosing a great Deal and must continue so to do – on the whole it is the worst conducted Public Work I ever saw.

The works were not, as one might think from Rastrick's scathing comments, under the control of some incompetent amateur, but were being overseen by none other than John Rennie. What is notable is just how quick Trevithick was to respond to the situation and how speedily he came up with a solution to at least one of the problems that were afflicting the works. He must have been encouraged by the contractors, for he was supplied with blocks of local stone for experiments back at Hayle. He worked quickly and in two months he was able to write in enthusiastic terms to the contractor, Robert Fox.[7] Trevithick may have leapt in the moment a new idea struck him, but that does not mean that he was slap-dash. He had quite enough sense to realise that what worked with the local granite – moorstone as he called it – would not necessarily work in the same way with limestone. He was keen to explain the differences as he had found them by experiment.

I can bore holes five times as fast with a borer turned round than by a blow or jumping-down in the usual way, and the edge of the boring bit was scarcely worn or injured by grinding against the stone, as might have been expected. I think the engine that is preparing for this purpose will bore ten holes of $2^{1}/_{2}$ inches in diameter 4 feet deep per hour. Now suppose the engine to stand on the top of the cliff, or on any level surface and a row of holes bored, 4 feet from the edge of the cliff, 4 feet deep, and about 12 inches from hole to hole for the width of the piece to be brought down at one time, and wedges driven into the holes to split the rock in the same way as they cleave moorstone, only instead of holes 4 inches deep, which will cleave a moorstone rock 10 feet deep when the holes are 14 or 15 inches apart, the holes in limestone must go as deep as you intend too cleave out each stope, otherwise the rock will cleave in an oblique direction.

He concluded the letter:

If this plan answers, the whole of the stones would be fit for service, even for building, and would all be nearly of the same size and figure. Each piece would be easily removed from the spot by an engine on a carriage working a crane, which would place them into the ships' hold at once. It would all stand on a plain surface, and might be had in one, two, three, or four tons in a stone, as might best suit the purpose, which would make the work from beginning to end one uniform piece. Steam machinery would accomplish more than nine-tenths of all the work, besides saving the expense of all the powder. I find that limestone will split much easier than moorstone, and I think that a very great saving in expense and time may be made if the plan is adopted.

He followed up this letter with further accounts of more trials and suggested that with the engine he was using at Hayle and a crew of four, they could cut 100 tons of stone a day and load it on the ship. It was puffer versatility seen in practice once again. He estimated that they could get stone at 9d a ton (3.7p). That may have been a trifle optimistic, but shortly after the engine was sent, the cost of stone fell from 2s 9d (14p) to one shilling (5p) a ton. This was good news for Fox, who was on a fixed-price contract, and good news for Trevithick who had learned one lesson from Boulton and Watt – he was to receive a share of the costs saved. Just how much Trevithick's work contributed to the breakwater is not known, but anyone who visits it will be struck by the fine work and regularity of the massive stone blocks.

The Plymouth interlude was a typical piece of Trevithick opportunism. He had accepted a casual invitation to join Rastrick on the visit to the breakwater, with no idea that he would necessarily find anything of either interest or profit. Then, the moment he saw that things were going badly, he at once applied his mind to thinking up improvements, and in a very short time those ideas had materialised into a valuable contract. These were heady times for him.

The first commercial successor to Trevithick; the Middleton Colliery railway opened in 1812, here seen passing Christ Church, Leeds. (*Anthony Burton*)

The crowded scene in the Pool of London in 1810, with ships waiting for loading, unloading and ballasting: a lucrative market for the "nautical labourer".
(by courtesy of Museum of London PLA Collection)

The threshing engine, built at Hayle, remained in use right up to 1879. *(SCNPOW Science and Society Picture Library)*

The town and mines of Cerro de Pasco around 1850. *(Tony Morrison, South American Pictures)*

A nineteenth century ore carrier at Cerro de Pasco. *(Tony Morrison, South American Pictures)*

Portrait of Jane Trevithick. *(The Trevithick Trust)*

The White Hart, Hayle, 1900. The present hotel opened in 1838 to the right of the picture, the older where Jane Trevithick presided is to the left of it. (*Hayle Community Archive*)

Jane Trevithick in 1861 surrounded by her sons and daughters. They are from left to right Richard, Anne, John, Francis, Elizabeth and Frederick. *(The Trevithick Trust)*

The statue of Richard Trevithick clutching a model of the Camborne engine, erected in the town in 1932. *(Simon Cook)*

He had never been at a loss for ideas, if anything they came too readily, but now not only could he see them translated into work, but what was even better, profitable work. That does not mean that because he had a lot of schemes on the go he stopped looking for new applications for high-pressure steam, or that he had abandoned old and grander plans. There was, it seems, no area he was not ready to explore. Having achieved success in such different works as mining and harbour construction, he now turned to a quite new subject – agriculture.

Sir Christopher Hawkins had shown little interest in mine investment but, as an important land owner, he was a great enthusiast for improvements in agriculture. An obvious candidate for mechanisation was threshing, separating the grain from the straw and chaff. This had always been a filthy, back-breaking job. The wheat or barley was piled up in barns and beaten with flails, the men working in ever-thickening clouds of dust. This was the universal practice in Britain until 1786 when a Scots inventor, Andrew Meikle, built the first satisfactory threshing machine. It was a simple device consisting of a drum rotating inside a concave plate. Corn was fed into the narrow space between drum and plate, and the rubbing action separated out the grain. The drum was generally turned by horse power, with four horses being used at a large mill and two for a smaller version. Arthur Young, who travelled throughout Britain reporting on the state of agriculture, visited Oxfordshire around 1812 and found nine mills at work in the county.[8] These were expensive items, costing as much as £120 to build – enough to pay the wages of three farm workers for a year. Trevithick recognised an obvious candidate for steam power. Horses walking in a circle to turn a machine had already been replaced at the mines by whim engines, and there was no reason why the same should not be done here. The engine was simple, turning a flywheel, which carried a rope drive to the threshing drum. He gave a full description to Hawkins.[9] The 9-in. cylinder engine was said to do the work of four horses. It worked at 30 strokes a minute, which gave 360 revolutions a minute to the 3 ft diameter drum. He gave the building costs at £90, and the running costs, together with the interest that would have been earned on the capital if it had been invested instead, at £9 per annum. Machinery for a four-horse mill was cheaper at £60, but was subject to greater wear and tear so that costs came out at £13. The

Fig 7: *Francis Trevithick's drawing of the steam cultivator, based on his father's sketch.*

real savings were in daily costs – 2s 6d (12.5p) for steam against £1 for horses.

Trevithick's claims for the work done by steam were verified a week later by independent witnesses.[10]

> We hereby certify that a fire was lighted under the boiler of the engine five minutes after eight o'clock, and at twenty-five minutes after nine the thrashing mill began to work, in which time 1 bushel of coal was consumed. That from the time the mill began to work to two minutes after two o'clock, being four hours and three-quarters, 1500 sheaves of barley were thrashed clean, and 1 bushel of coal more was consumed. We think there was sufficient steam remaining in the boiler to have thrashed from 50 to 100 sheaves more barley, and the water in the boiler was by no means exhausted. We had the satisfaction to observe that a common labourer regulated the thrashing mill, and in a moment of time made it go faster, slower, or entirely to cease working.

We can actually make a direct comparison with a horse-powered mill, for Arthur Young provides his own equally independent statistics. He went to see a mill at Brightwell Grove near Watlington, which was actually designed by none other than Rastrick. It was a variation on the standard in that it had two drums. The first at $3\frac{1}{2}$ ft diameter was slightly larger than Trevithick's, but slower at 260 r.p.m. It appears that it did not thresh completely clean, so a rake automatically carried the straw to the second drum to recover the last of the grain.[11]

> I observed the horses to labour considerably. They work four hours, in which time it does eight quarters of wheat. It thrashes every thing perfectly clean; and does not break the straw more than flails ... I numbered the sheaves as delivered, and found that it thrashed 43 in ten minutes.

He produced his own set of costs, similar to those supplied by Trevithick. For the four-hour day, the cost was 10s (50p) for the horses, 3s 9d (18.75p) for three men, three women and a boy, calculated at half a day. The comparative work rate was 316 sheaves an hour for Trevithick, 258 for Rastrick. This was all very impressive, and Trevithick was quick to publicise the fact by placing this advert in the *Royal Cornwall Gazette*, 10 October 1812.

THRASHING MACHINE

To be SOLD by PRIVATE CONTRACT, a Two-Horse THRASH-
ING MACHINE, allowed by mechanics to be the best in the
county. Apply to me; (my reason for selling the Horse Machine is
that I am about to have a Steam Engine to grind for the poor, and
the same power will work the Thrashing Mill;) the Mill is adapted to
grind 150 bushels corn per day.

RICHARD TREVITHICK
Engineer

This was another success, and further orders soon followed.
Meanwhile, he was already planning the next obvious step, to
adapt the engine so that it could do other jobs on the farm, such
as grinding corn and sawing logs. The thrashing engine was reck-
oned to be an improvement on earlier puffers, and with no
adaptation at all, it could also be used as a portable whim engine
at the mines. He went further even than that, proposing an engine
that would "*go itself* from shaft to shaft".[12] He also designed what
he described as a plough, but was rather more like a modern roto-
vator for tearing up the soil. It consisted of a wooden wheeled
frame with gearing to drive a vertical wheel set at one end. The
rotating wheel had a set of shovel-like blades set round the rim.
The new engine was to be built at Bridgnorth, but Rastrick had
clearly had doubts about the tractive power of the engine.
Trevithick reassured him:[13]

> There is no doubt about the wheels turning around as you suppose, for
> when that engine in Wales travelled on the tramroad, which was very
> smooth, yet all the power of the engine could not slip around the
> wheels when the engine was chained to a post for that particular exper-
> iment.

Here we have Trevithick describing an engine that could move under
its own power, and once it arrived on site could work machinery. He
was, in effect, inventing the traction engine. Once again he was
leading where others would follow, if rather slowly, behind. The lag
was partly due to the conservatism of the farming community, especially in areas where, unlike Cornwall, people were not used to seeing
steam engines at work. Partly it was the reluctance of manufacturers
to move on from what was still a small beginning. Portable engines
slowly found acceptance, but it was not until 1859 that Thomas
Aveling took out a patent for a traction engine that would haul a

threshing drum from farm to farm – nearly half a century after Trevithick had first proposed it.

Trevithick was doing his best to spread the news, and Sir Christopher Hawkins recommended that he write to Sir John Sinclair at the Board of Agriculture to discuss his inventions. He took the advice, but also included notes on other ideas which had nothing to do with agriculture, in the hope that such an eminent man might have the ear of other men of influence. It was a scatter-gun principle. If he shot out enough ideas, there was a chance that he might get public funding for at least one of them. As he explained later in the correspondence, he had spent quite enough of his own time and money on public demonstrations, and now he had to look after family interests. One can imagine Jane nodding in agreement as that letter was sent off in the mail. Among the old ideas he resurrected was the development of steam for shipping. He found it very galling when he knew what could be done that Britain had "to be shown the way by Americans".[14]

There is an interesting footnote to this letter. Among the many companies who built high-pressure engines for Trevithick was Fenton, Murray and Wood of Leeds. We have already met Matthew Murray as the builder of the Middleton Colliery Railway locomotive, but in 1813 he was approached with a different request. A Yarmouth gentleman, John Wright, had acquired a captured French privateer, *L'Actif*, a wooden vessel, 52 ft (16m) long. He wanted to have it converted into a paddle steamer, and the firm set to work installing a Trevithick engine. The vessel set off down the Aire and Calder Navigation and out into the Humber for the sea voyage to Yarmouth, mostly under sail because of insurance problems. On 9 August 1813 she made a trial run on Breydon Water watched by thousands. This was so successful that, under a new name, the *Experiment*, she began a regular passenger service between Yarmouth and Norwich. A second vessel, the *Telegraph*, also with a Trevithick engine, was added to the service. It was to have a tragically short life. The success of the enterprise encouraged competition, and in 1816 a rival, the *Nelson*, appeared on the water. By now the *Telegraph* had been given an overhaul, and the boiler end plate, which had corroded from using sea-water, was replaced. The two rivals set off to race for Norwich, and the *Telegraph* engineer decided to give himself an advantage by weighing down the safety-valve to increase the pressure well above the recommended 30 p.s.i. The result was disaster. The newly-fitted end plate blew

out, the fragments bursting through the passenger compartment,
leaving nine dead and six injured. It was a sad end to what had
otherwise been a very successful experiment, and it is worth noting
that the *Telegraph* had, during her short life, actually made a
genuine sea-voyage under steam from Yarmouth to the Medway –
so that the honour of designing the first steam engine to put to sea
may well lie with Trevithick. It was a bold venture, particularly
when one compares Trevithick's 30 p.s.i. with the engine built for
Brunel's famous ocean-going vessel, the *Great Western*, for which
Maudslay designed engines working at a very modest 5 p.s.i. It was
yet another pioneering effort, but sadly little is known about the
details of just how the vessels were driven – though it is a fair bet
that no one used Trevithick's air pumps for the paddle box.[15]
Predictably, nothing came of Trevithick's attempts to get public
funding, so he turned back to another idea that had been mooted
some years earlier with his first patent – making engines for sugar
mills on the plantations of the West Indies. There is no record of
how many were sent out, but one at least, intended for St Kitts, got
caught up in the debacle at Hayle, and its manufacture had to be
transferred to Bridgnorth. In the event, it was not finished in time
for shipment, but it was destined to go even further afield. But that
is a story that will be told a little later.

The return from London, and the recovery of his health,
galvanised Trevithick. Ideas flowed from him at an astonishing
rate. He also seemed to have learned some very useful lessons from
the London experience. He was no longer so keen on sinking his
own funds into research projects, from which he might never
receive any financial advantage. Nor was he willing to pass on his
ideas for free. During 1812 he corresponded with the Irish brewers
Robinson and Buchanan of Londonderry. They were interested in
a water-pressure engine, but Trevithick suggested that as they only
had a 30 ft head, this was not very practical. He suggested using a
small steam engine, which would probably have rather more power
than they needed, but they could use the exhaust steam for heating
the liquor during the brewing process. He also made some rather
vague suggestions for other improvements, which the brewers
quickly pounced on. But this was a new, canny engineer they were
dealing with.[16]

I find by your letter that you have been trying practice on the hint I
gave you about the Chain & Bucketts and that you expect it will

answer if properly executed. You are not the first that have catched my hints and stuck fast in its execution. I allways make it a rule never to send a drawing untill I have received my fee.

By the end of 1812, he could look back with considerable satisfaction on the revival of his fortunes. His mind was as active as ever, and he was already contemplating an idea for a machine which he was convinced would finally provide the reward he had worked towards for so long. And a fresh challenge was about to appear that would hold out even more glorious prospects of wealth and fame. He had never felt so optimistic nor so confident.

CHAPTER THIRTEEN

The Man from Peru

Of all Trevithick's inventions and adaptations made during those fruitful years following his return from London, the one that gave him the most personal satisfaction and pride was the plunger-pole engine. It had the virtue, shared by so many good designs, of being essentially very simple. It derived directly from his first successful experiments with the expansive use of high-pressure steam. He already had the plunger-pole pump established as a powerful weapon in the endless battle against water in the mines, and perhaps his mind turned back to his younger days when he had worked with Bull in defiance of the powerful Watt empire. Then they had inverted the engines directly over the shafts to work pump rods. This was what he was about to do with the plunger-pole, but with even greater economy of effort. In the new engine, the case of the plunger-pole itself became the steam cylinder. The pole was then connected via crossheads to the pump rods in the shaft (see drawing page 159). Two boilers were used to produce steam at 100 p.s.i. The pole inside the case was 16 in. in diameter with an 8-ft stroke, and this is how it worked.

The steam was admitted into the case, below the pole, cut off early and allowed to expand. At the end of the up-stroke, pressure had dropped to around 20 p.s.i., when the exhaust valve opened and the steam escaped to be condensed. As in the Wheal Prosper engine, a partial vacuum was created in the case, and the pole descended for the down-stroke. Movement was evened out through a balance bob, which also served to control the air pump. This was, in fact, the engine over which Rastrick had enthused on his visit. Shortly afterwards, Trevithick wrote with even greater enthusiasm: "That new

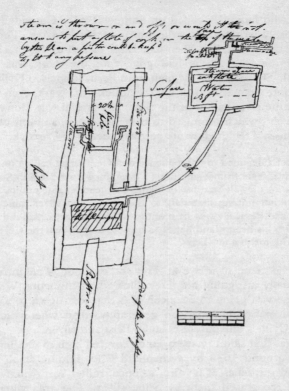

Fig 8: *The original 1815 sketch of the plunger-pole engine. At the top right is the steam pipe with inlet and exhaust valves. Steam is admitted into the water vessel with the cork floating on top. The expanding steam pushes water down the curved pipe to the pole-case supported on a beam across the shaft, cross-hatched in the drawing. The rising water lifts the pole, with its two side-rods moving outside the case. As they rise so the pump rod (marked as shaft rod) also rises. When the exhaust valve is opened, the plunger falls again.*

engine you saw near the sea side with me is now lifting forty millions 1 foot high with 1 bushel of coal, which is very nearly double the duty that is done by any other engine in Cornwall".[1]

He was obviously keen to get on with building more engines and working on improvements, and he was still in full inventive flow. Then, in the middle of all this excitement, there was an interruption. It was rather reminiscent of the arrival of the "Man from

Porlock" who famously called on Samuel Taylor Coleridge as he was feverishly writing down the words of *Kubla Khan*. The man came, the man went, but when Coleridge picked up his pen again, he found that the words had gone too: the work was never completed. The arrival of the man from Peru, Francisco Uvillé had an even more dramatic effect on Trevithick's life work, even if that was not quite so apparent at the time. His arrival was, however, a notable event, which promised to bring in a huge amount of well-paid business. Trevithick wrote enthusiastically to Rastrick.[2]

> I have been detained in consequence of a Gentleman calling on me who arrived here from Falmouth 11 days since from Lima in South America for the sole purpose of taking out steam engine pumps and sundry other mining materials to the Goald and silver mines of Mexico and Peru. He was six months on his passage, which did not agree with his health, and hopes to be able to go down the Cornish mines with me in a few Days.

Just how he came to arrive at Trevithick's door is an intriguing story. Equally intriguing are Trevithick's first thoughts. Why did he think he was going to Mexico? Was that just down to a shaky knowledge of South American geography? And where did gold come in? Uvillé's only interests lay in Peru and silver.

Silver was first said to have been discovered high in the Peruvian Andes in around 1630 by a shepherd who, finding small white particles in the ashes of his fire, at once, rather surprisingly for a shepherd, recognised them as being silver. The area where the metal was found was the plateau that lies between the eastern and western range of the Cordilleras. Prospectors and miners soon arrived and the first excavation was dubbed the "Discovadora". Here the mining town of Cerro de Pasco grew up, and soon the wealth pouring from the ground earned the town a new popular name – "El Opulent". Not that the opulence spread to the town itself, set in a horribly wind-swept, barren waste, 14,200 ft (4330 m) up in the mountains. The American Consul to Peru visited the town in the 1820s and wrote this gloomy account.[3]

> The place is most irregularly built, houses of one story, thatched roofs, with no windows, except of paper; no chimnies, though they say it snows by force eleven months in the year, and voluntarily the other ... they use braziers in which coals from burnt turf are put; this creates such a bad air that they are always obliged to leave the

door open, to prevent suffocation, though many die in this way every year. This place shows very strongly the miserable habits of the Spanish government and people, and their opposition to all improvements. With all the immense wealth that was drawn from this place, they lived here in the most comfortless manner.

The Consul might have wondered, more usefully, where the wealth had gone but that is another story that we shall be coming back to later. The first workings were very basic. The miners dug down as far as they could and, when they could go no further, started another hole somewhere else. The result was a town that was bewilderingly redesigning itself all the time, and constantly creating new dangers to add to the filth and squalor.[4]

> The suburbs are nothing more than a confused collection of dirty-looking mud cottages, which are hastily erected when required for the convenience of the mines, near any new mine that is opened, whilst those that are near a mine that has done working are deserted; consequently the town is constantly altering its form. The mouths of the mine are frequently in the middle of the streets, which makes walking at night very dangerous, as there is no barricade or light hung near them. They are sometimes enclosed in the courts and yards of houses; in the house we occupied there was one turned to a very ignoble purpose.

This ramshackle arrangement did well enough for poor scrapings, but it soon became obvious that such surface workings could not last for ever, and as ever-deeper shafts were sunk, so the old enemy duly appeared – water. What made this even more frustrating was that the deeper the miners went, the richer they found the silver deposits to be. Uvillé, a man of Swiss origin, formed a partnership with two prominent Lima merchants, Pedro Abadia and José Arismendi, to investigate the possibility of bringing steam engines and pumps to the Andes. Britain was the acknowledged world centre for steam engine development, so Uvillé set off for England to make enquiries. The obvious first call was at the greatest manufacturer of them all, Boulton and Watt. The results could not have been more discouraging. One look at their giant beam engines must have been enough to convince him that such monsters could never be hauled up narrow mountain tracks. And even if they could be brought to the mines, Boulton and Watt broke the dispiriting news that they would never be able to work in the rarified atmosphere at that altitude. It seemed his journey had been in vain.

Uvillé went back to London and the story would have ended there if he had not chanced on a model steam engine in a shop window near Fitzroy Square. No one seems to know how the model got there, nor even which type of engine it represented, except that it was high pressure. The shop was owned by a model maker, William Rowley, so it is possible that he made it after seeing a Trevithick engine at work. A much more likely explanation is that it was indeed one of Trevithick's own models, one of those seized by the bailiffs and put up for sale to clear the debts of the bankruptcy. In any case, Uvillé was given a demonstration, bought it for 20 guineas and hurried back to Peru in a rather more optimistic frame of mind. Of course, it had to be put to the test, so the model was carried on the long, difficult journey to the mines and fired up. It worked and now the grand scheme for developing Cerro de Pasco could begin. A new partnership was formed with capital of $40,000. Abadio and Arismendi were the senior partners, having two-fifths of the shares each. Uvillé had the remaining fifth, and he was also awarded $2000 for his work in finding and bringing back the wonder engine. Now all he had to do was go back and find the inventor. His brief was very clear. He was authorised to spend up to $30,000 in acquiring two engines – roughly £600 – and he was to hire two suitable workmen to return with him to Peru to oversee their erection and set them to work. Deals had already been made with the local mining interests on how the expected profits should be divided, so he was quite expressly forbidden to offer any form of partnership to anyone in Britain. All the instructions were soon to be blissfully ignored. One cannot really blame Uvillé. Communication between Britain and Peru could take months, and as the man on the spot he had to take the decisions that were absolutely necessary to get the work done. It was all rather symptomatic, however, of what was to prove a somewhat rickety partnership.

For a man who, from Trevithick's letter, seems to have been prone to sea-sickness, yet another journey round notorious Cape Horn and out across the Atlantic can hardly have been welcome. It says a great deal for his enthusiasm and tenacity that he was willing to undergo the ordeal, even though all he had to go on was the name "Trevithick" and the information that he could probably be found somewhere in Cornwall. He was fortunate enough on the final stage of his long voyage, the packet from London to

Falmouth, to meet on board a cousin of the engineer's. The man
was a relation on his mother's side called Teague, a name that
Trevithick was later to come across in less agreeable circumstances. So it was that the two men finally met, and now things
began to move with extraordinary speed. Although he had only
been authorised to buy two engines, here he was, scarcely a week
into the visit, placing orders for six. And he was soon to find that,
in meeting Trevithick, he had set an unstoppable force in motion.
Trevithick at once set out to put the work in hand. Enquiries were
made to Bridgnorth and to the Neath Abbey iron works in South
Wales. The Welsh letter explained something of his thinking on
what was needed, and why only high-pressure steam would answer
– "because the place they are for has a very deep adit driven into
the mountain and lifting condensing water to the surface would be
a greater load than the whole of the work under the adit level".[5] He
also gave details in both letters of what was needed. The main
items were six 24 in. engines, each to be supplied with 25 fathoms
of 12 in. pumps and 10 fathoms of 3 in. water-supply pipes. He
stressed the urgency of the orders.[6]

> six full setts of the same kind I want delivered in Cornwall as early
> as possible, a part of the Wrought Iron for the pitwork and boilers I
> have agreed with som smith in Cornwall, now I want your immidate
> answer saying part of these materials you will enter in to an engage-
> ment to deliver on Bristol Quay within four months from the time
> the drawings are sent you, I will lodge in a bank the money to pay
> for the whole of the matls and it shall be inserted into the same
> agreement that you shall draw every week for your money as you
> turn it oute at Bridge North immidly on receipt of yours you will
> hear from me again.

He was also writing to Uvillé setting out just what had already been
done.[7]

> I have begun your job. Yesterday I engaged a great many Smiths
> and boiler builders who sett to work this morning and have also
> engaged all the boiler plates in the County which will be sent to day
> to the different workmen, the master Smiths that I have engaged
> which are the best workmen in this Kindom and I have obligated
> them to find the best quality Iron and to be delivered to Falmouth
> within four months. I have been obliged to give them a greater price
> than I expected but otherwise they would not turn aside their usual
> employment for so short a job as four months.

Uvillé was back in London, no doubt reeling under the great wave of activity spreading from Cornwall out to Shropshire and Wales. He might also now have had some time to sit back and contemplate just what he had done, which would certainly have left him feeling a little nervous. He had authorised far more work than his senior partners had deputed him to order, and he must have known that he probably did not have sufficient funds to pay for the orders already placed in his name. But there was no stopping it now, not with Trevithick driving everything along at a furious pace, and soon he was setting off with the engineer on a round of visits to get first-hand reports on work in progress, and this it seemed was going to involve yet more sea-crossings. One cannot help feeling rather sorry for the man. It was quite bad enough contemplating sea-sickness, but he was travelling at a time of war, when privateers were cruising the coast, looking for dainty morsels like unarmed packets to pick off. Trevithick who had already been chased once by the French, was now also threatened by new predators, marauding Americans. It was no longer just France that was the enemy for, thanks to British high-handedness in trying to dictate what neutral vessels could carry and where they could trade, America had joined in as well. Trevithick was typically blasé about the threat: Uvillé may well have been too busy feeling ill to care. In any case, everything seems to have gone off well, with a good deal of what we would call corporate entertainment.[8]

I have your favor of the 10 Inst containing the invoice of sundrys from Bristol to Cornwall with pipes and Ale all of which being very necessary tools for engineers and miners, the Ale and pipes we are very thankfull for and shall not forget to remember each your health often over a glass of good Shrop Shire ale which will be chearfully joined by my rib as long as we find the can all continue to run. Mr Uville remains at my house and Spends the greater part of his time in the mines which he is much pleased with, was underground at Whl Alfred last Monday. We arrived at Swansea the Saturday after we left Bridge North. I did not meet the gents in the Coal mine but they are now on the Spot. We sail'd from Swansea on Monday Morning and arrived at Portreath on Wednesday morning. An American ship two days after took three Swansea coal ships for Cornwall. We saw a Ship of this description near Lundy Island abt 4 miles from us but did not suspect her at that time, however, a miss is as good as a mile.

To Trevithick, the war may have been no more than an occasion for a little adventure, but it had a real effect as far as getting engines to South America was concerned. There was no question of any vessel making a voyage to South America without an armed escort. News arrived of a Spanish man-of-war that could take the machinery, but first everything had to be carried to Cadiz. Pressure was being put on Trevithick to get everything ready, and he in turn was passing it on to the manufacturers. But they were disinclined to hurry, as the promised funds were not coming through at an acceptable rate. Trevithick pleaded and cajoled, even threatening to turn up in Shropshire himself to oversee the work if promises were not kept – "you will be very much annoyed with our company unless we fiend your assertions grounded in fact". Trevithick had to fight on two fronts. As well as pressurising the iron works he also had to keep nagging Uvillé for money. He impressed on him that the tradesmen working on the boilers had to be paid every week, and that they were not prepared to accept promises instead of cash, especially when the promises were being made by a stranger from a foreign country. Typically, he made it clear that he had no doubts at all about Uvillé's honesty and was not worried about his own payments coming in eventually. The Swiss seems to have made a quick assessment of the engineer's character, and realised that there was a way round his chronic shortage of funds. He could get Trevithick himself to help out by offering him a partnership. The document setting out the terms is an extraordinary affair.[9] Uvillé freely admitted that "several of the bills brought by him to England not having been honoured, by reason of the absence from England of the parties upon whom they were drawn, the said Francisco Uville hath not at present sufficient funds to answer the engagements he has entered into in this country". Trevithick agreed to pay approximately £3000 for a $12,000 share in the company, which would entitle him to one fifth of the profits. If anyone really believed that Trevithick had abandoned his old ways and settled down to a regular way of doing business, here was sad disillusionment – it was pie in the sky time again. And there was an additional clause added almost as an afterthought. It was signed by Uvillé and on behalf of his two partners "who will ratify these presents in the capital of Lima as soon as it shall be produced to them, to which the said Uvillé holds himself bound". He presumably neglected to mention to Trevithick that he had left Peru under strict orders not to offer any such partnership, and really had not the slightest idea whether they would agree to any such thing or not. Francis Trevithick bitterly summed up the agreement his father had entered into: "So Trevithick paid 3000*l.* and received nothing for his engineer's work, to be made a partner, contrary to Uville's limit of authority, in a speculation that proved to be not worth a farthing". He was being wise after the event, and things were not quite as bad as they seemed. Trevithick was able to pay off his engineering costs by selling part of his share. And was it a worthless venture? The answer to that question will emerge later. One thing at least is clear – he was taking an awful lot on trust – trusting that Uvillé really could get the partnership signed, trusting that there really were more funds in Peru and, above all, trusting that there really was a fortune in silver waiting to be unearthed high in the Andes.

The suggestion has always been made that Uvillé was untrust-worthy and acting dishonestly. On balance, it seems likely that he was simply a man far from home, constantly harassed, forced into making decisions to meet a rapidly-changing set of circumstances and generally overwhelmed by the press of events. And it has to be said that Uvillé, at least, really did believe wholeheartedly in the venture and was convinced of the value of the investment. And if it was a bad deal for Trevithick, it was one he entered into voluntar-ily with huge enthusiasm. In the meantime, Uvillé faced unexpected troubles of his own, and a situation which at one time descended into farce.

Among the many who had been drawn into the frantic efforts to have everything ready on time was a certain John Teague from Penryn. He was soon spreading malicious gossip about Trevithick, and was also claiming that Uvillé owed him money for work he had carried out. He was sufficiently persuasive for the authorities to put the unfortunate Swiss under arrest. Trevithick made it quite clear that Teague had done very little; that what he had done was of even less use; but that he had nevertheless been paid in full for it. He appeared at the Launceston Assizes to testify – to Teague's discomfort but his own considerable pleasure. It must have made a change to be on the winning side in a court case. He wrote to put Uvillé's mind at ease.[10]

Teague's Attorney informed Mr. Edwards that he was present at Penryn when you informed him you acknolidged Teague's debt and that he would give such evidence at the Assize in consiquence of which Mr. Edwards sent a supena to both me and my whife to give evidence in court that Teague acknolidged when you paid him the £15 that he had no farther demand on you. We both attended the Assize and when the rascal of Attorney saw us both in court he dropd the case. Mr Edwards said that as he new him to be in the habit of making false oaths that he would have done the same hear, if it had not been for two oaths direct against him. Teague had another sute there for Debt which he also lost which was equally as rascally as that of yours, Smith Truman of Penryn was bail for him and Teague have absconded from his bail and the poor old Smith will have all his furniture taken to pay Teague's debt and Cost which will be above £80. A more compleat fool and rogue than Teague was never. Jane return'd in big Spirits from the Assize and begs her best respect and services to you in every occasion when call'd for. Your Cornish Shipmates are anxiously waiting your call.

As preparations for despatching the machinery neared completion, Trevithick began recruiting men to go to Peru. He chose Thomas Trevarthan, with William Bull to act as his assistant. This was what Uvillé had asked for, but Trevithick was concerned that although he had undergone a crash course in engineering, he might still have difficulty in coping once he got up in the mountains. He suggested it would be prudent to take a third man along. "It will give you an opportunity of attending more generally to the concerns and not be confined on any one spot as a working engineer which will expedite the work very much as well as making a certainty of getting on instead of trusting entirely on your own health & extra exertions which I fear might otherwise be impaired."[11]

The man who was eager to take the third place was Andrew Vivian's brother, Henry, who had married Trevithick's younger sister, Thomasina. He was suitably qualified, but was unfortunately prone to "making too free with an evening glass". Trevithick was not prepared to push Henry's application in case things went wrong in Peru: he had no need of any more disagreements in the family. In the event, Henry Vivian did join the party, which set off on the South Sea whaler, *Wildman*, on 1 September 1814. With them went four pumping engines, four winding engines, two crushing mills and four boilers. There was also a ninth engine, intended not for the mines, but for the Mint at Lima. This was the portable engine originally built for the St Kitts sugar mills – what a splendid example of versatility that it could be instantly adapted

from processing sugar in the West Indies to making coins in Peru.
The other engines were all in the form of sections that could be
loaded onto mules and assembled on site. That such a huge
amount of material should have been specially designed, built and
shipped in such a short time – less than a year and a half after the
very first meeting – is a tribute to Trevithick's enthusiasm and
convincing proof that he had fully recovered all his old powers
after his desperate illness. The cost was enormous, nearly £7000
for equipment, with freight charges of £1500 and a startling £2300
for insurance.

The Peruvian affair had totally absorbed Trevithick, and even
pressing family concerns had to be put to one side until everything
was done, and the ship had sailed. His eldest son Richard was, it
seems, in poor health and his father was considering taking him
away from school.[12]

> At the end of this month I intended to have taken my son under my
> care to try for a short time what effect a change of education and
> outdoor exercise would have had on his mind and constitution, but I
> shall be obliged to go to the North and return to London where I
> expect the Shipping the engines for South America will call my atten-
> tion two or three months for which reason I should esteem it a favour
> if you would be so good as to keep him with you one more quarter.

Other things, too, had been put on hold, and now at last he could
return to his plunger-pole engine, which he finally got round to
patenting in 1815. He was now eager to build more and better examples of the wonder machine. But although everything seemed to be
going so well, not everyone was overjoyed at his success. Having been
forced to take work away from Hayle for a time, he had shown no
enthusiasm for going back again. He had found in Rastrick a man
who shared his own love of invention, a man who could not only
produce the iron work for his machines, but who was also ready with
useful criticism and helpful advice. It created a much happier atmosphere than the air of disapproval that perpetually hovered around his
brother-in-law. And Harvey, to make matters even more uncomfortable, was showing a distressing tendency to look with favour on the
work of the arch rival, Arthur Woolf. Turning away from Harvey also
meant, to an extent, turning his back on his old friend and partner,
Andrew Vivian, who had invested time and money, along with
Trevithick, in taking out the original patent for a high-pressure

engine. He had seen no return at all on that investment which, on the contrary, had brought him close to ruin. Now he could only stand by and see his former partner bustle through the world, pushing through new plans, developed out of their joint work, in which he no longer had any part to play and for which he could expect no reward. It would have required the character of a saint not to have felt some resentment. Harvey, too, could have expected more consideration after his stalwart support of the family in their time of crisis. It rankled that none of the work carried out for Peru was placed at Hayle. Here were two men who had been of great help to Trevithick in the past, and could have been again in the future. He was dangerously close to making enemies out of old friends. But Trevithick was in too much of a rush to worry about personal relationships and damaged sensibilities. He had engines to build, new ideas to investigate.

He was soon at work on what he was later to describe as one of his finest achievements, the plunger-pole engine for Herland Mine. Other engines of a similar type were being built, but this was to be the best of them all, and he was ready to challenge all comers. The engine had a 48 in. diameter steam case, and he was ready to back it against a 72 in. Boulton and Watt beam engine or any of Woolf's compounds. In fact he offered a wager to Woolf at odds that showed his confidence, £10 to £500 that his engine would have a higher duty rating than any of Woolf's. The challenge was not accepted. Trevithick, brimming with confidence, explained to Gilbert just what he thought he would achieve.[13]

> This engine, every thing new, house included, and sett at work at the surface will not exceed £700 and 2 month erecting. The Engine of Woolf's, at Whl Vor, which is but two thirds the power of a 72 In Cylinder, single power, cost £8000, and was two years erecting.

As usual he worked out what could happen and then blithely assumed that it would, making no allowance for what others were doing and certainly not expecting to face any local opposition to his plans. Because the engine was now his main preoccupation, he tended to assume that everyone else would also give it first priority. Not, however, on this occasion: Rastrick was concentrating all his efforts on a major project of his own, the iron bridge he was building across the Wye at Chepstow. In his absence from the foundry, work went neither very quickly nor very well. This fact was not lost on Harvey and Vivian. Not having been given the order themselves, they now went around crowing that the "iron ore was not yet raised" for making the castings. They denigrated the engine, and Andrew Vivian even turned up at Herland and, presumably with the agreement of at least some of the adventurers, dismissed the men working for Trevithick. Relations between the old close friends and partners had completely broken down. Trevithick retrieved the work situation, but then had new, exasperating problems to face when the castings finally did arrive from Bridgnorth. The pole could not be made to fit into its casing. It was in Trevithick's own words "most shamefully fitted up" and had to go back to the foundry. It was December 1815 before everything was finally ready, and even then it had to be left to the vigorous engineer himself to set everything in motion. Fortunately, we have an eyewitness account of what must have been a dramatic, not to say melodramatic scene, all enacted amid clouds of steam like dry-ice in a horror movie.[14]

> I was a boy working in the mine, and several of us peeped in at the door to see what was doing. Captain Dick was in a great way, the engine would not start; after a bit Captain Dick threw himself down upon the floor of the engine-house, and there he lay upon his back; then up he jumped, and snatched a sledge-hammer out of the hands of a man who was driving in a wedge, and lashed it home in a minute. There never was a man could use a sledge like Captain Dick; he was as strong as a bull. Then, he picked up a spanner and unscrewed something, and off she went. Captain Vivian was near me, looking in at the doorway; Captain Dick saw him, and shaking his fist, said; "If you come in here I'll throw you down the shaft". I suppose Captain Vivian had something to do with making the boilers, and Captain Dick was angry because they leaked clouds of steam. You could hardly see, or hear anybody speak in the engine-house, it was so full of steam and noise.

In the event, the engine seemed to be a great success. Gilbert was asked to calculate the duty and measured it at the very high level of 58 million. Trevithick had triumphed over his opponents. Apart from Harvey and Vivian, he had also antagonised Joseph Price of the Neath Abbey iron works, who had also presumably been aggrieved at not being selected for making the Peruvian engines. Now Trevithick was threatening to horsewhip him, "for the falsehoods that he with the others had reported". In the event, he was content to let the engine itself do the arguing for him, which it did in stentorian tones, according to one who remembered it at work.[15]

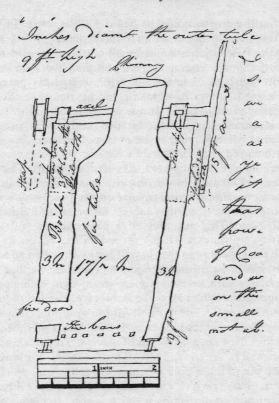

Fig 9: *The recoil engine of 1815. The drawing shows a large vertical boiler, with fire door, fire bars and vertical flue narrowing to the chimney. The water-level is shown as 3 ft below the top of the boiler. An axle is mounted above, with a pipe on the right admitting steam to the 15 ft diameter, hollow rotor. The steam escapes through a hole at the rotor tip, shown here at the bottom of the arm. A belt and pulley system is shown at the far end of the axle.*

When a young man, living on a farm at Gurlyn, I was sent to Gwinear to bring home six or seven bullocks. Herland Mine was not much out of my way, so I drove the bullocks across Herland Common toward the engine-house. Just as the bullocks came near the engine-house the engine was put to work. The steam roared like thunder through an underground pipe about 50 feet long, and then went off like a gun every stroke of the engine. The bullocks galloped off – some one way and some another.

It was said that the engine could be heard 5 miles away. In time, the steam pressure was raised to an unprecedented 150 p.s.i. It seemed that the new engine would be all conquering, and might even replace the beam engine for all pumping work at mines. There was no shortage of orders. Trevithick had his patent to ensure that he got the reward, which he and his family could hope to enjoy for many years to come. It was not a dream that was to be realised, but it seemed very realistic in 1815, and it is important to bear that in mind when looking at the events of the next few years. He sincerely believed that the family's fortune was fully restored, and no matter what else happened they had an assured income. Over the next year or two, however, problems started to appear. The violent action caused irregular wear on the pole, which made it difficult to pack, with an inevitable loss of steam. Efficiency began to fall away. This accentuated a basic design fault. The plunger cooled very quickly when exposed to the air on its long travel outside the cylinder, so that loss of heat was added to loss of steam. The stories of steam-filled engine houses indicate that there were still problems with keeping boilers steam-tight at high pressure and temperature. When all these factors were added together, the result was a steady decline in duty. All too soon, the claims that these were the finest engines in Cornwall were heard no more, and one after another they were taken out of service. Trevithick was no longer in Cornwall to see the sad fate of his favourites for himself.

Just because the plunger-pole engine was such a success at first does not mean that Trevithick was prepared to drop everything else and concentrate on perfecting it. He was still fascinated by the idea of steam boats, and started thinking about a new type of engine and a new way of driving a vessel through the water. This led him to a bizarre experiment, which has been compared to the Sphere of Aeolus or Aeolopile, designed by Heron of Alexandria around the end of the first century AD, in so far as both were forms of reaction turbines. In the first version, Heron used a jet of steam to pass into a hollow ball to drive it round. He also used hot air passing through a swastika-shaped pipe and out at the end of the arms, which whirled round to rotate a disc with dancing figures. These were intended as nothing more than amusing toys. It is highly unlikely that the Cornishman knew much if anything about Roman steam toys. With the amount of steam whistling around his many engines, some of it would inevitably have made something move by accident and he hit on the idea on his own.

Basically what he built was rather like a giant propeller, a 15ft-long hollow armature, pivoted at its centre. Steam was admitted at the centre of the arm at a pressure of 100 p.s.i. and escaped through a tiny opening at one end of the arm. The effect was similar to that of a catherine wheel – the whole thing whizzed round at about 300 revolutions a minute. He soon abandoned the idea of using this to drive a boat, and not being able to think of any other use for what he called his "werling engine" he gave it to the works foreman at Bridgnorth. What he was supposed to do with it was never explained, perhaps it ended up as a giant version of Heron's aelopile, a monstrous toy to amuse the children.

Even if he could find no use for the machine, he patented it anyway in November 1815, together with a small collection of other devices. One of these related to a notion that he had for finding a better device for moving ships than the paddle wheel. Perhaps he had developed an interest in ancient mechanics after all, for what he now described was an idea based on the Archimedean screw – the screw propeller. He would not, in fact, have had to delve in ancient manuscripts to learn about the Archimedean screw, for it was already widely used for pumping water. Operated either by hand or machine, it consisted of a helical screw in a cylindrical case. As the screw turned, so it drew water up the cylinder. It was a small, but vital, leap of the imagination to realise that if the screw, when firmly based, would move water, then if it was afloat it would necessarily be itself moved along as it turned. He made a number of experiments with different types and sizes of screws, and designed a double screw that he intended to fit to a Thames barge. In the event, it seems the full-scale trial never took place, or if it did, Trevithick was not around to oversee it. His other new design at this time was a boiler designed for use with the reaction engine. It was an early form of multi-tubular boiler. In place of the familiar U-tube, the water to be heated was contained in three horizontal tubes, with three vertical tubes descending from the bottom of each of them. Again, there was to be no real development of this idea.

He may have had a great deal to get on with, but Peruvian affairs were still very much on his mind, and it was with a good deal of relief that he heard that the whole party had safely arrived at Lima, and what brought even greater relief was the arrival of the money to pay for the engines.[16]

Aboute a fortnight since, I recd Letters from Lima, and also letters to the friends of the men who sail'd with the engines. They arrived the 29 Jany after a very good passage and withoute one hour's sickness. Both theirs and my agreements was immid'ly ratifyde and they are in big spirits. The ship finish'd dissg the 11 Feby which was the day these letters sail'd from Lima with 12000 Dollars for me which is all arrived save. I shall make another fit oute for them immidly. I expect that all the engines will be at work before the end of October. Half of them must be at work before this time. The next day after their letters sail'd for Europe, they intended to go back to the mines.

Somehow, whenever one reads a Trevithick announcement that something is sure to happen by a certain date, one knows that things are bound to go wrong. But no one could have foreseen that the difficulties in Peru would be so serious as to demand his own immediate presence to sort them out. Even then, he would probably never have gone if he had not entered the partnership. It was his own profits that were being threatened by incompetence in South America. Historical "ifs" are notoriously futile: what happened happened and nothing can change it now, but sometimes speculations have a point. If Uvillé had never seen the model in the shop window and had simply returned to Peru to report failure, what would Trevithick have done? He would have seen the problems of the plunger-pole engines for himself, and either devised a solution of sorts, or abandoned them to concentrate on other ideas. He was very enthusiastic about steam on the water, and given any time at all he would surely have worked out how to use the screw propeller. It was not a great mechanical problem. In fact, its successful development was not even down to a professional engineer, but was the work of a farmer, Francis Pettit Smith, using models on his duck pond! But that was still twenty years in the future, and as soon as Pettit Smith had shown what could be done, the notion was seized by Brunel for the first true, modern liner the SS *Great Britain*. Events in South America cancelled all the other options.

CHAPTER FOURTEEN

Silver Mines

It is almost impossible for us to imagine the difficulties involved in getting Trevithick's engines to the mines at Cerro de Pasco, never mind the problems to be faced in getting them to work in the thin air of the Andes. The only route was a mule track, a narrow ledge hacked out of the mountain side. It was not an ascent that anyone looked forward to with very much pleasure.[1]

> The perils of the journey were very considerable. He had to pass over deep ravines, along bridges not more than five or six feet wide. The passage along the precipitous sides of the mountains was still more frightful. The mule always walks close to the edge of the precipice, and at times his leg was dangling over a descent alarming to look at.

The writer noted that some travellers to the mines could only manage it by keeping their eyes shut most of the time and relying on the sure-footedness of the mules. And this was the route that had to be used to move the heavy machinery. It was a project, however, of such immense importance to the whole of the Peruvian economy that immense resources were made available.[2]

> To effect the great work, the whole power of the viceroy was neces-sary, assisted by the means and co-operation of the richest men in Peru. Three thousand mules and four thousand Indians, were put in requisition by the government, and by dint of the most extraordi-nary exertion ever made in any undertaking in South America, one of the engines was put together.

Fig 10: *A somewhat imaginative drawing of the mule track to Cerro de Pasco.*

The various accounts have concentrated, not surprisingly, on the immense effort needed to get the engines up to the town high in the Andes. The engines had to be supplied in parts, none of which could weigh more than 300 lbs (136 kg) nor be longer than 7 ft (2 m). Once the parts arrived, they had to be assembled under the direction of Uvillé and the three Cornishmen – that is, one amateur engineer, two ordinary workmen and a drunk – relying on a workforce who had never seen a steam engine in their lives before, and with whom three of the four directors of operations were totally unable to converse. And these were not just ordinary engines. They could only be worked using high-pressure steam, which meant that everything had to fit together very precisely, even after it had all been hauled up a rough mountain track by mules.

What this meant in practical terms can perhaps be best explained by looking forward to 1870, when yet more steam engines were being sent to the same mines, this time provided by, of all people, Harveys of Hayle. Technology had improved vastly in half a century – but not the track up the Andes. Edward Hodge was the man in charge, whose forebears included Richard Hodge, who was famously upended by Trevithick and had his boot prints stamped on the Dolcoath count house ceiling. Later Captain Hodge, also a relative of Edward's, was to work with Trevithick in Peru. In his diary, Edward described some of the problems that had to be met in order to produce the parts for the engine he was now to erect at Cerro de Pasco.[3]

> It may be mentioned that the cylinders, thirty seven inches in diameter and nine feet in length had to be subdivided into twenty two half rings or segments, and the joints so carefully wrought that their faces should be brought into mathematical contact to ensure their being eventually steam tight, while offering no inequalities of surface to impede the fair action of the pistons. To effect this important object no known machinery was capable of finishing the segments with the required accuracy; but each face of every segment was, with an incredible amount of labour and skill "hand fitted" until the surfaces had acquired the polish and perfection of a mirror, and could be brought into a perfect mathematical contact. The accuracy in preparing the faces permitted the making of every joint during the subsequent erection by the simple application of a coating of the finest paint, so that the divisions became impalpable to the touch on the completion of the cylinder. So great was the amount of labour expended on the preparation of the cylinder joints, that about fifty skilled mechanics were occupied during the greater part of a year in scraping and handfitting the faces, after they had been fitted as accurately as possible in the lathes etc of the factory.

To supervise the construction of just two engines with their pumps and boilers, a party of seventeen men and a foreman was sent out as an advance guard, and Hodge joined them later to supervise the actual erection. Trevithick had designed his sectioned engines at a time when sophisticated machining was not possible and, as his experience with the Herland engine had shown, at a time when foundries could not be relied on to produce castings that fitted together even roughly. No advance party had been sent out, and the work-force that did go was less than reliable. And they had a huge task in front of them. Between them, they were supposed to set up the plant for the Lima Mint and oversee the transport and erection of not two, but six engines. It would have been a miracle if all had gone well. Yet, at first, it really did seem that there were no real problems. By the summer of 1816 Trevithick was enthusing over the reports that were reaching him; one engine was at work at the mines, the mines themselves were proving to be even richer than promised and he looked forward to "Dollars and work plenty". Soon, however, problems did start to surface. Vivian was proving as unreliable as expected, and Trevithick sent him a stern note.[4] "Your very great neglect in not writing both me and your family have made it very unpleasant for all partys & your friends suppose you are dead ... I cannot help saying to you that I am much hurt at your cold treatment to your family as well as to me onely one letter since you arrived". This, in light of future events, was a bit rich, coming from Trevithick.

Soon there were more mixed reports coming back from Lima. Trevithick knew what needed to be done, but communicating his ideas across such a distance was next to impossible. The simplest things could hold up a project, things that had he been there on the spot, he could have sorted out in minutes, not in the months that it took to send a letter by sailing ship. He had sent out a Cornish boiler for use at the Mint with, he thought, very clear instructions on how it was to be used. If coal was available, it could be put in the fireplace at the end of the boiler tube, as was done in the Cornish mines. But if no coal could be had, they would have to use wood, and he explained that there was not enough space in the tube to fit sufficient wood to reach the required temperature. In that case, it would be necessary to go back to old-fashioned practices, and light a fire under the boiler instead of inside it. So what happened? There was no coal, so they tried to use wood in the boiler and then announced that the boiler was faulty and could not raise enough steam for the engine. If something as simple as that could go wrong in Lima, where all sorts of facilities were available, what on earth was going to happen up in the mountains? It was clear to Trevithick that to protect his own investment, apart from anything else, he would have to go to Peru himself. In fact, he was now so concerned about the state of affairs, that he was contemplating taking a ship that could not guarantee to take him anywhere near Lima, but which offered to drop him off in Buenos Aires. Quite how he proposed to make the cross-country journey of around 2000 miles was never explained, but then he had earlier planned a trip that was to take in both Peru and Mexico: it was probably bad geography again.

There was good news to set beside the bad, and it was widely publicised in Cornwall, where these foreign adventures were arousing a great deal of interest. A report from the *Lima Gazette* of 10 April 1816 was reproduced in the local newpapers.[5]

Immense and incessant labour, and boundless expense, have conquered difficulties hitherto esteemed altogether insuperable; and we have, with unlimited admiration, witnessed the erection, and astonishing operation of the first steam engine. It is established in the celebrated and royal mineral territory called the mountain of Yaüriacocha, in the province of Tarma; and we have had the felicity of seeing the drain of the first shaft in the Santa Rosa Mine in the noble district of Pasco. We are ambitious of transmitting to posterity the details of an undertaking of such prodigious magnitude, from which we anticipate a torrent of silver, that shall fill surrounding nations with astonishment.

The Cornish, overwhelmed by the flowery language, were even more astonished to find that the only Englishman singled out for praise was the workman, Bull. No one, however, dared question the authenticity, when it came under the auspices of Don Domingo Gonzales de Casteñeda and Don José Lago y Lemus, Commissaries and Territorial Magistrates in the Royal Military Territory.

The good news could not deflect Trevithick from his resolve to go to Peru, and he began putting his affairs in order. He moved the family to Penzance, so that it would be easier for the children to attend school. In a final flurry of intense activity, he worked hard at perfecting and finding new uses for his various inventions. The most important change involved adapting the plunger-pole for use with existing Watt engines. New boilers were built to provide steam at a higher pressure, and the steam case and pole were added alongside the existing cylinder, effectively compounding the engine. Now that he was sure that he had covered all possible variations of the pole engine, he sold half his patent off to one of the leading engineers in Cornwall, William Sims, trusting him to look after his interests while he was away. He felt completely confident that what he saw as the glorious future of his greatest invention was in good hands, and that whatever might happen to him in South America, his family was assured of a solid income for as long as he

chose to stay away. He also sold off the one mine in which he was
the main adventurer, Wheal Francis, though as the industry was
very depressed he could hardly have got a very high price. But,
with scrupulous fairness, he recommended that any would-be
purchaser get an independent report on the mine from a competent engineer – "Anyone but Captain Andrew Vivian". That
breach had not healed.

Now Trevithick felt everything really was in first-class order, and
with copper prices still collapsing he was not too sorry to be leaving
Cornwall for a land where silver flowed free. One minor problem
does seem to have crossed his mind, as he wrote to Uvillé.[6]

> The newspapers say a great deal aboute the State of Peru being
> disturbed by factions contending for independence. I think it ought
> not to injure as you have not a wish or parshallity either on the one
> side or the other.

Trevithick's plans seem on the surface to be well-formed and
unusually well executed. Two factors were, however, to have a
profound effect on the life of himself and his family. The first we
have already met, the failure of the plunger-pole engine to live up
to expectations. The second was the political upheaval that was
already under way in South America, and this was a situation
where the politics of Uvillé were of no concern to anyone. Silver
mines, however, had a vital role to play. To understand what was
going on calls for the sort of short history lesson that would have
been invaluable to Trevithick before he became involved in the
venture. The first silver had been extracted from the Potosi mines,
now in Bolivia. As they declined, so Cerro de Pasco grew. Wealth
poured from the mines, but only the Spanish benefited. A vast
bureaucracy was built, Spanish noblemen crossed the ocean to buy
up land and then did little more than count the revenue. Churches
of great splendour were endowed. It was an age of prosperity –
unless one was unlucky enough to be a native Peruvian Indian.
They had never forgotten that they had once had a great empire of
their own, and the Chota women of Paso were still wearing mourn-
ing for the last Inca ruler, Atahualpa, three centuries after he was
killed by the Spanish. Now, however, they were little better than
slaves. Spanish law allowed the mine-owners to impress one in
every seven adult men to work for a year in the mines.
Theoretically they were paid for the work, but payment was often

on the basis of meeting productivity levels set down by the owners, and many owners made sure those levels were impossible to reach. Half-starved, kept going as much by chewing coca leaves as by the wretched food they were given and often working for nothing, the Indians' hatred of the Spanish grew and festered. A bloody rebellion under the Indian leader Tupac Amaru II broke out in 1780 and was just as bloodily repressed.

The Spanish were engaged in a futile attempt to stop the world from changing and developing. In the eighteenth century, the works of libertarian writers such as Diderot and Voltaire were banned and the church even managed to have Newtonian physics removed from the science syllabus at the University of San Marco. Ideas are not that easily suppressed. A new movement was under way, which erupted as an easily-suppressed rebellion in 1814. More ominously, as far as the old regime was concerned, a much greater movement was gaining momentum with a vision of a new republic, "Great Colombia" that would embrace the whole subcontinent. Its leaders included Simon Bolivar and Bernardo O'Higgins, both of whom had made considerable headway long before Trevithick planned his journey. And there was a third liberator, José de San Martin. He was to lead his Army of the Andes all the way from Argentina to Peru. It was an unstoppable force, and anyone who believed that the revolutionaries would simply allow the engineers to get on with their work at the mines, which had come to symbolise the worst of Spanish oppression, was living in fantasy land. But that was one country where Richard Trevithick was not a stranger. Perhaps the position in Peru at that time was best summed up by one of its historians who described how, thanks to "misconceived colonial economic policies', the country had "governments without authority, ministers without prestige, treasuries without funds, militia without honour, citizens without patriotism".[7] The fate of his Peruvian fortune had been sealed before he even set sail.

On 20 October 1816 Trevithick embarked on the South Sea whaler *Asp*, sailing from Penzance, not to Buenos Aires, but to Callao, the main port of Peru adjoining Lima. He probably prided himself on having personally seen to all the necessary arrangements. He told his wife he had paid a year's rent in advance on the Penzance house: six months later she was to receive a rent demand. He had only paid for half a year. Aware of the dangers of sea-voyages and foreign lands threatened by civil war, he realised that he needed life insurance to protect his family's future: he forgot to pay the premiums, leaving Jane to settle the matter later out of her own meagre funds. So he sailed away, leaving a characteristic muddle in his wake. With him went a boilermaker, Sanders, to add to the small English contingent and Richard Page, the attorney who had drawn up the partnership agreement with Uvillé. It was Jane who encouraged him to take him as a companion for the long journey, but Trevithick neither liked nor trusted him. On this occasion he was the one who had the right instincts.

The ship arrived off the coast of Peru and Page rhapsodised over "the stupendous Andes, far higher than the clouds". Even more rhapsodic was the welcome given in the *Lima Gazette* of the 12 February 1817. After reporting that a second engine was at work at the mines and that ore was already arriving of unprecedented richness the account continued.[8]

> To this agreeable intelligence we have the happiness to add that of the arrival of the British ship Asp, from London, having on board a large quantity of machinery consigned to the royal Mint of this City, and for constructing eight engines equal to those already erected on the Santa Rosa and Yauriacocha Mines in Pasco, with this advantage, that they are of the latest improvement. But that which is of still greater importance, is the arrival of Don Ricardo Trevithick, an eminent professor of mechanics, machinery and mineralogy, inventor and constructor of the engines of the last patent, and who directed, in England, the execution of the machinery now at work in Pasco. This professor, with the assistance of the workmen who accompany him, can construct as many engines as shall be wanted in Peru, without the necessity of sending to Europe for any part of these vast machines. The excellent character of Don Ricardo, and his ardent desires to promote the interests of Peru, recommend him to the highest degree of public estimation, and make us hope that his arrival in this kingdom will form the epoch of its prosperity.

The "professor" was no doubt greatly flattered and perhaps a little amused. A more interesting and less amusing welcome was provided by his first meeting with his two partners Abadia and Arismendi. The story they had to tell was not quite the same as that being put around in the official notices. Expenses had risen, and it had been necessary to bring in new investors and expand the company, affairs were in a poor state with the engines running quite badly, while Uvillé now considered himself master of all aspects of steam and mine engineering, and was developing a fine line in megalomania. The good news was that the Mint was working well, turning out 5 million coins a year. The new machinery now being unloaded at Callao would soon, according to Trevithick, raise this to 30 million. But there was a great deal still to be sorted out, as he explained to James Smith of Greenwich who had shares in the venture.[9]

There are still two engines to put up for lifting water and two for winding ore, and those at work to be put to rights. They are raising ore from one mine which is immensely rich, and from what I can learn, a much greater quantity will be got up, when the whole are at work, than these people have any idea of. Several other mines will also be set to work by engines that we shall make here. We have been received with every mark of respect, and both Government and the public are in high spirits on account of our arrival, from which they expect much good to result.

Mr Vivian died the 19th of May. I believe that too much drink was the cause of it. Uville, I think, wished him gone, and was in great hope that I should not arrive. His conduct has thrown down his power very much, which he never can again recover.

They all say that the whole concern shall be put entirely under my management, and every obstacle shall be removed out of my road. Unless this is done, I shall soon be with you in England. I am very sorry that I did not embark with the first cargo, which would have made a million difference to the company. The first engine was put to work about three months since, the other about two months; but they are as much at a loss in their mining as in their engineering. The Mint is the property of our company, and Government pays us for coining, which gives us an immense income.

The letter ends with a typical Trevithickian touch.

If you wish your dividends in this company to be applied to further advantage in any new mines I may engage in, in preference to having it sent to England, I will, as the dividends are made, do everything in my power to improve the talent. On this subject I must have your answer before I can make any new arrangement under this head.

He had scarcely set foot on shore, had only second-hand reports on what was going on but was already planning to invest dividends that had not yet been earned.

The Mint had proved so successful in producing gold and silver coinage, that new machinery was now required to meet the

demand. It was agreed to install new water wheels to work the
rollers brought from England, but there was a difficulty. The
water-course that needed to be investigated ran through the
grounds of a convent, and no amount of pleading by Abadia had
yet produced permission to go inside. Trevithick, never a great one
for niceties and formal applications, simply turned up with his
interpreter.[10]

> I walked up and knocked, in my blunt way, at the nunnery court door,
> *without knowing there were any objections to admit men*; it was opened by
> a female slave, to whom the interpreter told my name and business.
> Very shortly three old abbesses made their appearance, who said I
> could not be admitted. I told them I came from England, for the
> purpose of making an addition to the Mint, and could not do it without
> measuring the watercourse; upon which a council was held amongst
> them; very soon we were ordered to walk in, and all further nunnery
> nonsense was done away. We were taken round the building and were
> shown their chapel and other places without reserve.

Trevithick received the most flattering attention. He had, he
realised, arrived just in time to prevent the whole enterprise from
faltering. The engines were in a wretched state and the authorities
were near to despair. Now he was hailed as a saviour: the Viceroy
offered him a military escort through the mountains, the bells were
rung at Cerro de Pasco and the Lord Warden, who had control of
the mining region, proposed erecting a silver statue to the
Cornishman. And even while he was expressing his own criticisms
of Uvillé's engineering ability, he was very happy to assume that
his own welcome came with no reservations.[11]

> On my arrival Mr Uville wrote me a letter from Pasco, expressing
> the great pleasure he had in hearing of my arrival, and at the same
> time he wrote to Mr Abadia that he thought Heaven had sent me to
> them for the good of the mines.

Once again, life seemed set fair, and once again Trevithick failed to
notice some ominously dark clouds. In England, Uvillé had shown
huge enthusiasm for the venture, but very little regard for the
solemn promises given to his partners. Helped by Page, he had
drawn up an agreement which he knew he was not entitled to do,
and on the basis of which the responsibility for payment for essential machinery had been passed on to Trevithick. We know that the

engineer already distrusted the lawyer, whose close alliance with the Swiss entrepreneur would have sounded a warning note that should have been heard by any prudent man. No one has ever claimed even elementary caution for Trevithick, let alone prudence. Off he went to the mines, as full of confidence as ever.

When he arrived he was able to assess the problems for himself. The best account of the mine comes from Edward Hodge's diary. As well as describing the situation he found in the 1870s, he also gives a good account of what Trevithick achieved in his day. He saw the Cornishman's survey that showed the silver ore being distributed in beds, rather than veins, and quantified the differences found by going deep. At the surface, yields were quite low. Measurements were given in terms of a 6000 lb (2724 kg) "box" of excavated material. At the surface, this produced 40 to 80 oz (1.13 to 2.26 kg) of silver; at the greatest depth then being worked the yield could be as high as 800 oz (22.6 kg). Drainage mostly depended on the great adit. Trevithick had already spoken of this back in Cornwall, but Hodge although he had seen no official papers noted that "I was assured in the Cerro that it is his work. It was certainly admirably carried out, draining from all three existing shafts at a depth of 282 feet [86 m] below the surface. It is capacious, arched in a most endurable manner, and discharges in a lake a mile below the Cerro". Whether this was the adit Trevithick found when he reached the mine, whether he improved it or started a new adit is not known. What he certainly found were problems very different from those he had encountered in Cornwall.

He found that the only available fuel for the engines was turf, and there appeared to be no way at all that coal could be supplied. Even bringing in the peat presented a major problem. There was no food available for the animals anywhere near the mines, so the mules had to be sent down to pasture where they were fattened up. Once they were suitably filled out, they came back up to the mines where they were able to work for a week relying on their reserves of fat before being sent down again for the next feed. The surprising thing is that there are actually coal deposits quite nearby, but they were not discovered until 1819. Hodge again filled in the details.

One of these coal deposits, close to the town, was discovered by my relative previously referred to, but he, wanting silver and despising coal presented his discovery to his major domo, one Sanchez, from whose descendents I purchased large quantities, while growling at my uncle's stupidity in not retaining it, and making me his heir!

Most of the coal was brought in by llamas, creatures for whom Hodge showed little affection – "a villainously, ill-tempered brute, who when angry, his cronic condition, ejects an acrid saliva aimed at its opponents eyes, causing excruciating pain". Just as worrying for mining engineers was the total lack of timber for shoring the mine and construction. The nearest sources were 60 miles away and by the time a log had been dragged over the rough ground by mules it was half the diameter it had been when it had started the journey. Trevithick was never fazed by such problems, which he regarded as difficulties to be overcome, welcome tests for his ingenuity. He was a good deal less well adapted to cope with the convoluted dealings of human affairs. There was a pleasing directness about the man. He said exactly what he thought, and meant what he said. Sadly, such direct honesty too often arrives with a certain naivety, an assumption that others act in the same way. He set about restoring order to the mines, bringing the new machines into working order and overseeing a spectacular increase in the amount of silver emerging from the depths. That was what he had arrived to do and in achieving it he assumed he was making everybody richer and happier.

Uvillé and Page had needed Trevithick to put matters right, but now that everything was up and running they felt his presence was no longer necessary. Uvillé, in particular, had had a taste of being the man in charge, and he very much fancied the idea of being so again. John Miers heard much of the story from Abadia's family when he visited Peru in the 1820s. It was obvious to Trevithick that extra funds were going to be needed, but it was equally obvious from the results already obtained that any improvements would soon pay for themselves and yield handsome profits. This was unwelcome news for the various shareholders, including those in London, who were so alarmed that they sent an agent to Peru to report on what had gone wrong. In fact, things were going rather well – it was simply a case that estimates of what would be needed to work and drain the mines and operate machinery in the Mint had been made in Cornwall by a man who had never seen Peru. It was not too surprising that, when he was able to assess the situation for himself, he found that more resources were needed. But no one ever welcomes news of rising costs, and a whispering campaign orchestrated by Page and Uvillé pushed all the blame on to Trevithick, accusing him of gross mismanagement.

Never in his life was Trevithick prepared to stand for this kind of treatment. One remembers the abortive salvage operation back at Margate, when he was ready to throw away everything he had gained rather than haggle or give way on what he saw as his rights. Now, in Peru, just as the mines were moving into serious profitability, he walked away. Abadia, the one man who emerges as steadfast through all the Peruvian dealings, was also the one man who really did appreciate Trevithick's unique contribution. He offered him $8000 a year, with all his expenses paid if he would only stay at the mine. His reply was firm: "On no conditions would he consent to contend with the jealousies and ill-treatment of the persons with whom he had to deal". [12]

Trevithick was never a man to sit and brood over what had happened, and he set off straight away to see what other opportunities the area might offer. As far as the authorities were concerned, he was still the man whose opinions mattered, whose judgement was valued and who had shown himself more than capable of mastering all the problems of mining in the high Andes. He had the written permission of the Viceroy to prospect and develop mines and he later wrote his own account of those times.[13]

> In this way I travelled through many of the mining districts, and although I met with several unoccupied spots which would have paid well for working, yet, being a considerable distance inland, and requiring more capital to do them justice than I could then advance, I abandoned for the time all ideas of undertaking them.
>
> To this, indeed, there was but one exception, and that was a copper and silver mine, the ores of which are uniformly united, in the province of Caxatambo.

Huge deposits of copper ore were indeed found, and are still being worked in the mountains to the south of Cerro. But before Trevithick could think much more about his discoveries, news arrived that Uvillé had died in August 1818 and that Bull too was dead. Abadia was quick to move and soon Trevithick was reinstated and placed in sole charge of affairs at Cerro de Pasco. Only one enemy now remained. Page was still trying to stir up trouble among the London shareholders but there was no need to have any more fears from that quarter. He had an ally back in Cornwall who was more than ready not only to rise to his defence but to launch a full scale attack on his opponent – his wife Jane.

Jane Trevithick does not feature as much as she deserves in this story simply because we know so little about her, but whenever she does appear she does so as a steely character, well-endowed with the true Harvey grit. She held the family together through all the years of fluctuating fortunes, coped admirably with the drama of her husband's near fatal illness combined with bankruptcy, and she was not about to be defeated by the likes of Page. In an undated letter to the shareholders, she accepted her share of blame for encouraging her husband to travel with Page, and also suggests that if she had not been ill and unable to cast her own eye over the various agreements, things would have turned out very differently. This is just one of several hints that she might have been a good deal more capable of looking after the financial side of the business than her husband. She rehearsed the story of the plot and elaborated on the details.[14]

> Captain Hodge informed me that when the news of Mr T.'s arrival reached Pasco, Uville set out with a party intending to intercept him in his progress to the mines; in this however he was disappointed, and having reached Lima, he was obliged to receive him as others did, and this appears to be confirmed by a series of letters from Uville, Bull and Sanders at Pasco to Page at Lima, which were brought with him to England and sent to Cornwall for my perusal; these doubtless you have seen. Thus had the friends time to consult and consider such means as were put into immediate execution on their reaching the mines. Under such circumstances could your letter of the 16th of October in which you speak of the haughty imperious and brutal conduct of my husband fail to arouse indignation? Even the money which you were given to understand he was about to undertake some new project of his own account, Mr Abadia in his letter to Mr Tyack allowed he had never received. I am not informed of what Mr Tyack wrote to you, but I should suppose he proved Page's falsehood by asserting the boiler plates and iron to be his uncle's not his own as Mr P. affirmed.

She was clearly a firm, businesslike lady. Life in Peru was, it seemed, back on an even keel. Even Trevithick's time away from the mine had not been wasted, as he had located new sources of mineral wealth. He had what he had wanted from the first, full control of the mines and a share in the substantial profits from the Mint. Page was discredited, and the only man he had to deal with was the trustworthy Abadia. What could go wrong? The answer lay in events far outside the control of any of the participants.

CHAPTER FIFTEEN

Golden Opportunities

Abadia was one of the few men of real influence in Lima who saw that if the Spanish were not to lose Peru to the patriots of the independence movement, they would have to shake off their lethargy and introduce meaningful reforms. He "exerted all his influence to prevail upon the government to open the port to free trade, which event he promised would not only win the confidence and hearty support of the people, but would supply the treasury with means of resisting the enemy, should an invasion be threatened".[1] Nothing was done, the dithering continued and by the time the authorities had decided that perhaps they should do something after all, it was already far, far too late. By 1819 Sir Thomas Cochrane was leading the Chilean navy into battle, routing the Spanish and setting up a blockade of Lima. Cochrane was a splendid, maverick figure. After a highly successful naval career, in which he won high honours as much through daring as skill, he returned to Britain and entered politics. His main target was Admiralty incompetence and corruption, a popular cause with many, but one which brought powerful enemies in high places. The upshot was imprisonment on a trumped-up charge, and the removal of his hard-won and well-merited Order of the Bath. When the Chileans invited him to come and reorganise their navy, he had no hesitation in returning to arms. He soon showed that he had lost none of his old panache. With the sea under his control, the way was open for San Martin to advance into Peru with his troops.

The Peruvian campaign was unusual for an independence movement in that it was largely directed by foreigners, taking their inspiration from Bolivar, who saw the war as part of a concerted campaign against all Spanish interest in South America, rather than being a matter of interest only to Peruvians. San Martin, however, was not completely won-over to The Liberator's politics. He favoured some form of constitutional monarchy, an idea that was never going to be accepted in Peru. Bolivar was blunt: "Thrones will not come back into fashion as long as there are men who love freedom and feel repelled by glamour of that sort".[2] It all made for a very confused situation. Men such as Abadia, who were motivated by love of their country rather than allegiance to any one faction, were always likely to end up antagonising both sides. The royalists suspected him of sympathising with the rebels, simply because he had argued in favour of reform, and were inclined to believe reports that he was using the wealth of the mines to finance their campaign. But they were in retreat and in 1821 they abandoned Lima, at which point San Martin promptly declared himself "Protector of Peru".

Having been mistrusted by the old regime, Abadia might have expected to find favour with the new. He soon found that San Martin had little sympathy for would-be supporters. Captain Hall, who had come down to Peru with Cochrane's fleet, described San Martin's character. "This vigorous chief wanted no adviser; he directed eveything himself and, with the decision of a soldier, admitted no appeals; he swept classes away; established new laws and institutions; and entirely altered the general aspect of society."[3] Others were less flattering, describing him as a vacillating general who finally had to call in Bolivar and his army to finish the work he himself had started. But one part of the description is certainly accurate: he did not enjoy having influential men around him. In the early days, when Abadia was still a man worth courting, the patriots had been keen to try and win him to their cause. Now he was disposable, a relic of the old regime, and a plot was hatched against him. He was approached by two friars claiming to have a message from the Spanish Viceroy up in the hills. He was to supply intelligence on the state of affairs in Lima, and if he refused all the machinery at the mines would be destroyed. It was a crudely executed trap. The friars took one of Abadia's books from his library and brought it out as evidence of their visit when they trotted round to the Lima authorities with their story. The result was inevitable, and he was arrested. Open season had been declared on the Cerro de Pasco mines. The company was in some disarray, and accounts of what happened next are muddled.

According to one source, Arismendi saw what was happening, took whatever profits he could lay his hands on from both mining and the Mint, said to be as much as $600,000, and fled. Everything he left behind was then confiscated by San Martin.[4] The money and property that disappeared almost certainly included some which should have gone to Trevithick. With his support in Lima gone, he had to fend for himself up in the mountains, with both sides now convinced that the mines were being used by their opponents.[5]

> The Cerro fell into the hands of different parties, and was long in the possession of the Royalists, who did everything they could to destroy the engines; they carried away all the wrought iron and bars to make horse-shoes and spurs, and it was supposed they had ruined the engines irretrievably.

However, Trevithick had managed to bury some of the parts, and when the forces moved on they were able to reassemble the main engine and set it back at work. It was no more than a reprieve. Trevithick gave his own account of what happened next as the fortunes of war fluctuated around Cerro de Pasco.[6]

> When the patriots arrived in Peru, the mine was deserted by all the labourers, in order to avoid being forced into the army. In this state it remained for a considerable time; but on the Spaniards retreating into the interior, I recommenced working; and to secure my right to this mine under the new Government I at the same time transmitted a memorial and petition to the established authorities, accompanied by a plan and description of the mine, the result of which was the formal grant, as exhibited in the Spanish document now in your possession. It was not my good fortune to be allowed to follow up my plans, which almost warranted a certainty of success. I had scarcely commenced a second time when the Spaniards returned, and everyone again was obliged to fly.

The course of the whole war was altered by the arrival of Bolivar and his men on the scene, as was Trevithick's life. Bolivar had heard, as everyone of note in Peru had, of the ingenious Cornish inventor and mechanical genius. He had no need of steam engines, but he was short of firearms for his cavalry, so he asked Trevithick to design and make a suitable gun. Trevithick had no choice but to agree. He came up with a short-barrelled carbine, in which barrel and stock were cast as a single piece in brass. It fired an early type of dum-dum bullet.

Bolivar, a canny man, who had probably seen his share of allegedly brilliant new firearms that did more harm to the user than the enemy, promptly "recruited" Trevithick into his army. He was to be given the privilege of testing the new gun for himself. The Cornishman may have been a man of many talents, but marksmanship was not one of them. Bolivar decided the army would be a safer place without him, and allowed him to return once again to the mines.

A bizarre incident occurred at about this time, where it seems he drew on the more gruesome experiences of spending time on a battlefield. One of the miners had his arms crushed in an accident, and there was no possibility of getting medical help. Trevithick realised that unless something was done, the man would die. He offered to amputate the arms himself, and the patient agreed. According to eye witnesses, the result would have been a credit to any surgeon, and the man survived. It was one of the few things that managed to go well in that troubled time. He had scarcely resumed work at the mines before another turn of fortune saw battle raging round Cerro de Pasco itself. Now it was the patriots who appeared at the mines, and decided that help had been given to their opponents. It was their turn to set about wrecking the machinery.

This was the final blow for Trevithick. When disaster finally struck, he had about 300 tons of ore waiting for shipment to England, with an estimated value of £24,000. It was never sent, and he never saw it again. Trevithick was not the only one to be bitterly disappointed by the turn of events. Back in England, young Francis Trevithick had been getting ready to join the ore ship on its return journey to Peru for a reunion with his father. One of the charges levelled against Trevithick was that he never kept in touch with his family while he was away. He may not have written many letters himself, but it is clear that the family were kept fully informed of what was going on, and that Jane knew all the details of the ore shipment and her husband's situation. She was hardly going to send her young son, scarcely ten years old, all the way to Peru on the off chance that he might bump into his father somewhere. The only reference to the trip seems to be in Francis' biography of his father, where he describes his disappointment at not setting off for exotic lands. He makes no mention of anyone else being included in the trip, but that does not mean that he was expected to go alone, which is surely unlikely. It raises the intriguing possibility that the whole family was planning to go. Obviously, the changed situation in Peru made such a trip impossible.

This is a good point to pause and try and assess what, if anything, Trevithick had achieved in Peru. In the silver mines, the engines had done their work and, until the war reached the region, productivity was good and getting better. Unfortunately, the two sides were less concerned about using the mines than they were with making sure they were no use to their opponents. With Abadia arrested, Arismendi decamped and the machinery wrecked, all hopes of profit had ended. For Trevithick it was a total disaster. There has never been a shortage of detractors ready to criticise his decision to go to Peru, in what even his own son dismissed as a worthless enterprise. But, if war had not intervened, he would have emerged as a very wealthy man. The mines had proved far richer than he had dared to hope. He could have stayed in Peru and brought the family over to enjoy a life of luxury, or he could have returned to Cornwall as rich as any eighteenth-century nabob. Even though none of this happened, the enterprise as a whole cannot be written off as a failure. Thanks to his intervention, Peruvian mining was transformed from an industry that had scarcely changed for centuries into one that was modern, efficient and profitable. He may have been forced to abandon the silver mines himself, but others were eventually able to restart the work and they flourished once more. He had found copper deposits which he estimated as worth $12 million, and those mines are not yet exhausted. If you judge success by the amount of money one individual makes from an enterprise, then Trevithick failed. But if, instead, you think in terms of what he contributed to the economy of the newly independent country, then he triumphed. He may never have got his silver statue, but he earned it.

The impression has been given that the end of mining left Trevithick virtually penniless, but this was almost certainly not the case. Although all his income had stopped, he had been paid well over the previous years. How much he invested in mining equipment and how much he put by is not known, but we do know that he had the will and resources to enter into new ventures. He was not beaten yet. The obvious question to ask is – why did he not simply give up and go home? There seemed to be two reasons, and both derive from his character. He was a proud man, who hated being defeated in anything. He would have dearly loved to have arrived back in Cornwall loaded with riches to silence his detractors. Equally he would have hated to have returned defeated, to the sly glances and "told you so" comments.

Whenever things had gone seriously wrong in the past, when a grand scheme had failed, he had simply pushed it away and started again. And that was what he planned to do now. One fortune had been won and lost: now he would win another. The other characteristic that shines through in everything that he ever did was his total inability to turn away from a challenge. Whenever the chance came for patiently building on the foundations he had laid, some new idea would present him with a lure he could never resist. In South America he had found the greatest challenges of all and he had not yet finished with them. He was drawn to new horizons, literal and metaphorical. In that short period between first leaving Cerro de Pasco and Uvillé's death, he had roamed the wild mountains as eagerly as any gold prospector and he had found incomparable riches. Peru was just one country. There was a whole sub-continent, much of it unknown and unexplored. He was fifty years old when work at the mines came to an end, but he still had the enthusiasm of youth.

We know a great deal about what Trevithick did over the next couple of years, even though the chronology is vague. At some stage he made a long journey south down the Andes chain into Chile, where he began a copper-mining venture near Valparaiso. A Cornish miner, a Mr Waters, on returning to Camborne reported that Trevithick's name was still remembered there many years after he left. Simon Whitbarn of St Day described seeing copper ore said to belong to Trevithick to the north of Valparaiso at Copiopo and Coquimbo. Incredibly, around 1830, a miner turned up in Cornwall to claim back pay for having guarded Trevithick's ore. The years had passed and when no one claimed it, he finally decided to give up and come home. One other venture from those years is better documented. Cochrane's fleet was now safe in harbour at Callao, following the Spanish flight from Lima in 1821. There they were joined by a British warship HMS *Aurora*, with a young lieutenant John Liddell on board. He told Francis Trevithick how he was introduced to his father by Hodge.[7]

> I remember your father delighting us all on board the "Aurora" by his striking description of the steam-engine, and his calculation of the "horse-power" of the mighty wings of the condor in his perpendicular ascent to the summit of the Andes. Your father's strong Cornish dialect seemed to give an additional charm to his very interesting conversation.

He then continued to describe the events that happened in, he thought, 1822 when an old frigate the *San Martin* sank in Chorillos Bay 10 miles from Callao. Trevithick offered to salvage the brass cannon on board, provided he got the cargo of copper and tin. He was finally to make use of the lessons he had learned in the abortive salvage effort at Margate but this time at a profit.

This was a very successful speculation, and in a few weeks your father realised about 2500*l*. I remember visiting the spot with your father whilst the operations were carried on, and being astonished at the rude diving bell by which so much property was recovered from the wreck, and at the indomitable energy displayed by him. It was Mr. Hodge, and not I, who then urged in the strongest manner that at least 2000*l* should be immediately remitted to your mother.

Trevithick inevitably had other ideas for using the money to make the fortune that he still sought. There were new lands to explore, new adventures beckoning. In an earlier age Trevithick would have made a great buccaneer, in later years he could have been one of the great explorers. There was something of both in his make-up. Having mined for copper and silver beneath the ground he now proposed to set off to find riches under the sea. He was planning to turn pearl fisher. The idea was born out of the successes with the diving bell and he was now eager to leave Peru. He had made good connections there, particularly with Cochrane, and an unconfirmed story has it that he once swam out to the latter's ship to warn him of an assassination attempt. It is an unlikely tale, as Trevithick was a poor swimmer, but it would be no surprise to find two such unconventional characters enjoying each other's company. But Bolivar was also beginning to make demands on him which he was not eager to meet: his short army experience had given him a healthy caution in dealing with The Liberator. It was time to move on.

He had purchased a brig, a two-masted square rigger, the *Devan* and he set off up the Pacific coast heading for Colombia. He appeared to have some unspecified mission for Bolivar in Bogota, but was destined never to get there. He reached Guayaquil in Ecuador, where he heard stories of rich mines having been discovered in Costa Rica. It all seems very muddled, and Trevithick's own account is little help. It is probable that his disappointments in Peru had soured his view of that country. He took the opportunity of accepting the mission for Bolivar to get away, hoping to find new challenges. The pearl-fishing idea was an obvious development since he had the necessary equipment, but he was just as ready to try his hand at anything else that looked as if it might show a profit. Costa Rica now seemed to hold out the best possibilities, so on he sailed, arriving there some time in 1823.

The man Trevithick had met and who had set him off in this new direction was a Scot, James Gerard, who was also something of an opportunist wanderer, trading up and down the South American coast in whatever commodity looked likely to make money. He had called in at Puntarenas intending to sell a load of cotton and to use the proceeds to buy sugar. Here he heard about gold mines being opened up by a man called Castro at some time in 1821. The very name of Costa Rica, "rich coast" pointed to the wealth that the Spaniards had found when they first arrived, and it seems remarkable that the wealth had been ignored for so long. Gerard put it all down to Spanish apathy, without considering the other possibility: that experience had shown that deposits that looked promising were often quickly exhausted. He went to investigate and found a new system in use that was making processing a good deal easier. The gold from the mines was not like the familiar nuggets of other goldfields which could be separated by panning. Here it appeared as the ore. The process of winning the metal by amalgamation with mercury had been known since Roman times, but a local man Alverado had produced what he called an "Ingenio" which involved an efficient, continuous process. The ore was brought by some form of conveyor to a water-powered crusher, after which it was blended with mercury to form an amalgam with the gold. The mercury was filtered, then distilled. The gold was left behind as pure metal, while the mercury was condensed and re-used. This meant that, unlike the situation at the Peruvian mines, there was no need to transport vast quantities of ore over difficult tracks. This was good news, as the Costa Rican mining area was also high in the hills, based on Monte del Aguacate, which form a southern spur to the main Cordillera ridge, rising to a height of 1541m and looking down on San Mateo.

It was an area that certainly offered a more pleasing prospect than the Andes, Where the latter region was barren, miserable, cold and windswept, this area enjoyed a pleasant climate. The forest was rich in fruit and even in the severe rainy season it seldom rained for more than two days at a time, even if, for those days, the downpour was startlingly torrential. Gerard found a few disadvantages. The region had poisonous snakes. There are, in fact, over a hundred species of snake in Costa Rica; but although they sound alarming, they prefer to keep well away from man and are seldom seen. The mine area, however, is volcanic and given to occasional small eruptions and earthquakes. When Trevithick was told about this new mining region it must have seemed close to paradise, after what he had experienced in Peru. Even the political situation was now stable. Independence had already been achieved, and Costa Rica was now part of the new Central American United Provinces. It was a chance not to be missed and Trevithick hurried on to set up business as gold-miner and pearl-fisher.

Trevithick was never a man to do one thing when he could do two or, better still, three. His time in Costa Rica was no different. He added a little trading with the *Devan* to his other activities. On his arrival he set about trying to put all his plans into operation. He already had his diving bell that he now proposed to use for the pearl-fishing. It was a perfectly reasonable idea that would allow the fisherman far more time on the seabed than they ever had when diving in the traditional way. He wanted the government to grant him exclusive fishing rights for a set period of time, preferably seven years, during which he would instruct locals in the use of the diving bell and at the end of the period hand over all his equipment. It all sounded quite reasonable and the Costa Ricans were enthusiastic, but he had not allowed for the slow grindings of the bureaucratic machine. In April 1824 he wrote to the Junta to say that in spite of an agreement made that February "I am unable to fish for pearls because I have no document of agreement with the government which establishes me in the right".[8] He reiterated that he was ready to start work at once. The government officials confirmed that they were still wholly in favour of the scheme, but there was a snag: "it conflicts with the approved and sworn principles of the Federal Constitution of these States". Then came the note of doom. A report would be made and properly debated, and only then could an answer be given. Ominously, no date was given for when these deliberations might end.

It was as well that he did have other lines to pursue. Contrary to what most commentators have written, he had lost nothing at all by following up his pearl-fishing plan. He already owned the equipment so there had been no expense there, and he still had his ship which could be a valuable asset in trade. In the meantime he had been up to the mining area and discovered that, as well as

gold, there were large quantities of silver. He wrote an official
report to the government in March 1824.

> To extract efficiently all that the veins are able to produce, it is neces-
> sary to get a great deal of material, bronze, copper and iron, from Lima
> for the pumps and also for steam engines, since there are no rivers here
> which can be utilised for water power, and it is indispensable that the
> mines be drained. There are several foundry workers in Sanapasca
> who have worked for me on the bronze parts of steam engines and it is
> absolutely necessary that I have those workmen here. The possibilities
> of the veins are such that I must remain in the province in order to
> accomplish all the tasks that need to be done, and it is also indispens-
> able to send the brig for the workmen. All the expenses, the necessary
> materials, and the conduct of operations shall be at my expense, and to
> my account. It is also necessary to construct mills to pulverise the ore
> and extract the gold, of which there ought to be a considerable amount
> intermixed with the silver, enough to pay for the expenses of the best
> silver mine. The same mills which pulverise the gold ore can be used to
> pulverise the silver ores.

There now followed a complex series of negotiations in which
Trevithick was looking for ways to raise money for all the equipment he needed as well as the very expensive mercury for the
amalgamation of gold. It all centred on sending the *Devan* back to
Peru where she would be loaded with muskets for the government,
equipment to establish a mint as well as the materials and men for
the mines. He had established friendly relations with the head of
state, Juan Mora Fernandez, but that did not relieve him from the
torture of going through the endless bureaucratic process. All the
surviving documents are very proper and courteous, and whoever
wrote them in Spanish for Trevithick did so with a formality that
was hardly Trevithick's style. One can hardly imagine him choos-
ing to sign off as "Your attentive and obedient Servant Who Kisses
your Hands"! None of it seems to have got anywhere and
Trevithick, no doubt hoping to cut through at least some of the red
tape by a change of status, even applied for Costa Rican citizen-
ship. The answers all came back with the same dispiriting phrases –
"it is not in the power of the government", "it is a matter to be
decided by the National Assembly". None of this actually stopped
him from prospecting and putting in claims for mines. Moreover, it
seems from a memorandum from Gerard that a lot less machinery
was actually needed than Trevithick claimed.[9] He wrote that the
two mines, Coralillo and Quebrada-honda, could both be

completely drained by adits, which could also be used for bringing out the ore.

> The veins would be worked upward from the adits, and thus no expense would be incurred for ages to come in lifting either water, ore, or rubbish to the surface. Padre Arias Mine is an exception, requiring a powerful water wheel, or an hydraulic pressure-engine, for which there is a fine fall of water of 135 feet. The mines in Quebrada-honda are those in which an interest has been procured. Captain Trevithick has an interest in the mine of Coralillo; the great watercourse is also his.
>
> It will be seen by the plan that there are 75 fathoms fall to the point where his present mill is situated, and other 75 fathoms to the junction of the rivers of Quebrada-honda and Machuca. The whole length does not amount to two miles, within which it is estimated that sufficient power may be commanded to stamp 500,000 of quintals [25,000 tonnes] annually. To bring it up to that pitch, the waters of Machuca must be brought to join those of Quebrada-honda at Trevithick's mill, and then 40 tons of water per minute could be delivered in the dry season.

Trevithick did not find life easy in the Cordillera. He was constantly writing to complain about the workforce. He entered into contracts with carpenters who failed to arrive, or when they did come, left before the work was finished. One of the workers made off with his mule, and abandoned it, half-starved, many miles away. Charcoal burners arrived, left their fires unattended and burned down some of the property. He tried to persuade the government to act on his behalf, employing a mixture of cajolery and bluster.[10]

> I am under the sad necessity of begging Your Excellencies for your immediate protection without which it will always be impossible for foreigners, particularly those who are not able to speak the language, to understand the customs of the country, and to do anything for the public good, and referring to this I can assure Your Excellencies, that I have a great deal of feeling which will force me to do something quick and disagreeable and unprofitable, and for someone or other that will be a loss. I cannot waste more time in a strange country without having protection to aid me in the completion of the contract which I have entered into with its government, and I ask to be excused to leave. I beg pardon of Its Excellency, the Government; and second, the pardon of Your Excellencies; for my work, it is necessary that everything be straightforward; and it will have to be the same with my contracts, or I shall depart for England.

Trevithick was indeed very much a foreigner in Costa Rica. In spite
of the years he had spent in South America, he still could not speak
Spanish and he displayed a certain nostalgia for home in the name of
his mill in the mountains – Britania Works. And if he complained
about the Costa Ricans, they also complained about him. The
government soon became bored with his list of often trivial
complaints, which they blamed, probably with a good deal of truth,
on the "lack of an accurate interpreter". They pointed out, with a
sarcasm that comes through even the politest phrasing, that they did
not believe that the temporary loss of a mule was actually about to
drive him out of the country. His bluff was well and truly called. They
were, however, a good deal firmer when it came to more serious accu-
sations levelled against Trevithick, and he received a sharp rebuke.[11]

> The Supreme Chief of State has received complaints that on a
> number of occasions you have attempted to hinder the use by others
> of timber land which is to be used freely by all, and to hinder them
> in the use of the road you were allowed to construct to transport
> minerals from the mine to the reduction works. The road passes by
> the mine entrance, ore crushing area, and machinery which are
> legally conceded to and being worked by Citizen Cruz Alvarado.
> The legality of his claim is not impaired by the fact that you have
> been permitted to build the road across it. The Government
> intended that all miners in the area should have free passage over
> the land, of which fact you have had repeated reminders. It cannot
> be considered less than astonishing that there should be an occur-
> rence despite the warnings which were issued previously in this case
> of which you were expressly warned.

The most serious dispute of all was with Father Vincente Castro,
who had first opened up the gold-silver mines in the area. He now
claimed that Trevithick's activities in the Monte del Aguacate
region were damaging his own interests. This one was left with the
lawyers, who began the usual battle of claims, counter-claims and
writs. It was an issue that resolved itself; for while the legal battle
continued, Trevithick and Gerard decided to leave the country. It
was, by then, clear that they lacked the capital to develop the
mines in the most profitable manner, and that their efforts to get
money out of the government were doomed to founder in a sea of
procrastination. Their only hope was to go to Britain and raise the
finance there. Trevithick had been away for more than ten years. It
was time to go home.

CHAPTER SIXTEEN

Coming Home

There are some mysterious circumstances surrounding the departure of Trevithick and Gerard from Costa Rica. What arrangements did they make to protect their considerable investments in that country? Why did they decide to take two young boys with them? And why did they not make use of Trevithick's stout sea-going vessel, the *Devan*? Once home, he could either have sold it or stocked it with mine machinery and other cargo for the return.

But Trevithick and Gerard were looking to the future. They had decided to make their homeward journey into what they hoped would prove to be a profitable expedition. The principal markets for their gold and silver were likely to be in Europe, and the machinery they needed to develop the mines would have to be brought from Britain. As things then stood, the only possible passage was long and dangerous. Wherever men have sailed, the voyage round Cape Horn is still regarded with awe, on which one might face some of the worst seas in the whole world. Although the mines were on the eastern flank of the Cordillera Ridge, offering an easy journey to the Pacific port of Puntarenas, they were also not much more than 60 miles from the Atlantic, in a direct line. Unfortunately, there was no direct line. The two men felt, however, that if they could find a suitable route through the Cordillera, they could then head off to find the headwaters of the Sarapiquí river, and follow it north to the point where it became navigable. They would then have a good route up to the San Juan River, which forms the boundary between Costa Rica and Nicaragua. After that, it would literally be plain sailing down to the port of San Juan del Norte and the Caribbean.

It was largely uncharted territory, so that this really was a trip into the unknown. The party consisted of the two partners, Gerard's servant and six local men, three of whom were brought along specifically to hack a way through the forest until they reached the river. Work completed, they were to return. Then there were the two young boys. José Mariá and Mariano Montelegre, who were on their way to school in England, the first native Costa Ricans ever to be sent for education in Europe. Were there ever two boys who had a more exciting start to a journey to a new school? José Mariá was to go on eventually to the Royal College of Medicine at Edinburgh, while his brother may well have been inspired by his travelling companions, as he spent his adult life as a very successful engineer. Eventually they returned to Costa Rica, and they served their country well. They had seen the enthusiasm for coffee-drinking in Europe, and came home to encourage the local growers to meet the demands of this market, the first step in establishing what was to become a vital export trade and the mainstay of the country's economy. The climax to José Mariá's career came when, in 1860, he was elected President of Costa Rica. Their parents were obviously ambitious and saw great futures for their two boys – and were willing to send them off, through unknown territory, to a country they did not know and a school that had not even been chosen before they left. But would they have been so keen to send them off in the charge of the two engineers if they had had the least idea of just how close they were to come to disaster and even death? Perhaps they regarded the whole thing as some sort of character-building initiative test in the best upper-class, stiff-upper-lip English tradition. In the event, it did the boys no harm at all.

The first task facing the party was to find a route from the mines across the Cordillera, which could be developed into a mule track, or perhaps even a decent roadway. With only Francis Trevithick's description of what he described as his father's "rough map", it is difficult to work out just where the party went on the first part of the journey. It seems that their first idea was to look for a way down to the existing mule track between San Mateo and San José, but the route down the mountain proved too steep, so that plan was abandoned. They headed instead for the high pass that separates the two volcanos, Poás and Barva, which formed the spectacular backdrop to the mines. At times, the spectacle could be a little too exciting. Poás, in particular, is quite active and there was a minor eruption as recently as 1989. Records do not go back quite as far as 1827 when the party passed this way, but it seems likely that it was bubbling and grumbling even then. The area is now a National Park where visitors follow well-marked and cleared trails to see the volcanoes and admire the wildlife, which includes the startlingly beautiful crimson-breasted humming birds. This party had little time for scenery or for bird-watching. They had quite enough to do in finding a way through the forest, where the trees dripped with exotic mosses and lichens. At the top of the pass at around 2000m they would often be overwhelmed by the clouds that sank down to blanket the hills. Their compasses told them which way they wanted to head eventually, but not which route to take down through the complex of gullies and ravines that rippled down the face of the mountains. Conditions were harsh, often hot and humid by day, falling to freezing point, or below, at night.

A whole succession of small rivers have their origin on the eastern slopes of the Cordillera, and they eventually merge to form major rivers, one of which was the party's main objective, the Sarapiquí. Now they had to decide which of the tributaries to cross and which to try and follow – there was a bewildering array of choices. Once down from the ridge, they were confronted by soft, swampy ground and decided to send the mules back with three of the men. Trevithick, in his own notes on this part of the expedition, describes how they waded across shallow rivers, taking what they hoped was the best route down to the headwaters of the Sarapiquí. The going was very difficult, but he was convinced that if only they had allowed themselves a little more time, they could have found a better route, one which would have been passable by the mules. He particularly liked the look of a ridge, clearly visible from the valley floor, which led down from Poás. But having reached the Sarapiquí there was no question of retracing their steps up the slopes to try an alternative route. They had quite enough problems ahead of them.

The original idea had been to make a trail along the riverbank until they reached the navigable section, which traditionally begins, as the name suggests, at Puerto Viejo. They soon found that forcing a route through the dense vegetation that swept down to the river's edge, was slow and tiring work. The river ran fast as it teemed down from the Cordillera, but it looked very much better than endlessly hacking on through the trees. They built what must have been a very substantial raft to take themselves, their supplies and provisions and launched themselves out on the water. They had no means of knowing what lay ahead and almost no means of controlling their ungainly craft. At first, it must have seemed very pleasant, speeding along with the current, but it was not long before they heard an ominous roar of water. Nowadays, the river is a sporting route for experienced canoeists, but even the best of them would hesitate to tackle the rapids on a home-made raft. Down it dashed through the rocks and churning water. More than once they nearly capsized, and the waves rushing over them carried away a lot of their food and provisions. Now all they could do was drift uncontrollably – and hope. Long before they reached the next rapids their way was blocked by a fallen tree. Trevithick and two of the men leaped ashore, but before the rest could follow, the lightened craft drifted off and was caught by the stream to run against the opposite bank.

No one suggested getting back to rafting after that experience, but now they had a dilemma. All were safely ashore, but on opposite banks. There was no question of their simply continuing on parallel tracks each to their own side of the river, for their remaining provisions and the one firearm which represented their best hope of getting food were with Gerard. The other three would have to cross the dangerous waters. One man leaped in and swam across. The second was not so lucky: unable to cope with the strong current he was swept away and drowned. Now it was Trevithick's turn. He simply had no choice. He could not stay where he was, there was no way he could carry on by himself and in spite of the horror of just having seen one of his companions drown, he had to get across somehow. He was at best a poor swimmer, so he gathered up a bundle of sticks, lashed them together and with these as a float he too jumped in. The sticks were fine for keeping him afloat, but they acted like a small raft, swinging and turning with the flow and eddies. Trevithick did his best, but he was getting weaker and weaker. Gerard came to his rescue, wading in as far as he dared and holding out a creeper like a safety rope. The exhausted man just managed to grab it and was hauled ashore. Their troubles were still very far from over. They now had to live off the country on whatever they could find. Then the powder got damp, making the fowling piece useless. They tried to dry it out by the fire, and all they succeeded in doing was blowing it up. They were reduced to foraging until they finally got out of the forest and on to the inhabited lands.

The latter part of their journey was a good deal easier. The lower Sarapiquí, still navigable by small craft, once formed a trading route to the coast, and the inland port of Puerto Viejo had developed at the head of navigation. Using rafts and canoes, it was now just a matter of heading north to the San Juan River, where they could turn east to the Caribbean. This is a popular route for the more adventurous tourists who can enjoy the wealth of wildlife from the crocodiles turning an interested eye on passers-by, to the sloths and monkeys in the riverside trees. With no more disasters, they eventually reached the sea at San Juan. They had achieved their objective, and proved that it was possible to make a route from the mines to the Atlantic coast. Trevithick had no doubts about the matter.[1]

> On a regular decline for perhaps 7000 or 8000 feet in height, down to near sea-level, which would in that distance have given a fall of about half an inch in a yard [1 in 72], four men in ten days would make, I have no doubt, this ridge passable for mules on a regular descent to where the Serapique River is navigable. I have no doubt if we could have spent one week more on our journey we might have passed mules the whole distance with us. To carry machinery from where the Serapique is navigable to the mines is about one-third farther than from the port of Arenas on the south, on which the carriage is two dollars per mule load; three dollars might therefore be charged per mule from the Atlantic side, a much less cost than by way of Matina, or by going around Cape Horn. It would give a speedy communication and a great accommodation to the province of Costa Rica, which I doubt not would gladly contribute to its making.

The Costa Rican government showed no such inclination either then or later, and San Juan today has little more to offer than a military post on the Costa Rica-Nicaragua border.

The next stage of the journey is lost. All we know is that Trevithick, Gerard and the boys somehow made their way down the isthmus of Panama to Colombia and the port of Cartagena. There was to be one more adventure and near disaster, and an astonishing meeting. This extraordinary episode was told to Francis Trevithick by James Fairbairn, who, in turn, had heard it from a third party.[2]

> Mr. Trevithick had been upset at the mouth of the river Magdalena by a black man he had in some way offended, and who capsized the

boat in revenge. An officer in the Venezuelan and the Peruvian services was fortunately nigh the banks of the river, shooting wild pigs. He heard Mr. Trevithick's cries for help, and seeing a large alligator approaching him, shot him in the eye, and then, as he had no boat, lassoed Mr. Trevithick, and by his lasso drew him ashore much exhausted and all but dead.

It must have seemed an extraordinary piece of good fortune that the huntsman was on hand, and even more fortunate that he turned out to be British, and ready to help the unfortunate Trevithick who declared himself "half drowned and half hanged, and the rest devoured by alligators". He helped him back to Cartagena, and now the story becomes almost surreal. There was another Englishman there, waiting for a ship back to Britain, and that man was also to become known as one of the greatest engineers of the railway age – Robert Stephenson. Fairbairn continues the story.

> Thus it was that he fell in with Mr Stephenson, who, like most Englishmen, was reserved, and took no notice of Mr. Trevithick, until the officer said to him, meeting Mr. Stephenson at the door, "I suppose the old proverb of 'two of a trade cannot agree' is true, by the way you keep aloof from your brother chip. It is not thus your father would have treated that worthy man, and it is not creditable to your father's son that he and you should be here day after day like two strange cats in a garret; it would not sound well at home". "Who is it?" said Mr. Stephenson. "The inventor of the locomotive, your father's friend and fellow-worker; his name is Trevithick, you may have heard it," the officer said; and then Mr. Stephenson went up to Trevithick. That Mr. Trevithick felt the previous neglect was clear.

The officer was Bruce Napier Hall, who confirmed the story of the rescue but gave a rather different interpretation of the meeting.

> I will just say that it was quite possible Mr. R. Stephenson had forgotten Mr. Trevithick, but they must have seen each other many times. This was shown by Mr. Trevithick's exclamation, "Is that Bobby?" And after a pause he added, "I've nursed him many a time".
>
> I know not the cause, but they were not so cordial as I could have wished.

Cordial or not, Stephenson took pity on the man who had suffered so much in his journey to Cartagena. He must have started with funds for the journey, for he and Gerard were not without means in Costa Rica, but they had lost a good deal on the way. They could hardly go back to get fresh funds, and the young engineer gave the older man £50 to help him on his way home.

This meeting was a coincidence that almost defies belief, and is desperately poignant. Robert Stephenson had, like Trevithick, arrived in South America hoping to make a fortune in the silver mines, not in Costa Rica but here in Colombia. He had signed on as engineer for three years, but had found the experience deeply depressing. He had, in any case, an infinitely brighter prospect waiting for him at home. His father was in the process of building what was, in effect, the world's first main line, inter-city railway, the Liverpool and Manchester, and debate was raging over how passengers and freight were to be moved on the new line. The steam locomotive, even at this late date, was still not fully accepted, and the more conservative backers favoured a system using stationary engines that would haul the trains, a stage at a time, by cable. To the Stephensons such an idea was ludicrous, and it was to be Robert's task to build a locomotive that would prove once and for all that this was the way forward. As we know, he succeeded with the *Rocket*, which triumphantly performed all it was asked to do and more. He knew as he headed for home that he was to do great things. Trevithick had only hopes and dreams to show for eleven years' absence. As Stephenson was probably little more than a baby on the last occasion when he had seen Trevithick, he can hardly be blamed for failing to recognise him now. And as he thought about what he was planning for the future of the locomotive, it is not really surprising that he felt uncomfortable in the presence of the sadly bedraggled man who had begun it all.

The story is remarkable enough in itself, but without it we would probably never have known that there was a direct contact between the two great pioneers, Trevithick and George Stephenson. And it raises the very interesting question of how they ever came to meet in the first place. When he visited Tyneside in the years between 1805 and 1810, Trevithick was already an engineer with a very considerable reputation, whereas Stephenson was simply the brakeman at the West Moor colliery near Killingworth. There was no reason for Trevithick to notice him, but there was every reason for Stephenson, who was already showing signs of ambition, to seek him out. If this is so, and it is difficult to think of any alternative explanation, then we have another direct connection in the chain that led from the first tentative experiments in Cornwall and Wales to the locomotive that established the basics for all steam locomotives that followed it, *Rocket*.

Gerard and the Montelegre boys left Cartagena with Stephenson on a brig bound for New York. Troubles certainly followed the two adventurers from Costa Rica, and now it was Gerard's turn to suffer near disaster. The brig was wrecked, but fortunately within sight of land and all the passengers were rescued. He then dawdled home, taking in a trip to Niagara Falls, and only reaching Liverpool in November 1827. Trevithick had by then arrived home, having travelled back via Jamaica. He had a good deal of news to catch up on, not just of the great changes that had been happening in the world of engineering while he had been away, but also on news of his own family that he had not seen for eleven years. He had probably never been unduly worried about them, always being inclined to work on the assumption that all was well and would be well until he heard anything to the contrary. His family, on the other hand, had no idea if he was alive or dead, prosperous or a pauper. Even Davies Gilbert, who was one of the few friends with whom Trevithick had never quarrelled, finally lost patience and sent out a stern letter to Panama in the hopes that somehow or other it might reach the engineer in his wanderings. It probably never did.[3]

> Although many years have now elapsed since any direct communications have reached me from you, or since those who had much stronger reasons for hoping that you would not neglect to inform them at least of your proceedings, have known any thing about them: yet I entertain a firm opinion of your still continuing the same honest, thoughtless, careless man that I ever knew you, and that in the event of such success attending your exertions as would prove satisfactory to your own mind, that you would return and share Prosperity with those most nearly connected and most entitled to your kindness and protection. But while this uncertain attainment is in progress, Human Life has advanced and is wearing away. Mrs Trevithick is advanced beyond the middle Period of Life, your children are become Men and Women – and their very support and maintenance has been owing to the kindness of Mr Harvey.
>
> I believe that no Woman ever conducted herself in a more exem-

plary manner than Mrs Trevithick during the whole of your absence or with greater care and attention to her children. Suppose only the case of her having abandoned them! And some years since when a report was current in the West of Cornwall and generally believed, that you had a second Family in South America, Mrs Trevithick declared to me in the strongest Terms that she never did, and never would believe it: but on the contrary she promised herself if you were successful that she herself and her Family would partake of it with you. I enclose her two letters, the second was written in consequence of my having in answer to the first recommended the plan of sending out one of your Sons without delay.

The rumours of a second family in South America could only have been malicious, since no one had any more notion of what he was doing than any of his family or friends had. His interest in his first family had always come second to the fascinations of his working life, and it is doubtful if he even considered starting another. When would he have had the time?

As Gilbert wrote, the older boys were children no longer, and they were fortunate in that, whatever else might happen to them, the Harvey connection would always ensure that they could look forward to decent employment and good prospects. Richard, the eldest, was taken on in the foundry and soon showed that he had inherited both his father's enthusiasm and aptitude for engineering. An entry in the Hayle books for March 1819 reads "Channel; Paid Rd Trevithick Jnr for his artendance fom the end of June last to this time, 9 months at £30 £22 10s 0d." – nine months share of a pay rate of £30 per annum.[4] This was all part of an ongoing process to improve the shipping access to Hayle by deepening the channel of the Penpol River. This proved an exciting time, as Harvey's old rivals, the Cornish Copper Company at Copperhouse, took a very dim view of anything that looked like giving him an advantage in trade. They sent out a gang of, no doubt suitably brawny and intimidating, men who, as fast as the Harvey men dug out the mud, shovelled it back in again. Harvey responded by bringing in still more men and hiring all the carts in the neighbourhood, which were filled and removed before the opposition could get their spades on the spoil. For a time, it looked as if it could end in a vast brawl, but the Copperhouse brigades were withdrawn. It seems to have been just the place for a Trevithick!

The second son, John was found a place in the other side of the business that dealt with their considerable trading interests, their farm, timber yard, ropewalk and grain mill. He had been given the middle name of "Harvey", and it seems to have been a good choice. He proved to be every bit as good a businessman and merchant as his brother was an engineer. He became an important figure in the shipping business that the Harveys were beginning to develop. In 1833, they became involved in fitting out the *Idas* and after that began as shipbuilders themselves. By the 1840s there were five schooners registered in the name of John Harvey Trevithick. In time, Francis and Frederick would also receive their initiation into the working life as apprentices at Hayle.

The older boys had been set on their way, but as the years went by, Jane, her daughters and the two schoolboys were finding it inceasingly difficult to cope. She had made strenuous efforts to collect money due on the plunger-pole. When Trevithick had sold a share in the patent, it had been on the clear understanding that he would get a quarter of all savings above a duty of 26 million. It had been taken up by William Sims, acting for Michael Williams of United Mines. Richard Edmonds, the solicitor acting for Trevithick, noted that the mines using Trevithick's invention were all showing massive increases in duty, but only two were actually making any payments.[5]

> In 1819 I attended at the account-houses of Treskerby and Wheal Chance, of which the late Mr John Williams, of Scorrier, was the manager, in consequence of some of the adventurers objecting to continue the allowances on the savings to Captain Trevithick, when Mr Williams warmly observed, that whatever other mines might do, he would insist, as long as he was manager for Treskerby and Wheal Chance, the agreement made should be carried into effect.

That was all very well, but others were refusing to pay, and Jane was forced after years of fighting the adventurers herself and with the help of her brother, Henry Harvey, to appeal to Davies Gilbert, to see if he could use his influence.[6]

> I beg the favour of your writing to Mr John Williams Junr respecting the savings of the Engine on Mr Trevithick's plan at the United Mines. When my Brother meets him, he promises a speedy settlement, and when he has written to him he has given him an evasive answer. This has been the case three years; to his last letter,

however, he has received no reply. I have also written to him, but with no better effect. Mr Michl Williams regularly pays the savings on the Treskerby Engine and I had hoped the Agents of the other Mines would have been induced to follow his example. Mr Sims is the acting partner and he being entirely in the power of Messrs Williams prevents one having recourse to Law.

Gilbert was at least able to get an answer, but not a very satisfactory one. John Williams argued that because the plunger pole had not been as successful as anticipated, it was generally felt that nothing was due to the Trevithicks. He was, however, willing to go over the figures with Gilbert. There was a real problem here, in that much of the increase in duty was due to another Trevithick invention, the Cornish boiler, but that was not covered by any patent. Working out just how much improvement was due to which invention was almost impossible. In the event, Jane got nothing.

Henry Harvey once again came to his sister's rescue. It had been a source of irritation to him for some time that businessmen who called at Copperhouse had the choice of three inns where they could stay, while those who came to Hayle could only be offered a room in a private house. He decided to build premises of his own in Foundry Square. A simple but handsome building, with a high, hipped roof, it was first described in the records of 1824 as Foundry Public House. That description would surely have offended Harvey, who did not even want it to be known as an inn, but called it the White Hart Hotel. From the start, it was intended as a hospitality centre for the foundry where important visitors could be entertained, with Jane Trevithick installed as hostess. She seems to have taken to the life, for she remained in charge right up to 1836, when at the age of sixty-four she probably felt she had deserved a rest.

This was the family situation when the prodigal returned, unannounced and totally unexpected. He reached Cornwall early in October, and the *West Briton* for 12 October 1827 was able to record his arrival at Hayle from Falmouth, and had heard enough about his travels to be able to inform the readers that he had come from "scenes and dangers, which none but a man of his courage and fortitude could support". He walked back into everyone's lives as if he had just been away on a short business trip, assuming that he could simply carry on as if nothing had happened. The only written record of the family reunion is a rather touching account, written by Francis, who at the time of his father's return was a fifteen-year-old schoolboy.

In the early part of October, 1827, the writer, then a boy at Bodmin school, was asked by the master if any particular news had come from home. Scarcely had the curiosity of the boys subsided, when a tall man with a broad-brimmed Leghorn hat on his head entered at the door, and after a quick glance at his whereabouts, marched towards the master's desk at the other end of the room. When about half-way, and opposite the writer's class, he stopped, took his hat off and asked if his son Francis was there. Mr. Boar, who had watched his approach, rose at the removal of the hat, and replied in the affirmative. For a moment a breathless silence reigned in the school, while all eyes were turned on the gaunt sun-burnt visitor; and the blood, without a defined reason, caused the writer's heart to beat as though the unknown was his father, who eleven years before had carried him on his shoulder to the pier-head steps, and the boat going to the South Sea whaler.

The father had not returned with a fortune: all he had was drawing compasses and a magnetic compass; the only gold was his gold watch, the only silver a pair of silver spurs. A friend had even had to pay for the final part of his journey back to Falmouth. But nothing could dampen his spirits nor stem his enthusiasm. He wrote to Gerard as soon as he heard of his return.[7]

We had a very good passage home, six days from Cartagena to Jamaica, and thirty-four days from thence to England; and on my return was so fortunate as to join all my family in good health, and also welcomed home by all the neighbourhood by ringing of bells, and entertained at the tables of the county and borough members, and all the first-class of gentlemen in the west of Cornwall, with a provision about to be made for me for the past services that this county has received from my inventions just before I left Peru, which they acknowledge to be a saving in the mines since I left of above 500,000*l.*, and that the present existence of the deep mines is owing to my inventions. I confess that this reception is gratifying, and have no doubt but that you will also feel a pleasure in it. I should be extremely happy to see you down here; it is but thirty-six hours' ride, and it will prepare you for meeting your London friends, as I would take you through our mines and introduce you to the first mining characters, which will give you new ideas and enable you to make out a prospectus that will show the great advantages in Costa Rica mines over every other in South America.

One thing is clear from the letter. Whatever might have happened to Trevithick over the past few years, nothing in his character had changed. There is not even a hint that anything might go wrong. He would be recompensed, the mine shares would sell. But there had been changes. He was now fifty- six years old, and although he had not yet realised it, he was going to have to pick up his life, and prepare for yet another fresh start. Even for a man of his fortitude and genius that was asking a great deal.

CHAPTER SEVENTEEN

The Final Years

Trevithick wasted no time in getting back to work. In his November letter to Gerard he had mentioned that he had already made a model of his latest invention. He may have looked back with distaste on his time as a reluctant soldier in Bolivar's army, but at least it gave him first-hand experience of designing firearms. It was a new subject to explore. The long voyage home had given him a great deal of free time, and he always thought that the best way to use any free time that did happen to come his way was to spend it in dreaming up new inventions. So on this occasion he turned his mind to naval gunnery.

Naval gunnery had changed little over the last century – indeed, nothing changed very much in that age: the most famous ship of them all, *Victory*, was already almost half a century old by the time she fought at Trafalgar. The cannon that fired the broadsides were remarkably crude. Weighing perhaps as much as 2 tons and mounted on wheeled carriages, they recoiled back each time they were fired with immense force. They were only stopped by the recoil ropes running through blocks. They then had to be sponged out, reloaded through the muzzle and reprimed before they were ready for firing again. It required a nine-man crew to work one pair of guns.

Trevithick's gun was very different. There was just one gunner responsible for aiming and firing. When it was fired, instead of shooting back horizontally across the deck, it ran up a 25° incline, which absorbed the recoil, while a simple mechanism reprimed and cocked the gun. It was then swung vertical by a lever, reloaded and allowed to drop back under gravity, ready to be fired again. He claimed it needed just two men instead of nine and could be fired at five times the rate of any existing armament. This time, he had high hopes of having his invention taken up, as his old friend from Peru, Lord Cochrane, was back in England, and he was sure that his influence would prevail at the Admiralty. He was, however, to have no more success with the powers that ruled the Navy than he had ever had. The Select Committee of Artillery Officers, based at Woolwich, looked at the model and rejected it without more ado: "wholly inapplicable to practical purposes". As well as the gun, he had also sent drawings of a wrought-iron ship with a new type of steam engine, which he hoped to have built at Hayle. The recoil gun was never heard of again, and the ship never appeared on the stocks. He did, however, build an experimental ship's launch in iron. The Admiralty rejected that as well. In spite of it all, Trevithick never really gave up hope of getting something out of the Admiralty, and he was to make one more attempt to interest them in his ideas a few years later.

He would, no doubt, have been delighted to have had his gun taken up, but this was always a sideshow to the main event – raising funds for the Costa Rican mines. Certainly Gerard did not seem to be overwhelmed with disappointment when he heard the news, and wrote a jokey little letter back to Trevithick.[1]

> My poor mother, who I regret to say has been very delicate ever since your departure, and is now again confined to bed, desires me to say that she is very sorry she is not Master General of the Ordnance, to give it a fair *practical* trial, as she thinks Captain Trevithick's opinions, though she cannot pronounce his name, may be fairly placed in opposition to that of the special committee of artillery officers.

Unfortunately, things were going no better on the mine-promotion front either. There was an expression of interest from a London mining consortium, who wanted to send Trevithick back to Costa Rica with a second expert, appointed by themselves, to report on the prospects. Trevithick, not unreasonably, was not at all keen to go half way round the world to hold another engineer's hand, but declared himself quite happy to rely on any report made by an independent assessor. As he wrote to Gerard: "it would not only take off the responsibility from us, but also strengthen our reports, as the mining prospects there will bear it out, and that far beyond our report".[2] It was obvious that no one was going to invest a great deal of money in Costa Rica without some sort of independent report – unless they were prepared to gamble on striking a good bargain. One investor tried to do just that, offering Trevithick £8000 for his mining grant. He had chosen the wrong man. No matter how hard up he might be, he would never, under any circumstances whatsoever, accept less than what he considered a fair and honest valuation. The result was the inevitable, bad-tempered quarrel. Afterwards, one of the London consortium suggested, rather diffidently, that it might have been sensible to pocket the money first and pick the quarrel afterwards, to which Trevithick bluntly replied: "I would rather kick them downstairs!" One can be very sure that he meant it.

Efforts to raise money in Britain were getting nowhere, and a dispirited Gerard set off to try his luck at fund-raising in Holland and France. Unlike Trevithick, all his hopes were resting on this one venture, which was turning into a calamity. His efforts failed, and he died in Paris, a poor man. So many writers have written about the folly of the scheme, that it is perhaps worth pointing out that others did go on to develop the mines, and although production was never as high as had been hoped, they were rich enough to justify expenditure of $100,000 on new equipment in the 1880s.[3] The same review of the country's economy records that Trevithick's other money-making scheme was also thriving. Pearl-fishing was prospering, and there was an even better trade in mother of pearl. While Trevithick would no doubt have been pleased to hear that his opinions had been vindicated in the long-term, none of this was of any use to him now. It was all bitterly disappointing, but then he was well used to disappointments and always had the remedy at hand. Never waste time worrying about what might have been: if one plan fails, draw up another. Always be ready to move on.

His immediate priority was to get some money together. He had cheerily assured Gerard that the Cornish mine-owners and adventurers were going to be dashing forward to reward him for all the benefits his inventions had brought to the region. It soon became clear that no one was in any danger of being trampled in the rush to hand over money. He now had to try and sort out what had happened to the revenue from the plunger-pole, which he had relied on to supply the family income. He tried to get the money out of Williams, who controlled the patent, but had no more success than Jane and Davies Gilbert had enjoyed earlier. The one hope that he had lay with Williams' answer that he thought the patent had already expired. It had not, and was to run up to 1830. One can easily imagine the state of Trevithick's temper at the time, but for once he did the sensible thing and left it in the hands of his solicitor. The result was just one more disappointment to add to the failure of the recoil gun and the gold mine prospectus.[4]

> Yesterday I called on Mr Williams, and after a long dispute brought the old man to agree to pay me 150*l.* on giving him an indemnification in full from all demands on Treskerby and Wheal Chance Mines in future. He requested that you should make out this indemnification. I could not possibly get them to pay more, and thought it most prudent to accept their offer rather than risk a law suit with them.

It was clear that there was no more to be gained from the ungrateful adventurers, and now Trevithick's only hope of receiving anything from the debacle lay in a public appeal. Government grants to inventors who had failed to get a suitable reward for valuable work were not new. The basis on which they were handed out, however, could seem quite arbitrary. Samuel Crompton, for example, had spent all his resources on devising the spinning mule. It was a huge success, and instead of taking out a patent, he relied on a "gentlemen's agreement" with the leading textile manufacturers. They made fortunes out of increased productivity, and with a deep sense of gratitude they all clubbed together to raise a grand total of £60! The government awarded him £5000 in 1812. The clergyman Dr Edmund Cartwright was an amateur inventor, who devised a very crude power loom, which required a great deal of modification by others before it could be put to practical use. He got £10,000. In dealing with government, it was not so much what you had done, as who you knew. Trevithick was promised the full support of the Cornish adventurers, since it would cost them nothing, and he had his old friend Davies Gilbert, now Member of Parliament for Bodmin, to pilot him through Parliamentary waters.

The petition was drawn up and presented to Parliament on 27 February 1828. His main argument was that his boilers had been the most important factor in the improvements of steam engines and in their adaptation to new uses – which was very true. The old-style boilers were unable to withstand pressures higher than about 6 p.s.i., while the new could go up to 60 p.s.i. with ease, and he looked forward to pressure of 150 p.s.i. becoming common in the

near future. He described the situation in Cornwall as he had
found it when he returned from South America: "the old boilers
were falling rapidly into disuse, and when he returned he found
that they had been generally replaced by those of his invention,
and that the saving of coals occasioned thereby during that period
amounted in Cornwall alone to above 500,000*l*." He then went on
to list his other inventions – iron tanks and buoys, steam carriages
and locomotives, and high-pressure steam engines in general. It
was at least as good a case as Crompton's, and considerably better
than Cartwright's, but it failed anyway. He was, it seemed,
doomed for ever to invent and see others claim the reward.

Faced with the now certain knowledge that there was to be no
money from old ideas that had already been brought into use, the
only hope seemed to be to come up with new ideas. Even
Trevithick can hardly have thought the future looked rosy, but it
was not unrelievedly black either. One of the consolations of his
return was the rediscovery of his family. Francis tells a charming
story of how they studied together side by side, the schoolboy
trying his text book knowledge against his father's own unique
methods.[5]

> During the next six months father and son sat together daily, the
> one drawing new schemes and calculations, the other observing, and
> learning, and calculating the weight and size and speed of a poor
> swallow he had shot, that the proportions of wings necessary to
> carry a man's weight might be known. In these calculations cube
> roots of quantities were extracted, which did not accurately agree
> with Trevithick's figures, who, asking for explanations, received a
> rehearsal, word for word, of the school-book rule for such extrac-
> tions, which threw no more light on his understanding than did his
> own self-made rule on the writer's comprehension, though both
> methods produced nearly the same result.

This relationship was soon to be extended to a real working one, as
Francis was about to join his brother in an apprenticeship at the
Harvey foundry. Henry Harvey had made all the facilities of the
works available to his brother-in-law, so that he could continue with
his experiments. The ideas seemed to be flowing as freely as ever, and
as always they were tried against his regular sounding board, Davies
Gilbert. In June 1828, business brought Trevithick to London,
where he took the opportunity to visit St Katharine's Dock, which
was very near completion. The enclosed dock was to be served by

over a hundred cranes and hoists, and the idea was to work them all by a hydraulic system based on air pipes. The air was drawn through the lengthy pipe work, by means of a vacuum created by a steam-powered pump. This was an immense undertaking, for the wharves and warehouses enclosed 10 acres (4 ha) of actual dock. Trevithick was asked for his opinion, and he replied sensibly and honestly that he had grave doubts about the success of the scheme. He quoted the example of the iron master John Wilkinson, who had encountered great problems from loss of pressure, when trying to supply blast to his furnaces. The London men argued that he had been trying to push air through the pipes, whereas they were planning to draw it through, which would make all the difference, though they failed to explain why. Trevithick contented himself by offering the good advice that perhaps they should try a small experiment before committing themselves to major expense. But the experience set him thinking. He soon realised that a far better system could be devised by using water instead of air in the pipes.[6]

> At the time I was inform'd of this plan, a thought struck me that it might be accomplish'd by another mode preferable to this: by having one powerfull steam-engine to force water in pipes round the dock, say 30 or 40 pounds to the inch, more or less, and to have a worm shaft, working in to a worm wheel, exactley the same as a common roasting jack, and apply to the worm shaft a spouting arm like barker's mill horizontally, and the worm shaft standing perpenduclear would work the worm wheel thats on the chain barrell shaft of the crane, which would make the machine very simple and cheap, and accomplish a circulear motain at once, instead of a piston alternitive motain to drive rotarey motain. This report of mine had som weight with them; and an arrangement is on foot to make inquirey in to the plan propos'd by me, so as to remunerate me provided my plan is good.

It was not a new idea. Joseph Bramah had produced a very successful hydraulic press some years earlier, but there was still a long way to go before the technology would be available to transmit hydraulic power over such long distances. But the episode shows that Trevithick was as quick as ever at seeing to the heart of a problem, and coming up with solutions, even if those solutions would not appear in practice until very many years later. By the end of the nineteenth century, all kinds of machinery from dock cranes to elevators were being worked by water, supplied under pressure from central accumulators.

Sometimes, it needed no more than a chance remark to set him off on a new train of thought. Someone had told him that a huge amount of money was spent each year on shipping ice back from Greenland. Just a few days earlier, he had been worrying about the problems of hydraulic power, now he was to make an imaginative leap to pick on some of the elements in that problem and apply them to the very different problem of refrigeration.[7]

> A thought struck me at the moment that artificial cold might be made very cheap by the power of steam-engines, by compressing air in to a condencer surrounded by water, and also an injection in to the same, so as to instantly could down the verry high compress air to the tempture of the surrounding air, and then admitting it to escape into liquid. This would reduce the tempture to any state of cold required.

Once again, this was an idea a little ahead of its time, but if we look forward in the Trevithick story just a short way, we shall find him joining John Hall's engineering works at Dartford. And it was here, half a century later, that Everard Hesketh built just such a machine and, as J. and E. Hall Ltd., the business still thrives, manufacturing refrigeration units. It would be quite wrong to suggest that Hesketh drew any direct inspiration from Trevithick, but it was he who saw to the creation of the memorial to Trevithick that can now be seen in the church at Dartford. At the very least one can say that it was one more of those strange coincidences that seemed to pop up throughout the engineer's life.

His next excursion took him to Holland. Francis Trevithick gives a somewhat unlikely account of the start of the expedition.

> The Dutch, extending the use of steam on the Rhine and also in sea-going ships, wished Trevithick to see what was going on in Holland, where his nephew, Mr. Nicholas Harvey, was actively engaged in engineering. He had not money enough for the journey, and borrowed 2*l.* from a neighbour and relative, Mr. John Tyack. During his walk home a begging man said to him, "Please your honour, my pig is dead; help a poor man". Trevithick gave him 5*s.* out of the 40*s.* he had just begged for himself. How he managed to reach Holland his family never knew; but on his return he related the honour done him by the King at sundry interviews, and the kindness of men of influence in friendly communion and feasting.

His interest, however, was aroused not so much by the steamers as by the problems of flooding in the country. The old Dutch solution of windmills was no longer adequate, no matter how many they added. At Kindersdijk one can still see fourteen stretched out in a row, originally lifting water by Archimedean screws. To Trevithick the obvious answer was drainage canals and steam pumps, and he persuaded the authorities that the best way of proceeding would be by portable engines. And in that watery country, the best way of all would be by engines mounted in barges. He then proposed building a single-acting high-pressure engine of the type he had installed at Dolcoath back in 1812 (see page 91). It was to work his own version of the old rag and chain pump, which now became a ball and chain pump. Metal chains and metal balls rattling around in an iron barge must have made for an horrendously noisy working environment. A company was formed in London and work was put in hand at Hayle, where Francis was now apprenticed. It proved far more troublesome than Trevithick had expected, and Francis was recruited to help with the drawings after he had finished work at the foundry. He does not seem to have complained about the unpaid overtime tacked onto the end of a day that already ran from 6 a.m. to 6 p.m. By July 1829, the pump was ready for trial and was found to be capable of lifting 7200 gallons (33,000 litres) to a height of 10 feet.

At this point, Trevithick displayed his genius for turning triumph into disaster There are no details, just a few lines in the *Life*, but one can guess at what happened: a chance remark, a flare of temper and it was all over. It was a bitter disappointment to Francis, who had been anticipating a visit to Holland to oversee the erection, and one can guess at his embarrassment at his father's behaviour in the total lack of explanation of what really happened. He simply noted that before returning to London, the company representatives joined Trevithick for refreshments. "In those few minutes differences arose, resulting in the engine remaining for months in the barge, and then going to the scrap heap". It was the end of the Dutch connection for Trevithick, but not for Harveys. They were given the contract for building an engine to drain the Haarlem Mere. The first engine was installed at Leeghwater to be followed by a second at Cruquis. The first engine, which began work in 1845, had a vast 144-inch (3.66 m) diameter low-pressure cylinder. The Cruquis engine was the same size, and worked eight pumps. The latter survives, the biggest steam engine in the world.

Yet again, what Trevithick started, others finished.

Trevithick may have been ready to try his hand at most things but he always came back to his first love and main preoccupation. How could the steam engine be improved? A good deal had been done in Cornwall during his absence, notably by Samuel Grose. He had shown no great interest in complicated variations on the simple, single-cylinder beam engine. He concentrated instead on the basics, using high-pressure steam, simply designed pit-work and, most importantly, improving insulation to reduce heat loss. In 1825, John Taylor erected an engine which had what was then an enormous 90-in. (2.28 m) cylinder, which recorded an impressive duty of 47.9 million. Yet in 1828, Grose's 80-in. (2.02 m) engine, thanks to his simple improvements, recorded an astonishing 87.2 million. Grose, in a letter to Davies Gilbert, modestly attributed his success to "Mr. Watt for the engine and to Mr. Trevithick for the boilers".[8]

Such results were of huge interest to Trevithick, who set out to see just what had been done and was being done, and he began to apply his mind to what he might do in the future to make things even better. He spent a lot of time, with Francis in tow to take notes, observing and recording the efficiency of the best engines. It has to be remembered that at this time, there was still very little understanding of what heat was, so that he often worked as much by intuition as by experiment. This was an area where even the best scientists could offer little help, to Trevithick's considerable annoyance. "I am disappointed that you cannot give me a lift towards grabling my road in the dark, and am rather surpris'd that after so much have been said and reserches made by so many men of science that as yet that no certain data have been given or even a trace to such that can be relay'd on".[9]

One thing he had discovered was that the expansive qualities of steam could be greatly increased by raising it well above boiling point, what we would call "superheated steam". This experiment had been tried at Binner Down where, by heating the steam again after it had left the boiler, duty was increased by fifty per cent. He noted also that the amount of heat required to increase expansion decreased with increased pressure. He then realised that if that were the case, the opposite must also be true. Condensing high-pressure steam would not be a major problem. From these observations and deductions, he came up with the notion of the closed-cycle steam engine. Superheated steam was to drive the engine, and partially condensed steam would be fed back into the boiler. He sent Gilbert a sketch of the engine he was building at Hayle "for the express purpose trying the experiment of workg the same steam and water over and over again, and heating the returned steam by passing in small streams up thro' the hot water from the bottom of the boiler to the top". He realised that if such a system could be made to work, it had one immediate application, on board steam ships. Salt water has a disastrous effect on boilers, but with a closed system a small quantity of fresh water could be endlessly recycled. Long voyages would be possible, without any stops being necessary for boiler feed water.

While he was working on this model, he had also returned to an old idea, the portable puffer for use on board ship, the nautical labourer of 1806. This time a new engine was built, mounted on a wheeled carriage, that could do a rich variety of jobs. "I intend this engine to warp the ship, pump it, cook the victuals, take in and out the cargo, and do all the hard work. The captains are very anxious to get them on board every ship".[10]

Francis was present at the trials when the engine was set on the quay and used for unloading coal, with the idea of seeing how fast it would work. In the event it proved too fast for a stevedore used to more traditional methods, for the hook missed its target and swung him up out of the hold instead. Trevithick was still hoping to find a big market with the London colliers, but with limited success. The little engines did, however, prove very popular for hauling nets into fishing boats and even, paradoxically, for raising the sails of the big sailing steamers of the later part of the century. He was also still contemplating new ways of using steam to move vessels, and in the letter where he described the versatility of the puffer, he also suggested using a larger engine to drive the vessel by novel means. What he was proposing was a pair of paddles, set below the water line on either side of the rudder, which would act like a scuba diver's flippers. The advantage as he saw it was that they could be used on a sailing vessel. When there was plenty of wind and they were not needed, they would be set in a horizontal position to reduce water resistance. This bizarre idea was not, it seems, ever tried.

Although steam was his main preoccupation, he did find time to reverse the usual state of affairs, and give some practical help to his brother-in-law. Harvey was involved in yet another dispute with the Cornish Copper Company, this time over the rights to riverside wharves. It was a complex problem, that all rested on parish boundaries, historically set on the basis of the courses of the three rivers entering Hayle harbour, the Penpol, Copperhouse and Hayle. It was Harvey's contention that by building sluices, his rivals had altered the course of the Penpol, so that the boundary appeared to have shifted. If that was so, then wharves that they claimed were on Copperhouse land were really on Harvey land. Trevithick took it upon himself to carry out tests and then built a relief model to explain the true nature of the rivers once the case came to trial. In the event, Harvey won the day, but the question of just how much of the quays should be handed over to him was reserved for a second hearing. Relations between Trevithick and Harvey had never been better. It could not last.

Work was not going well on the closed-cycle engine. Another young apprentice had joined the Hayle staff, John Brunton, who was to go on to make a considerable name for himself as one of the pioneer railway-builders in India. In the meantime, he was deputed to work on the closed cycle engine.[11]

> I saw a good deal of him for he had persuaded Mr Harvey, his Brother in law, that he had invented a great improvement in Steam Engines – by which the Steam having passed through the cylinders was to be pumped back into the Boiler before it condensed. Mr Harvey consented for him to make a trial of his system in the works and I was appointed under his orders to erect the machinery. I soon saw that it was a mistake – but dare not tell Mr R. Trevithick so – for he was a very violent and passionate man. However the Boiler and Engine were completed and tested and then it was shown to be a failure on wrong principles. Old Richard Trevithick was very angry about this and it weighed heavily on his mind so as to derange his judgement.

Some time in February 1830, a major quarrel broke out between Harvey and Trevithick. As Brunton indicated, the failure of the new engine had put Trevithick in a foul mood, and in these circumstances he was always liable to erupt. All we know about the quarrel is contained in a wry note from Harvey to Gilbert.[12] "As you surmise, Trevithick did not leave here in a very satisfactory manner. When I have the pleasure to see you I will explain. However, be assured his own temper, always ungovernable, led to this last."

Trevithick stormed off to London. In quarrelling with Harvey he was turning away from the works at Hayle, where he had been given remarkable freedom to pursue his ideas and the resources to try them in practice. He was also turning away from his family. He could hardly have expected Jane to abandon her home, and the boys knew that their future lay with Hayle, not with their wayward father. Everything about the episode suggests that Trevithick was suffering from severe stress, and why should anyone be surprised at that? He had made and lost a fortune in South America, and since arriving home everything seemed to have gone wrong for him. He was ready to take offence at anyone and anything, as a result of which a valuable Dutch contract had been lost and he had broken with his brother in law. Harvey seems to have taken the whole affair with equanimity: he had been there before.

The case of the disputed wharf was coming up for arbitration, and as Trevithick had been called as an expert witness for the first hearing, he was expected to appear again. Harvey wrote to R.B. Follett who looked after his business affairs, asking him to call on Trevithick in London, but warned him that he would be unlikely to be able to persuade him to turn up for the hearings. It turned out to be even worse than that, with Trevithick now threatening to appear for the opposition. Harvey had known the Trevithick bluster too well over the years to worry about that one.[13] "We do not fear but what we shall make our case out without him & are of opinion with Mr. Follett that it is better to say no more to him on the subject. His threat of going over to the other side is a mere idle one and has no meaning". He knew his man: Trevithick simply turned up, bright and cheerful, and proceeded to give evidence in favour of Harvey as if nothing had ever happened.

Trevithick made his temporary London home at Lauderdale House, Highgate, which was the boarding school where Gerard had placed the two Montelegre boys. He wrote from there in March 1830, apologising to Gilbert for not having kept in touch, pleading ill health. He had arrived in London itself on 14 February, but after ten days had been forced to leave, because, it seems, of breathing difficulties. It seems likely that he had asthma or bronchitis, probably made worse by stress. Trevithick had never before complained about his health, so that when this robust man wrote that he was "afraid to enter the city", one can be very sure that the symptoms were severe. He had only just managed to stagger along for a meeting with the leaders of the coal trade to discuss the portable engine, but was obviously relieved to be back in the clean air of the hill-top village. Not that any of this stopped him from working. No one had done more to help and encourage Trevithick than Davies Gilbert, and he finally had a chance to do something for Gilbert in return. Trevithick had developed a steam heating system for Gilbert's house. But it was very rare for Trevithick to do one thing, without it suggesting another. This time his new idea was that, instead of using steam for domestic heating, he could use hot water. He described a portable boiler in which water could be heated, either out of doors, or in a fireplace. Once the water was boiled, the fire tube could be removed, and the boiler wheeled off into any room that needed heating. It was designed to be placed under a table, with curtains round to control the heat. As the water cooled, so the room heated, with no risk of fire. It was a prototype storage heater, and he was sufficiently convinced of its value to take out patents in both Britain and France. They proved quite popular, and instead of being hidden away behind curtains, they were often produced in extravagantly ornate styles.

It is ironic that an idea tossed off almost as an afterthought on a rather trivial topic should have proved profitable, while he was making no progress at all with what he regarded as the far more important schemes that were more and more dominating his life. He saw, quite rightly, that size and efficiency were the key elements in designing steam engines for ships. There was a limit to how big anyone could build a ship, as long as wood was still being used for construction, so there was also a limit to the available space for machinery and fuel. The work he had begun in Hayle was now coming together in a new design, which he was also to patent. Where Grose had been successful in raising duty by keeping things simple, Trevithick was cramming more and more new concepts into a single design. At the heart of the engine was a multi-tube boiler. The first element was simple, a conventional firebox and flue, producing steam. Then the steam was passed to the next region, where it was superheated, before passing to the working cylinder. The exhaust steam was then passed through another space, where it gave up some of its heat to the air that was feeding the firebox. In the last stage, it was condensed and returned to the boiler for reuse. In short he proposed a combination of multi-tube boiler, superheater, heat exchanger and condenser.

That would have seemed quite enough for most men, but he intended to ally this complex engine to an entirely new type of driving mechanism. In the past he had tried conventional paddles, the curious flippers and had even investigated the screw propeller. Unfortunately he did not return to either paddle wheels, which were proven, nor screw propellers, which were to represent the future. Instead he planned a system of pumping up water and shooting it out of the back of the boat. If he had calculated the power needed to make such a system work in practice, he might never have begun on it. But this was the arrangement he described in what was to be his last patent of 1832.

The usual problems now appeared. The idea had to be tested, but who was going to fund the experiments? Not Harvey, that was certain. Ever hopeful, he applied to the Admiralty yet again, this time with the idea that they might lend him a vessel for the trials. It was greeted as coldly as all his other requests had been. The next step was to form the New Improved Steam Navigation Company, a grand name, but the company proved to be of little use in actually getting anything done. Gilbert offered advice, which, if it had been given thirty years earlier, might have done some good. "Your plan unquestionably must be to appoint some one with you, as Mr. Watt did Mr. Boulton, and I certainly think it a very fair speculation for any such person as Mr. Boulton to undertake".[14]

Amazingly, a "Boulton" did appear – John Hall. He was older than Trevithick, having been born in Hampshire in 1764. He had followed his father in the trade of millwright, but then set off for Kent to make his own way in the world. He settled in Dartford, where he soon began to build up a thriving business. He was able to acquire a paper mill, to which he added a gunpowder mill in Faversham, and then more importantly he built up a foundry and engineering works. A letterhead of 1836 describes the concern as "Engineers, Steam Engine Manufacturers, and Millwrights, Iron and brass founders". Here was a versatility to match Trevithick's, and Trevithick was only too happy to come to the works to continue his experiments on jet propulsion. According to the local historian[15] "upwards of £1200" was spent, but nothing came of it. The problem was said to lie with exploding pipes, but it seems much more likely that it was lack of power. This was an idea that had to wait for the twentieth century and the technology that produced craft such as the hydrofoil. The suggestion was that Hall had wasted his time encouraging Trevithick, but that was not true. Whilst he was there, he also designed a new range of boilers, producing steam up to 150 p.s.i. Hall put these into production,

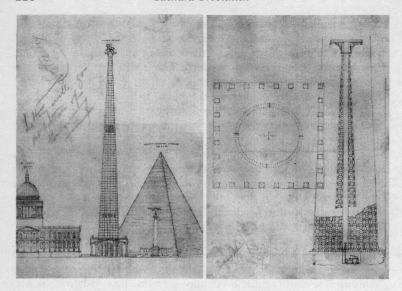

Fig 11: *The original drawings prepared for the published print of the Reform Monument. St Paul's, the Monument and the Great Pyramid are shown for scale. Note the tiny beam engine powering the lift in the right-hand drawing.*

and found a large number of customers.

Trevithick seems to have found a certain comfort here, working with a man who shared his enthusiasm and provided all the resources he requested. But his health remained a problem, and he went back as often as he could to enjoy the clean, clear air of Highgate. He even found himself able to walk up Highgate Hill, without becoming too breathless, in spite of what he called "the maggot" in his chest. At Dartford, he found a comfortable resting-place at The Bull in the centre of the town, as one old resident remembered.[16] "Twas almost nightly that the writer of this paragraph sat *vis-a-vis* in the Bull coffee-room and talked with him over the olden times in the far-western land of 'Jack, the Giant Killer', comparing it with the wild and weird world of the southern hemisphere".

He had one other fantastical scheme which came to him in the 1830s. This was the era of Reform, which was to banish the old corrupt system of rotten boroughs, and bring the vote to many men – though no women – who had previously had no say in the government of their country. The Reform Bill was introduced in 1831, becoming law in the following year. Trevithick had shown himself to be in sympathy with the revolutionary forces in South America, and he was no less enthusiastic about the more modest changes at home. This was an event to celebrate, and he designed a 1000 ft-high column of pierced cast-iron plates, with a massive statue at the top. He drew his own splendid picture of the edifice, soaring above St Paul's and the Pyramids to give it scale. A sectional drawing shows a lift, powered by a steam engine, that was to be used in the construction. If built, it would have been a touch taller than the Eiffel Tower, constructed half a century later. That famous monument spreads the load far more widely than Trevithick planned, but even so, it required concrete blocks 2 m thick to anchor it to the ground. Quite how the Reform Monument was to be stabilised must be forever a mystery. This must be the least practical of all his ideas, and it is just as well that no one tried to build it. He did send his plans to the King: not a very good idea since the King had never been in favour of reform in the first place. He received a formal acknowledgment on 1 March 1833. It was now all too late to worry about. Early in April he took to his bed at the Bull, and on 22 April he was dead.

Controversy stayed with him right to the end. It was widely reported that he went to an unmarked grave in the paupers' burial ground at Dartford Church. There is very good evidence that this was not the case. The major part of the funeral expenses were met by selling the gold watch, which he had brought back from South America and the balance was paid by Hall. The funeral itself was a very grand affair, with a party of pall-bearers drawn from the men at the works, who showed their respect for the engineer by mounting a vigil at his graveside to protect it from the resurrectionists, who might have hoped for a good price for such a famous body. Among those who were named as pall-bearers was a Mr Aldous. His grandson, Thomas Aldous, wrote to the local paper to describe how his grandfather used to take him as a boy and point out the grave of the engineer. He clearly remembered the grave as being by the north gate of the churchyard, and having a suitably engraved headstone.[17] Somehow it is comforting to know that the great man did not, after all, end up in an anonymous grave, huddled away in a dark corner. And what could be more fitting than that he should go to his grave, mourned by the men who knew him best and best knew his worth, his fellow engineers.

Epilogue

I have been branded with folly and madness for attempting what the world calls impossibilities, and even from the great engineer, the late Mr. James Watt, who said to an eminent scientific character still living, that I deserved hanging for bringing into use the high-pressure engine. This so far has been my reward from the public; but should this be all, I shall be satisfied by the great secret pleasure and laudable pride that I feel in my own breast from having been the instrument of bringing forward and maturing new principles and new arrangements of boundless value to my country. However much I may be straitened in pecuniary circumstances, the great honour of being a useful subject can never be taken from me, which to me far exceeds riches.

So, Richard Trevithick summed up his own life to his old friend, Davies Gilbert. There are men who find success in their chosen field, and end their days wealthy and basking in praise. Trevithick was never likely to be one of them. His temperament never allowed him to capitalise on the successes he did achieve, and the call of the new idea and the next experiment was always stronger than the muted, sensible voice that advised him to build patiently on the foundations he had laid down. Yet one can still only marvel at what he did achieve, even in those cases where others gained the reward. His fame has always rested on being the builder of the very first steam locomotive to run on rails, so that we tend to think that that was how he himself would have seen his life's work: this was the pinnacle, the high peak of his achievement. But that was never really the case. If he had been asked for just two words to form his epitaph, they would surely have been 'strong steam'. His life was devoted to exploring the almost infinite variety of uses to which high-pressure steam could be put. He shrank the vast beam engine to create a versatile, portable source of power. It could drive itself over the ground and can be seen as the forerunner of the automobile and the traction engine. Set on rails, it began a transport revolution. It could work on sea or on land, and load a ship or thresh corn. Almost every idea he tried, even when he failed to follow it through, was eventually to be taken up by others and to prove of immense value. Even the so-called wasted years spent in South America only seemed that way because we view them through European eyes. He came to countries that were fighting their way out of the old days of colonial rule and helped them build an economic future. A Peruvian or Costa Rican might well regard his years in their countries as being the most useful of his whole career.

Trevithick can hardly be held up as a model of the ideal family man, and his family seem to have thrived in spite of him rather than because of him. Jane lived on until 1868, able to watch with considerable satisfaction as her sons developed successful careers. And it is obvious that one, at least, had immense pride in his father, for he never had a greater champion than his son Francis. And, had Trevithick lived, he would surely have taken an equal pride in his son's career, for Francis went on to establish a reputation as one of the great Victorian railway engineers. His best known work was the engine he designed for the London and North Western Railway, named very appropriately, *Cornwall*. This remarkable engine with its huge pair of 8 ft 6 in. (2.6m) diameter driving wheels, brings a neat circularity to the Trevithick story. When Trevithick reached Cartagena he had met Robert Stephenson who was on his way to build *Rocket* that was to begin the service on the railway between Liverpool and Manchester. Now that same run was to be taken over by a Trevithick engine that was to stay on the route for almost half a century.

The Trevithick story has never been short of coincidences and they were to continue down the generations. Two of Francis' sons, Richard Francis and Francis Henry, went to Japan to help establish the Japanese railway system. Richard was to design the first locomotive actually to be built in Japan, which was wheeled out onto the tracks in 1893. It was not done to give credit to foreigners, and it was Francis Henry who saw the irony in the situation.

History repeats itself, as Richard Trevithick senior was branded with folly and madness by the late James Watt for bringing into use the high pressure engine, and even not known to the general public as

the builder and inventor of the first locomotive; so will Richard
Trevithick of Kobe never be known in Japan by the Japanese as the
designer and builder of the first locomotive, the credit already given
to a Japanese who had very little mechanical knowledge.

The two Trevithick brothers married and stayed on in Japan, and
their Japanese descendants are justifiably proud of their Cornish
ancestor. He may have been a wayward genius, but genius he
certainly was: a giant of a man, and a giant in the world of steam.

Notes

Chapter One
1. Quoted in F.E. Halliday, *A History of Cornwall*, 1959
2. Quoted in C.C. James, *A History of the Parish of Gwennap*, 1949
3. "Wheal" is the common Cornish name for "mine"
4. John Holland, *Fossil Fuel*, 1949
5. Quoted in A.K. Hamilton Jenkin, *The Cornish Miner*, 1927
6. As all steam engines were designated in terms of cylinder diameter, measured in inches, the practice is followed here.
7. Quoted in John Vivian, *Tales of the Cornish Miners*, 1970
8. Francis Trevithick, *Life of Richard Trevithick*, 1872. In future references this is referred to as *Life*

Chapter Two
1. *Trevithick Society Newsletter, August 1999*
2. *Life*
3. John Harvey to Joanna Harvey, his wife, 16 July 1776. Quoted in Edmund Vale, *The Harveys of Hayle*, 1966
4. John Robison's evidence to the Hornblower piracy case, 1796, quoted in Eric Robinson, *James Watt and the Steam Revolution*, 1969
5. Matthew Boulton to James Watt, 7 February 1769
6. Matthew Boulton to Thomas Innes, 3 July 1776
7. James Watt to Jonathan Hornblower, 15 December 1776
8. John Edwards to Matthew Boulton, 14 June 1777
9. John Budge to Boulton and Watt, 13 September 1777
10. Thomas Dudley to James Watt, 26 February 1778
11. Matthew Boulton to James Watt, 30 July 1781

Chapter Three
1. Quoted in H.W. Dickinson and Arthur Titley, *Richard Trevithick*, 1934
2. Charles Thomas, "Richard Trevithick: New light on his earliest years and family origins", *Journal of the Trevithick Society*, 1974
3. James Watt to Thomas Wilson, 27 January 1784
4. Matthew Boulton to Thomas Wilson, 11 July 1786
5. James Watt to Thomas Wilson, 9 May 1785
6. Letter from Boulton and Watt, 23 April 1787

7. James Watt to Thomas Wilson, 17 April 1788
8. Quoted in Jennifer Tann, "Mr Hornblower and his Crew", *Transactions of the Newcomen Society*, **51**, 1979-80
9. H.S. Torrens, "Some newly discovered letters from Jonathan Hornblower," *Transactions of the Newcomen Society*, **54**, 1982-3
10. Davies Gilbert to Jonathan Hornblower, 5 June 1791
11. Letter dated 20 October 1792
12. The anecdotes are taken from *Life*
13. Davies Gilbert to J.S. Enys, 29 April 1839
14. James Watt to Thomas Wilson, 10 October 1791

Chapter Four

1. *Mr. Hornblower's Case Relative to a Petition to Parliament for the Extention of the Term of his Patent, 1792*
2. *Short Statement on the Part of Messrs. Boulton and Watt, in Opposition to Mr. Jonatham Hornblower's Application to Parliament for an Act to prolong the Term of his Patent, 1792*
3. James Watt Jnr to F. Arago, 10 October 1834
4. Thomas Wilson to James Watt, 4 September 1791
5. James Watt to Thomas Wilson, 8 September 1791
6. James Watt to Thomas Wilson, 12 October 1792
7. Boulton and Watt *versus* Bull; copy of the shorthand writer's notes, June 1793
8. Erasmus Darwin to James Watt, 9 July 1795
9. *Life*
10. Thomas Wilson to James Watt, 27 February 1794
11. A. Weston to Thomas Watson, 30 June 1797
12. Alverton to Thomas Wilson, 2 July 1795
13. Thomas Wilson to Boulton and Watt, 16 July 1795
14. James Watt to Thomas Wilson, 23 July 1795
15. John Southern to Boulton and Watt, 22 September 1795
16. Thomas Gundry to Boulton and Watt, 6 July 1796
17. Thomas Wilson to Boulton and Watt, 3 September 1796

Chapter Five

1. James Watt Jnr to Thomas Wilson, 2 June 1797
2. James Watt Jnr to Thomas Wilson, 7 June 1797
3. James Watt Jnr to Thomas Wilson, 27 June 1797
4. G. Fox to Boulton and Watt, 29 November 1797
5. Trevithick to Thomas Wilson, 16 December 1797
6. Quoted in H.W. Dickinson and Arthur Titley, op cit.
7. *Life*
8. Trevithick to Davies Gilbert, 10 January 1805
9. Davies Gilbert to J.S. Enys, 29 April 1839
10. Details from Arthur Titley, "Richard Trevithick and the winding engine", *Transactions of the Newcomen Society*, **10**, 1929-30
11. *Life*

Chapter Six
1. John Griffiths, *The Third Man, The Life and Times of William Murdoch, 1754–1839,* 1992
2. Thomas Wilson to James Watt, 7 March 1784
3. Paper read to the Institute of Mechanical Engineers, October 1850
4. John Murdoch to James Watt Jnr, May 1815
5. Trevithick to Davies Gilbert, 1 October 1803
6. Aveling & Barford, *A Hundred Years of Road Rolling,* 1965
7. *Life*
8. The sketch is to be found in the Enys Papers in the Royal Institution of Cornwall
9. *Life*
10. Davies Gilbert *Pocket Book,* Enys Papers

Chapter Seven
1. Trevithick and Vivian to Davies Gilbert, 16 January 1802
2. Vivian to Trevithick, 23 February 1802
3. Davies Gilbert diary entry, 27 November 1801
4. Quoted in A.C. Todd, *Beyond the Blaze, A Biography of Davies Gilbert,* 1967
5. Vivian to Trevithick, 23 May 1802
6. Patent specification, *Steam Engines. Improvements in the Construction and Application thereof for driving carriages,* 26 March 1802
7. *Life*
8. *Ibid.*
9. Katherine Plymley diary entry, 15 December 1802
10. Trevithick to Gilbert, 22 August 1802
11. Quoted in Arthur Raistrick, *Dynasty of Ironfounders,* 1953
12. *The Coalbrookdale Iron-works and what they produce,* 1884. Quoted in Raistrick, op cit.
13. Trevithick to Gilbert, 1 October 1803

Chapter Eight
1. Homfray to Gilbert, 10 July 1804
2. Trevithick to Gilbert, 15 February 1804
3. Homfray to Simon Goodrich, 27 February 1804
4. Trevithick to Gilbert, 22 February 1804
5. *Ibid.,* 4 March 1804
6. *Ibid.,* 5 July 1804
7. *Life*
8. *Ibid.*
9. Oswald Dodd Hedley, *Who Invented the Locomotive Engine?,* 1858
10. *The Times,* 8 July 1808
11. Trevithick to Gilbert, 28 July 1808
12. Quoted in Dickinson and Titley, op cit.

Chapter Nine
1. Trevithick to Gilbert, 5 July 1804
2. *Ibid.,* 23 September 1804
3. Andrew Vivian to Trevithick, 22 May 1805
4. *Life*
5. Quoted in Edmund Vale, *The Harveys of Hayle,* 1966
6. William West to Trevithick, 7 September 1815
7. Gilbert to Thomas Trotter, 9 November 1805
8. *Life*
9. Trevithick to Gilbert, 5 October 1804
10. *Ibid.,* 10 January 1805
11. Humphry Davy to Gilbert, 22 October 1804

Chapter Ten
1. *Life*
2. Trevithick to Gilbert, 23 September 1804
3. *Life*
4. Trevithick to Gilbert, 18 February 1805
5. Report by Richard Trevithick to Trinity House, 20 May 1806
6. Quoted in Dickinson and Titley, op cit.
7. Rees's *Cyclopedia,* 1819
8. Trevithick to Gilbert, 11 August 1807
9. *Ibid.,* 28 August 1807
10. *Ibid.,* 5 January 1808
11. *Ibid.,* 2 February 1808
12. *Life*

Chapter Eleven
1. Trevithick to Gilbert, 23 July 1806
2. *Ibid.,* 22 February 1804
3. Specification for Trevithick and Dickinson Patent 3148, 5 July 1808
4. *Life*
5. *Ibid.*
6. Henry Harvey to Jane Trevithick, 1 June 1810
7. *Life*
8. Trevithick to Sir Christopher Hawkins, 10 March 1812

Chapter Twelve
1. John Murray, *Handbook for Travellers in Cornwall,* 1851
2. Trevithick to Sir Christopher Hawkins, 26 March 1812
3. Quoted in R.J. Law, "A Survey of Tank Boilers down to 1850", *Transactions of the Newcomen Society,* **48**, 1976–7
4. Trevithick to Hawkins, 20 March 1812
5. Richard Hosking to J.S. Enys, 17 January 1843
6. J.U. Rastrick to Goodrich, 15 November 1812
7. Trevithick to Robert Fox, 29 January 1813

8. Arthur Young, *General View of the Agriculture of Oxfordshire*, 1813
9. Trevithick to Hawkins, 13 February 1812
10. *Life*
11. Arthur Young, op cit.
12. Trevithick to Hawkins, 10 March 1812
13. Trevithick to Rastrick, 26 January 1813
14. Trevithick to Sir John Sinclair, 26 January 1812
15. The details are from Ronald H. Clark, "A Mystery and a Miscellany", *Transactions of the Newcomen Society*, **41**, 1968–9
16. Trevithick to Robinson and Buchanan, 5 December 1812

Chapter Thirteen
1. Trevithick to Rastrick, 26 January 1813
2. *Ibid.*, 20 May 1813
3. Quoted in Hugh Salvin, *Journal written on board His Majesty's Ship Cambridge*, 1829
4. Lt. W. Smyth and Mr. F. Lowe, *From Lima to Parà*, 1836
5. Trevithick to Mr Pengilly, 22 May 1813
6. Trevithick to Rastrick, 23 May 1813
7. Trevithick to Uvillé, 2 June 1813
8. Trevithick to Hazeldine, Rastrick & Co., 10 August 1813
9. Partnership Agreement, dated 8 January 1814
10. Trevithick to Uvillé, 31 March 1814
11. *Ibid.*, 15 March 1814
12. Trevithick to Mr Budd, 22 September 1813
13. Trevithick to Gilbert, 8 July 1815
14. Henry Phillips, quoted in *Life*
15. James Banfield, quoted in *Life*
16. Trevithick to Gilbert, 8 July 1815

Chapter Fourteen
1. Hugh Salvin, *Journal Written On Board His Majesty's Ship Cambridge, 1824 to May 1827*, 1829
2. John Miers, *Travels in Chile and La Platà*, 1826
3. Edward Hodge, *Reminiscences of a Veteran Engineer*, unpublished memoirs
4. Vivian is unnamed but Trevithick would have written to no else in such terms: letter dated 9 December 1815
5. Quoted in Henry Boase, "On the introduction of the steam engine to the Peruvian Mines" *Transactions of the Royal Geological Society of Cornwall*, 1818
6. Draft letter, Trevithick to Uvillé, 9 December 1815
7. Anibal Maurtua, *El Porvenir del Peru*, 1911
8. Henry Boase, op cit.
9. Undated letter in *Life*.
10. *Ibid.*
11. *Ibid.*

12. Miers, op cit.
13. Undated document, quoted in *Life*
14. *Life*

Chapter Fifteen

1. Capt. Basil Hall, R.N., *A Journal Written on the Coasts of Chili, Peru and Mexico, 1820, 1821, 1822,* 1824
2. Quoted in Emil Ludwig, *Bolivar, the Life of an Idealist,* 1947
3. Hall, op cit.
4. Salvin, op cit.
5. *Ibid.*
6. Undated document written by Trevithick, *Life*
7. James Liddell to Francis Trevithick, 3 November 1869
8. This and other translated Costa Rican documents are quoted from D.W. Davies, 'Richard Trevithick in Costa Rica', *Journal of the Trevithick Society* 5, 1977
9. *Life*
10. Document dated 12 June 1824
11. Document dated 21 July 1825

Chapter Sixteen

1. *Life*
2. *Ibid.*
3. Gilbert to Trevithick, 11 February 1827
4. Quoted in Vale, op cit.
5. *Life*
6. Jane Trevithick to Gilbert, 7 October 1820
7. Trevithick to Gerard, 15 November 1827, *Life*

Chapter Seventeen

1. Gerard to Trevithick, *Life*
2. Trevithick to Gerard, 30 January 1828
3. Paul Biolley, *Costa Rica and her Future,* 1889
4. Richard Edmonds to Trevithick, 24 January 1828
5. *Life*
6. Trevithick to Gilbert, 18 June 1828
7. *Ibid.*, 29 June 1828
8. D.B. Barton, *The Cornish Beam Engine,* 1969 (2nd ed.)
9. Trevithick to Gilbert, 27 August 1829
10. *Ibid.*, 24 January 1829
11. *John Brunton's Book 1812–1899,* 1939
12. Henry Harvey to Gilbert, 13 April 1830
13. Quoted in Vale, op cit.
14. Gilbert to Trevithick, 26 December 1831
15. John Dunkin, *The History and Antiquities of Dartford,* 1844
16. Undated cutting from *Dartford and West Kent Advertiser*
17. *West Kent Advertiser,* 7 January 1902

Select Bibliography

Beringer, John Jacob, *Richard Trevithick*, 1902

John Brunton's Book, 1812–1899, Cambridge University Press, 1939

Dickinson, H.W. and Titley, T.A., *Richard Trevithick*, Cambridge University Press, 1934

Dickinson, H.W. and Jenkins, Rhys, *James Watt and the Steam Engine*, 1927

Dunkin, John, *The History and Antiquities of Dartford*, 1844

Edmonds, Richard, *The Land's End District*, also *A Brief Memoir of Richard Trevithick*, 1862

Farey, John, *Treatise on the Steam Engine, Vol 2*, David & Charles, 1971

Griffiths, John, *The Third Man, The Life and Times of William Murdoch, 1754–1839*, Andre Deutsch, 1972

Harper, Edith K., *A Cornish Giant, Richard Trevithick, the Father of the Locomotive*, E & F.N. Spon, 1913

Hills, Richard L., *Power from Steam*, Cambridge University Press, 1989

James, C.C., *A History of the Parish of Gwennap*, 1949

Jenkin, A. Hamilton, *The Life of Richard Trevithick*, 1938

Jenkin, A. Hamilton, *The Cornish Miner*, George Allen & Unwin, 1927

Law, Henry, *Memoir on the Several Operations and the Construction of the Thames Tunnel*, 1857

Lean, Thomas, *Historical Statement of the Duty performed by the Steam Engine in Cornwall*, 1839

Miers, John, *Travels in Chile and La Platà*, 1826

Miller, Harry, *Hall's of Dartford, 1785–1985*, Hutchinson Benham, 1985

Owen-Jones, Stuart, *The Penydarren Loco*, The National Museum of Wales, 1981

Raistrick Arthur, *Dynasty of Ironfounders, The Darbys and Coalbrookdale*, David & Charles, 1970

Rees' Cyclopaedia, 1819

Robinson, Eric and Musson, A.E., *James Watt and the Steam Revolution*, Adams & Dart, 1969

Rolt, L.T.C., *The Cornish Giant*, Lutterworth Press, 1960

Salvin, Hugh, *Journal Written on Board His Majesty's Ship, Cambridge*, 1829

Smyth, Lt W. and Lowe, F., *Narrative of a Journey from Lima to Parà in 1834*, 1836

Stevenson, William Bennet, *Historical and Descriptive Narrative of Twenty Years Residence in South America,* 1825

Todd, A.C., *Beyond the Blaze: A Biography of Davies Gilbert*, Barton, 1967

Tregellas, Walter, *Cornish Worthies, Vol 2*, 1884

Trevithick, Francis, *Life of Richard Trevithick*, E & F.N. Spon, 1872

Vale, Edmund, *The Harveys of Hayle*, D. Bradford Barton, 1966

Vivian, John, *Tales of the Cornish Miners*, Tor Mark Press, 1970

Index